Exploring Classroom Discourse

MW00333886

Routledge Introductions to Applied Linguistics is a series of introductory level textbooks covering the core topics in Applied Linguistics, primarily designed for those entering postgraduate studies and language professionals returning to academic study. The books take an innovative 'practice to theory' approach, with a 'back-to-front' structure. This leads the reader from real-world problems and issues, through a discussion of intervention and how to engage with these concerns, before finally relating these practical issues to theoretical foundations. Additional features include tasks with commentaries, a glossary of key terms, and an annotated further reading section.

Classroom Discourse looks at the relationship between language, interaction and learning. Providing a comprehensive account of current perspectives on classroom discourse, the book promotes a fuller understanding of the interaction, which is central to effective teaching, and introduces the concept of classroom interactional competence (CIC).

Walsh makes the case for a need not only to describe classroom discourse, but to ensure that teachers and learners develop the kind of interactional competence which will result in more engaged, dynamic classrooms where learners are actively involved in the learning process. This approach makes the book an invaluable resource for language teachers and educators, as well as advanced undergraduates and post-graduate/graduate students of language and education, and language acquisition within the field of applied linguistics.

Steve Walsh is a lecturer in the School of Education, Communication and Language Sciences, Newcastle University, UK. He is the Editor of *Classroom Discourse*, a Routledge journal.

Routledge Introductions to Applied Linguistics

Series editors:

Ronald Carter, *Professor of Modern English Language*
University of Nottingham, UK

Guy Cook, *Professor of Language and Education*
Open University, UK

Routledge Introductions to Applied Linguistics is a series of introductory level textbooks covering the core topics in Applied Linguistics, primarily designed for those entering postgraduate studies and language professionals returning to academic study. The books take an innovative 'practice to theory' approach, with a 'back-to-front' structure. This leads the reader from real-world problems and issues, through a discussion of intervention and how to engage with these concerns, before finally relating these practical issues to theoretical foundations. Additional features include tasks with commentaries, a glossary of key terms, and an annotated further reading section.

Exploring English Language Teaching
Language in Action
Graham Hall

Exploring Classroom Discourse
Language in Action
Steve Walsh

'The innovative approach devised by the series editors will make this series very attractive to students, teacher educators, and even to a general readership, wanting to explore and understand the field of applied linguistics. The volumes in this series take as their starting point the everyday professional problems and issues that applied linguists seek to illuminate. The volumes are authoritatively written, using an engaging "back-to-front" structure that moves from practical interests to the conceptual bases and theories that underpin applications of practice.'

Anne Burns, *Aston University, UK*

Exploring Classroom Discourse

Language in Action

Steve Walsh

Routledge
Taylor & Francis Group

LONDON AND NEW YORK

First published 2011
by Routledge
2 Park Square, Milton Park, Abingdon, Oxon OX14 4RN

Simultaneously published in the USA and Canada
by Routledge
270 Madison Avenue, New York, NY 10016

Routledge is an imprint of the Taylor & Francis Group, an informa business

© 2011 Steve Walsh

The right of Steve Walsh to be identified as author of this work
has been asserted by him in accordance with sections 77 and 78
of the Copyright, Designs and Patents Act 1988.

Typeset in Sabon and Helvetica Neue by
Florence Production Ltd, Stoodleigh, Devon
Printed and bound in Great Britain by
TJ International Ltd, Padstow, Cornwall

All rights reserved. No part of this book may be reprinted or
reproduced or utilised in any form or by any electronic, mechanical,
or other means, now known or hereafter invented, including photocopying
and recording, or in any information storage or retrieval system,
without permission in writing from the publishers.

British Library Cataloguing in Publication Data
A catalogue record for this book is available from the British Library

Library of Congress Cataloging in Publication Data
Walsh, Steve.
   Exploring classroom discourse: language in action/Steve Walsh.
      p. cm. — (Routledge Introductions to applied linguistics)
   Includes bibliographical references and index.
   1. Language and education.   2. Oral communication.
   3. Discourse analysis.   4. Interaction analysis in education.
   5. Second language acquisition.   I. Title.
   P40.8.W34 2011
   370.1'4 – dc22   2010041937

ISBN: 978–0–415–57066–4 (hbk)
ISBN: 978–0–415–57067–1 (pbk)
ISBN: 978–0–203–82782–6 (ebk)

Contents

Series editors' introduction

The *Introducing Applied Linguistics* series

This series provides clear, authoritative, up-to-date overviews of the major areas of applied linguistics. The books are designed particularly for students embarking on masters-level or teacher-education courses, as well as students in the closing stages of undergraduate study. The practical focus will make the books particularly useful and relevant to those returning to academic study after a period of professional practice, and also to those about to leave the academic world for the challenges of language-related work. For students who have not previously studied applied linguistics, including those who are unfamiliar with current academic study in English-speaking universities, the books can act as one-step introductions. For those with more academic experience, they can also provide a way of surveying, updating and organizing existing knowledge.

The view of applied linguistics in this series follows a famous definition of the field by Christopher Brumfit as:

> The theoretical and empirical investigation of real-world problems in which language is a central issue.
>
> (Brumfit, 1995: 27)

In keeping with this broad problem-oriented view, the series will cover a range of topics of relevance to a variety of language-related professions. While language teaching and learning rightly remain prominent and will be the central preoccupation of many readers, our conception of the discipline is by no means limited to these areas. Our view is that while each reader of the series will have their own needs, specialities and interests, there is also much to be gained from a broader view of the discipline as a whole. We believe there is much in common between all enquiries into language-related problems in the real world, and much to be gained from a comparison of the insights from one area of applied linguistics with another. Our hope therefore is that readers and course designers will not choose only those volumes relating to their own particular interests, but use this series to construct a wider knowledge and understanding of the field, and the many crossovers and resonances between its various areas. Thus the topics to be covered are wide in range, embracing an exciting mixture of established and new areas of applied linguistic enquiry.

The perspective on applied linguistics in this series

In line with this problem-oriented definition of the field, and to address the concerns of readers who are interested in how academic study can inform their own professional practice, each book follows a structure in marked contrast to the usual movement *from* theory *to* practice. In this series, this usual progression is presented back to front. The argument moves *from* Problems, *through* Intervention, and *only* finally to Theory. Thus each topic begins with a survey of everyday professional problems in the area under consideration, ones that the reader is likely to have encountered. From there it proceeds to a discussion of intervention and engagement with these problems. Only in a final section (either of the chapter or the book as a whole) does the author reflect upon the implications of this engagement for a general understanding of language, drawing out the theoretical implications. We believe this to be a truly *applied* linguistics perspective, in line with the definition given above, and one in which engagement with real-world problems is the distinctive feature, and in which professional practice can both inform and draw upon academic understanding.

Support to the reader

Although it is not the intention that the text should be in any way activity-driven, the pedagogic process is supported by measured guidance to the reader in the form of suggested activities and tasks that raise questions, prompt reflection and seek to integrate theory and practice. Each book also contains a helpful glossary of key terms.

The series complements and reflects the *Routledge Handbook of Applied Linguistics*, edited by James Simpson, which conceives and categorizes the scope of applied linguistics in a broadly similar way.

Ronald Carter
Guy Cook

Reference

Brumfit, C. J. (1995) 'Teacher Professionalism and Research', in G. Cook and B. Seidlhofer (eds) *Principle and Practice in Applied Linguistics*. Oxford: Oxford University Press, pp. 27–42.

Note

There is a section of commentaries on a number of the tasks, at the back of the book from p. 235. The (TC) symbol in the margin indicates that there is a commentary on that task.

1 Introduction

Introduction

The central thesis of this book is that language teachers can improve their professional practice by developing a closer understanding of classroom discourse and, in particular, by focusing on the complex relationship between language, interaction and learning. The book provides a comprehensive account of current perspectives on classroom discourse, aiming to promote a fuller understanding of interaction, which here is regarded as being central to effective teaching. While classroom interaction has been the focus of attention for researchers for more than fifty years, the complex relationship between language, interaction and learning is still only partially understood. The case is made for a need not only to describe classroom discourse, but to ensure that teachers and learners develop the kind of interactional competence that will result in more engaged, dynamic classrooms where learners are actively involved in the learning process. The concept of classroom interactional competence (CIC) is introduced, described and problematised as a means of developing closer understandings of how learning and learning opportunity can be improved.

Rather than simply describing the discourse of second language classrooms – an enterprise that has been underway for more than fifty years – the concern here is to promote understanding and facilitate professional development. Chapter 1 focuses on the main features of classroom discourse and considers how it is typically structured. Chapters 2 and 3 look at the relevance of classroom discourse to teaching and learning, while Chapters 4 and 5 evaluate different approaches to studying classroom discourse. Chapters 6 and 7 introduce the SETT framework as a means of helping practitioners evaluate their own use of language while teaching. Chapter 8 focuses on the concept of classroom interactional competence. In Chapter 9 the main conclusions are presented.

This chapter considers some of the characteristics of second language classroom interaction, offering an overview of the more commonly found and widespread features that characterise classroom interaction throughout the world. Using extracts from a range of English language lessons, the aim is to offer a brief sketch of classroom discourse features rather than a detailed description. Many of the themes and issues raised here will be dealt with in more detail in the rest of the book.

The chapter is divided into three sections. In the first section, I present a description of the nature of classroom interaction in the context of language teaching. The following section deals in more detail with the underlying structure of classroom discourse, while in the final section, I point to the future by highlighting some of the challenges that face teachers and learners in relation to classroom interaction.

The nature of classroom interaction

When we reflect on classes that we have been in, either as teachers or learners, we quickly realise that classroom communication is both highly complex and central to all classroom activity. In the rapid flow of classroom interaction, it is difficult to comprehend what is happening. Not only is the interaction very fast and involves many people, it has multiple foci; the language being used may be performing several functions at the same time: seeking information, checking learning, offering advice and so on.

Personal reflection

Think about your own experiences as a learner or teacher. Why is communication in the classroom so important? In what ways can teachers make effective use of their language? What is the relationship, if any, between the language used by teachers and learners and the learning that occurs?

Given its complexity and centrality to teaching and learning, it is fair to say that any endeavour to improve teaching and learning should begin by looking at classroom interaction. Everything that occurs in the classroom requires the use of language. Like most human 'joint enterprise' language underpins every action, every activity. It is through language that 'real world problems are solved' (Brumfit 1995). Crucially, in a classroom, it is through language in interaction that we access new knowledge, acquire and develop new skills, identify problems of understanding, deal with 'breakdowns' in the communication, establish and maintain relationships and so on. Language, quite simply, lies at the heart of everything. This situation is further complicated when we consider that in a language classroom, the language being used is not only the means of acquiring new knowledge, it is also the *goal* of study: 'the vehicle and object of study' (Long 1983: 67).

Yet despite its obvious importance, until recently, little time has been given to helping teachers understand classroom interaction. While researchers have gone to great lengths to describe the interactional processes of the language classroom, few have used this knowledge to help teachers improve their practices. Most teacher education programmes devote a considerable amount of time to teaching methods and to subject knowledge. Few, I suggest, devote nearly enough time to developing understandings of interactional processes and the relationship between the ways in which language is used to establish, develop and promote understandings. Teachers and learners, arguably, need to acquire what I call 'Classroom Interactional Competence' (CIC, see Walsh 2006) if they are to work effectively together. That is, teachers and learners must make use of a range of appropriate interactional and linguistic resources in order to promote active, engaged learning. Classroom interactional competence is discussed in full in Chapter 8.

Let's go back to the three questions you were asked to consider on p. 2 and answer each in turn:

- Why is communication in the classroom so important?

- In what ways can teachers make effective use of their language?

- What is the relationship, if any, between the language used by teachers and learners and the learning which occurs?

To some extent, the first question has been answered: communication in the classroom is so important because it underpins everything that goes on in classrooms. It is central to teaching, to learning, to managing groups of people and the learning process, and to organising the various tasks and activities that make up classroom practices. Communication refers to the ways in which language is used to promote interaction; according to van Lier (1996), interaction is 'the most important thing on the curriculum'. If we are to become effective as teachers, we need not only to understand classroom communication, we need to improve it.

When we consider the second question, how can teachers make effective use of their language, we must first define what we mean by 'effective'. Given that the main concern of teachers is to promote learning, effective, here, means language that promotes learning. There are many ways in which teachers can influence learning through their choice of language and their interactional decision-making. We come back to this later in the chapter. For the time being, 'effective' simply means using language that helps, rather than hinders, the learning process (Walsh 2002).

Our third question is more difficult to answer. What is the relationship between the language used by teachers and learners and the learning that occurs? There is no clear and exact response to this question. According to Ellis (1994), this relationship can be seen as a strong one, where language use has a direct influence on the learning that takes place; a weak one, where there is some link between the language used and the learning that occurs; or a zero one, where there is simply no relationship at all between the language used by teachers and the learning that ensues. And of course, this relationship is difficult to assess given that there are so many other factors that influence learning. However, the very fact that this question is often asked does suggest that there is a relationship between classroom language use and learning. It is a question that underpins much of the discussion in this book and one that we will be returning to.

In the remainder of this section, I offer an overview of the most important features of second language classroom discourse. The discussion that follows presents these features largely from the perspective of the teacher who has the main responsibility for controlling the interaction. Later in this chapter, we take a closer look at the language used by teachers and learners (see below). Four features of classroom discourse have been selected, largely because they typify much of the interaction that takes place in classrooms and are prevalent in all parts of the world:

- Control of the interaction.

- Speech modification.

- Elicitation.

- Repair.

Control of the interaction

One of the most striking features of any classroom is that the roles of the participants (teacher and learners) are not equal, they are asymmetrical. This is true of all classrooms: primary, secondary, tertiary, monolingual, multilingual, with adult, teenager or very young learners. It is also true of many other contexts in which institutional discourse prevails and where roles are unequal: doctor/patient, solicitor/client, shop assistant/customer, and so on. In each of these settings, including classrooms, one party is in a position of power or authority; that person has control of the patterns of communication that occur and is able to direct and manage the interaction. In language classrooms, teachers control patterns of communication by managing both the topic of conversation and turn-taking, while students typically take their cues from the teacher through whom they direct most of their responses. Even in the most decentralised and learner-centred classroom, teachers decide who speaks, when, to whom and for how long. Teachers are able to interrupt when they like, take the floor, hand over a turn, direct the discussion, switch topics. As Breen puts it, it is the teacher who 'orchestrates the interaction' (1998: 119).

Learners, on other hand, do not enjoy the same level of control of the patterns of communication, although there will certainly be times when the roles of teacher and learners are more equal, allowing more even turn-taking and greater participation by learners. For much of the time, learners respond to the cues given by teachers: in the form of a spoken response, an action (such as opening a book, changing seats), or a change of focus (from a PowerPoint slide to coursebook, for example, or from listening to the teacher to talking to a classmate).

If we look now at some classroom data, we can see quite clearly how teachers control the interaction. Look at extract 1.1 below, in which a group of multilingual, intermediate adult learners are discussing issues about law and order in their respective countries. In line 1, we see how the teacher nominates a student (Erica), thereby determining who may speak. Her question, 'what happens if you commit a crime', both establishes the topic and provides a cue for Erica, who must now reply to the question, which she does in line 3. In line 5, we can see that the learner is experiencing some difficulty and the teacher interrupts in line 6, indicated by = (a latched turn, where one turn follows another without any pausing). Again, in line 6, the teacher is controlling the interaction, seeking clarification and correcting an error ('what's the verb'?). Not only does the teacher control the topic, she controls the precise content of the learner's subsequent utterance in line 8, 'they go to court'. Finally, in line 9, the teacher brings L1's contribution to an end 'they can go home', controlling participation by inviting a response from another student 'what happens in Brazil?' Breen's (1998) powerful metaphor of the teacher orchestrating the interaction is in evidence throughout this extract. Arguably, a teacher's ability to 'orchestrate the interaction' in this way not only determines who may participate and when, it influences opportunities for learning. It is also apparent when we look at extract 1.1 that teachers have control over the amount of 'space' learners have in the interaction. For every contribution made by the student, the teacher typically makes two: asking a question (in lines 1 and 6) and giving feedback (in lines 4 and 9). The consequence of this is that teachers clearly talk more and occupy more of the interactional space of the classroom. Learners' opportunities to contribute are largely controlled by the teacher. This three-part discourse structure, comprising a teacher question, learner response and teacher feedback is another feature of classroom discourse that exemplifies the ways in which teachers control the interaction. We discuss this in some detail under 'Exchange structure' – see page 17. (For a definition of the transcription system please refer to Appendix B, p. 220.)

Extract 1.1

1	T:	OK Erica could you explain something about law and order in Japan what
2		happens if you commit a crime?
3	L1:	almost same as Britain policeman come to take somebody to police station
4	T:	yes
5	L1:	and prisoner questioned and if he is (5 *seconds unintelligible*)=
6	T:	=yes what's the verb Eric Erica ... if she or he yes commits a crime they go
7		to
8	L1:	they go to court yes but if they he they didn't do that they can go home
9	T:	they can go home (...) very good indeed right what happens in Brazil

To summarise, we have seen that teachers, through their unique status in a classroom, and by the power and authority they have, control both the content and procedure of a lesson, as well as controlling participation.

Speech modification

One of the defining characteristics of all classroom discourse is teachers' modification of their spoken language. In some respects, teachers' use of a more restricted code is similar to the spoken language of parents talking to young children. Typically, a teacher's speech is slower, louder, more deliberate, and makes greater use of pausing and emphasis. Teachers also make a great deal of use of gestures and facial expressions to help convey meaning. The modification strategies used by teachers are not accidental; they are conscious and deliberate and occur for a number of reasons. The first, and obvious one is that learners must understand what a teacher is saying if they are going to learn. It is highly unlikely that learners will progress if they do not understand their teacher. A second reason is that, for much of the time, teachers model language for their students. That is, they use appropriate pronunciation, intonation, sentence and word stress, and so on in order to give learners an opportunity to hear the sounds of the target language. In many cases and in many parts of the world, a teacher's articulation of a second language may be the only exposure to the language that learners actually receive. It is important, therefore, that the L2 is modelled correctly and appropriately. A third reason for speech modification is the fact that there is so much happening at any one moment in a classroom that teachers need to ensure that the class is following, that everyone understands and that learners don't 'get lost' in the rapid flow of the discourse. In his 1998 paper, Michael Breen talks about the need for learners to 'navigate' the discourse and the fact that many learners do actually get lost from time to time. It is the teacher's responsibility to ensure that this does not happen by making frequent use of repetition, by 'echoing' an individual learner's contribution for the benefit of the whole class, by seeking clarification and so on.

An understanding of the ways in which second language teachers modify their speech to learners is clearly important to gaining greater insights into the interactional organisation of the second language classroom and to helping teachers make better use of the strategies open to them. What strategies do teachers use to modify their speech? We can look at modified speech in two ways. On the one hand, teachers employ a different range of linguistic resources to facilitate comprehension and assist the learning process. There are several features of spoken classroom language that teachers normally modify in some way. Perhaps the most obvious one is the use of simplified vocabulary and the absence of more idiomatic or regional variations. Grammar too is frequently simplified through the use of simpler and shorter utterances, the use of a more limited range of tenses and fewer modal verbs. Pronunciation is also often clearer, with slower articulations and wider use of standard forms. Of course, teachers may ask themselves if they are losing something of their identity by making all these changes. In my experience, this does not happen to any great extent, although teachers do employ their own particular 'classroom idiolect' (Walsh 2006): an individual way of talking that is normally based on their personal conversational style. There are times when a teacher's classroom idiolect may help learners and there are other times when learners simply do not understand because of the teacher's idiolect.

On another level, teachers modify their interactional resources to assist comprehension and help learners 'navigate the discourse'. Most notable is the use of transition markers to signal the beginnings and endings of various activities or stages in a lesson. Words such as *right, ok, now, so, alright* – typically discourse markers – perform a very important function in signalling changes in the interaction or organisation of learning. They function like punctuation marks on a printed page: consider how difficult it would be to read a newspaper without punctuation. The same applies in a classroom if teachers fail to make appropriate use of transition markers. This important category of discourse markers enables teachers to guide learners through the discourse, hold their attention, announce a change in activity, signal the beginning or end of a lesson stage. Crucially, they help a class 'stay together' and work in harmony.

In addition to the more obvious ways in which teachers modify their speech discussed above, there are other more subtle strategies that teachers use in order to clarify, check or confirm meanings. These

Task 1.1

Consider the extract below. To what extent does this teacher 'guide' learners through the discourse? As a learner in this class, in what ways might you feel 'lost' and how might the teacher address this problem?

66 T: =yes it's the result of INtensive farming they call it (**writes on board**) which is er (2) yeah

67 and this is for MAXimum profit from erm meat so as a result the animals suffer they

68 have very BAD conditions and very small erm they're given food to really to make

69 them big and fat and usually it's unnatural and as you said they HAVE to give them a

70 lot of anti-biotics because the conditions in which they're kept erm they have far more

71 disease than they would normally have so they give them steroids to make them

72 stronger and of course this is now being passed through to the HAMburger that you

73 eat is contaminated with er=

74 L: =sorry how do you spell anti- anti-biotics?

75 T: anti-biotics? anti-biotics yes? erm anti-biotics?

76 L: how to spell it?

77 T: oh how do you spell it right (**writes on board**) there's er I think I read a very shocking report

78 recently that nearly all for example chickens and beef now pigs all all these that are reared

79 with intensive farming they're ALL given anti-biotics as a matter of course and of course the

80 public don't hear this until quite a long time after we've been eating it and this this is what

81 makes me angry quite a scandal really . . . sometimes when I listen to these reports I think oh

82 perhaps I should be vegetarian and sometimes er you wonder about the meat=

83 L4: =how the people who offer food on the street how can you ((2))

84 T: =er you can't er check that they're=

85 L4: =no no I mean what the name?

86 T: er oh well street vendors? you could say yes (**writes on board**) er vendors from to sell yes?

87	people selling things on the street whether it's food or or anything else we call it street
88	vendors yeah? so of course you can't CHECK that that what their hygiene is so well you've
89	no choice you take a RISK if you buy a hamburger from someone who's selling on the street
90	((1)) I would think twice I think **(laughs)** be very very hungry before I actually bought a
91	hamburger in the street alTHOUGH some of course are very clean I wouldn't say they're all
92	unhygienic so yes just remember the words then er hygiene hygienic unhygienic I I'm going
93	to CHECK the spellings in a minute I'm not sure they're completely correct

include confirmation checks, where teachers make sure they understand learners; comprehension checks, ensuring that learners understand the teacher; repetition; clarification requests, asking students for clarification; reformulation, rephrasing a learner's utterance; turn completion, finishing a learner's contribution; backtracking, returning to an earlier part of a dialogue. These strategies operate at the level of interaction rather than solo performance; they are used to ensure that the discourse flows well and that the complex relationship between language use and learning is maintained. Interestingly, perhaps, teachers rarely ask learners to modify their speech, often relying instead on imposing their own interpretation. Very often this results in teachers 'filling in the gaps' and 'smoothing over' learner contributions, as a means of maintaining the flow of a lesson or in order to create a flawless discourse. Unfortunately, by so doing, learners may be denied crucial opportunities for learning. Arguably, by seeking clarification and requesting confirmation, by getting learners to reiterate their contributions, by paraphrasing and extending learner contributions, in sum, by 'shaping' what learners say, teachers are greatly helping learners' language development.

An example of how this works is presented in extract 1.2 on p. 10. Here, the teacher is working with a group of upper intermediate adult learners and the focus is academic writing. By seeking clarification and by negotiating meaning, the teacher helps the learners to express themselves more fully and more clearly. Note how learner turns are frequently longer and more complex than those of the teacher (122, 126). In the extract, this teacher works pretty hard to adopt a more facilitative role, seeking clarification (121, 123, 129) and eliciting from the learners descriptions of their writing strategies. Clarification requests are extremely valuable in promoting opportunities for learning since they 'compel' learners to reformulate their contribution, by rephrasing or paraphrasing. There is clear evidence in this extract that the teacher's unwillingness to accept the learner's first contribution (in 123, 125) promotes a longer and higher-quality contribution in 126. Note too how the teacher shows confirmation and understanding (in 121, 123, 125, 129) through the backchannels 'yes' and 'right'. Backchannels are very important in all human interaction since they tell the speaker that the listener has understood and is following what is being said. They 'oil the wheels' of the interaction and ensure that communication occurs. Consider how you feel during a telephone call when there is silence at the other end of the line – you have no way of knowing that you have been understood. The same is true in classroom interactions.

Extract 1.2

```
121  T:    =yes so tell me again what you mean by that?=
122  L:    =the first is the introduction the second eh in this case
           we have the ((3)) who you are to eh introduce yourself
           a few words about yourself and where you live and
           what I do [and]
123  T:    [so ] . . . yes?=
124  L:    =and then it's the problem what happened . . .
125  T:    yes=
126  L:    =and you need to explain it and why you are writing
           because probably you did something like you gave
           the information to the police but it didn't happen . . .
127  T:    so can I ask you why did you write it in your head as
           you said?=
128  L:    =I don't know it's like a rule=
129  T:    =right so it's like a rule what do you mean? . . .
```

We have seen, then, that modified speech is a key element of classroom interaction and one that can have profound effects on the quantity and quality of the learning that takes place. Effective speech modification ensures that learners feel safe and included and gives them the confidence to participate in the interaction. It also minimises breakdowns and misunderstandings and creates a sense of purposeful dialogue in which a group of learners is engaged in a collective activity. Although we do have some understandings of the role of speech modification in teaching and learning, there are a number of questions that remain unanswered:

- Do some types of speech modification create opportunities for learning?

- Do some hinder opportunities for learning?

- How might teachers help learners modify *their* speech?

- How might teachers gain a closer understanding of the relationship between speech modification and learner participation?

We shall return to these questions in Chapter 3.

Elicitation techniques

Elicitation techniques are the strategies used by (normally) teachers to get learners to respond. Typically, elicitation entails asking questions.

Task 1.2

Add as many reasons as possible to the following list of reasons why teachers ask so many questions. Then suggest alternatives to questions:

- To provide a model.

- To check comprehension.

- To test.

- To activate learners' responses.

- To stimulate practice.

Classroom discourse is dominated by question and answer routines, with teachers asking most of the questions, while learners ask correspondingly few questions. It is by asking questions that teachers are able to control the discourse, especially given that they know the answers to most of the questions they ask! Questions like these, where teachers already know the answer (for example, 'what's the past tense of *go*?') are called display questions since they require learners to display what they know. Classrooms are unique in that for most of the questions that are asked, the answer is already known. Imagine if you were to ask your friends or family questions to which you already know the answer – they would find this very strange, abnormal even! Yet in classrooms this practice is the norm. Display questions serve a range of functions, including:

- eliciting a response;
- checking understanding;
- guiding learners towards a particular response;
- promoting involvement;
- concept checking.

Essentially, the defining characteristic of display questions is to check or evaluate: understanding, concepts, learning, previous learning and so on. Responses tend to be short, simple, restricted, often comprising one or two words. Rather than opening up space for learning, they tend to close it down and result in a rather stereotypical, almost mechanical type of interaction that is often exemplified in IRF[1] sequences (see below).

Apart from display questions, teachers also ask genuine, more open-ended questions, designed to promote discussion and debate, engage learners and produce longer, more complex responses. These so-called referential questions result in more 'natural' responses by learners, often longer and more complicated, and resulting in a more conversational type of interaction. Referential questions often begin with a *wh-* question such as *who, why, what*, etc. From a teaching and learning perspective, the distinction between display and referential is less important than the relationship between a teacher's pedagogic goal and choice of question. If the aim is to quickly check understanding or establish what learners already know, display questions are perfectly adequate. If, on the other hand, the aim is to promote discussion or help learners improve oral fluency, then referential questions are more appropriate. The extent to which a question produces a communicative response is less important than the extent to which a question serves its purpose at a particular point in a lesson. In short, the use of appropriate questioning strategies requires an understanding of the *function* of a question in relation to what is being taught.

Consider the two extracts following. In extract 1.3 on p. 13, the teacher is working with a group of low-intermediate adult learners. The class has recently read a story and here, the teacher is simply recapping. It is immediately obvious that the turn-taking, participation and contribution of each learner are all tightly controlled by the teacher's use of display questions. In lines 11, 13 and 15, the teacher simply gets students to 'display' what they already know from what they have read. The interaction is rapid and allows little space for full responses, indicated by the latched turns (=: one turn follows another with no pausing or silence). Learner responses are short, typically two or three words and there is no space here for topic development (in lines 12, 14 and 16). We can surmise from this that the teacher's goal was to check understanding before moving on: her choice of display questions here is entirely in tune with her teaching goal. The ensuing discourse is 'classic IRF', with each teacher contribution serving to both evaluate a learner response and move the discourse forward with another prompt (again, in 11, 13, 15).

Extract 1.3

9	T:	I'll see if I have a (2) a photocopy (**looks for papers**) right you can't find it? look you
10		have this book and cos I've got another book here good ... so can you read question
11		2 Junya
12	L1:	(**reading from book**) where was Sabina when this happened?
13	T:	right yes where was Sabina? (4) in unit ten where was she?
14	L:	er go out=
15	T:	=she went out yes so first she was in the=
16	L:	=kitchen=
17	T:	=kitchen good and then what did she take with her?
18	T:	L: =er drug=
19	T:	=good she took the memory drug and she ran OUT

Compare extract 1.3 with extract 1.4 on p. 14. In 1.4, it is immediately evident that learners have more interactional space and freedom in both what they say and when they say it. This is a multilingual group of advanced learners, preparing for a reading activity on the supernatural. The teacher's opening question is perceived as a genuine one – he is seeking the opinions of the group. Note the two-second pause (in line 50) and the relatively short responses by learners in 51 and 52. But it is the question *why not* in 53, accompanied by the seven seconds of silence, which promotes the long learner turn in 54. Seven seconds of silence is very unusual in most classrooms; typically, the average wait time (the length of time that elapses between a teacher's question and learner response) is around one second. In line 54, and following seven seconds of silence, learner 3 produces an elaborated response and works hard to express herself. While to us, as outsiders, the meaning is not immediately apparent, the teacher seems satisfied with her contribution and moves on to another student, Monica, in 57. The teacher's comments (in 53 and 57) are non-evaluative, relating more to the content of the message than the language used to express it. By being non-evaluative, and by asking genuine questions and allowing pauses, the teacher succeeds in eliciting fuller, more complex responses from the learners and in promoting a more engaged, conversational type of interaction. His choice of questions is extremely important to the resulting extended learner turns and produces a more equal exchange, similar to casual conversation.

Extract 1.4

50	T:	I agree do you do you believe in this kind of stuff? We talked about UFOs and stuff yesterday (2)
51	L:	no . . .
52	L:	well maybe . . .
53	T:	maybe no why not? (7)
54	L3:	um I'm not a religious person and that's the thing I associate with religion and
55		believe in supernaturals and things like that and believe in god's will and that's so far
56		from me so no=
57	T:	I understand so and why maybe Monica? . . .
58	L4:	well I'm also not connected with religion but maybe also something exists but I
59		erm am rather sceptical but maybe people who have experienced things maybe=
60	T:	uh huh and what about you [do you]

Repair

Repair simply refers to the ways in which teachers deal with errors. It includes direct and indirect error correction and the ways in which teachers identify errors in the discourse. Clearly, there is a range of types of error correction available to a teacher at any point in time. As with all strategies, some will be more or less appropriate than others at any given moment. The basic choices facing a teacher are:

- ignore the error completely;
- indicate that an error has been made and correct it;
- indicate that an error has been made and get the learner who made it to correct it;
- indicate that an error has been made and get other learners to correct it.

These choices correlate very closely to the work of conversation analysts who recognise four types of error correction in naturally occurring conversation: self-initiated self repair, self-initiated other repair, other-initiated self repair, other initiated other repair (see Sacks *et al.* 1974).

It is apparent when we look at classroom transcripts that error correction occupies a considerable amount of teachers' time. According to van Lier, 'apart from questioning, the activity that most characterises language classrooms is correction of errors' (1988: 276). He goes on to suggest that there are essentially two conflicting views of error correction: one that says we should avoid error correction at all costs since it affects the flow of classroom communication, the other that says we must correct all errors so that learners acquire a 'proper' standard. As teachers, we need to decide on the type and frequency of error correction. Again, the strategies selected must be related to the pedagogic goals of the moment. A highly controlled practice activity requires more error correction than one where the focus is oral fluency.

It is perhaps also true to say that, within the classroom, learners do expect to have their errors corrected. While it may not be appropriate in more naturalistic settings for speakers to correct each others' errors, in classrooms, this is both what learners want and expect. As Seedhouse (1997: 571) puts it, 'making linguistic errors and having them corrected directly and overtly is not an embarrassing matter'. Rather than deciding whether we should or should not correct errors, teachers would do well to consider the appropriacy of a particular strategy in relation to their intended goals. By adopting more conscious strategies and by understanding how a particular type of error correction impacts on the discourse, teachers can do much to tailor their error correction to the 'moment' and promote opportunities for learning.

A sample of data is perhaps the best way to gain a closer understanding of the need to tailor repair strategy to pedagogic goal. Consider extract 1.5 on p. 16, in which the teacher is working with a group of eight pre-intermediate adult learners. Her stated aim is 'to improve oral fluency'. The most striking feature of the interaction is the overlapping speech (indicated [ ]). It is apparent from the data that this teacher believes that repair is necessary; there are examples of error correction in almost every teacher turn (277, 279, 281, etc.). The student is really unable to express herself adequately owing to the fact that the teacher interrupts so much in order to correct errors. It is only in line 286 that she is really able to produce an extended turn, presumably something the teacher wanted throughout given her stated aim of improving oral fluency. While it is apparently this teacher's intention to help the learner by correcting errors, it is also clear that over-correction is not very helpful. The flow of the exchange is disrupted to the point that the learner is unable to clearly articulate what she wants to say. While we are not claiming that this is a deliberate strategy on the part of the teacher, this extract does underline the need to match error correction strategy to the pedagogic goal of the moment. In extract 1.6, we see a mismatch between the teacher's intended goal and the language used to realise it. The result is interaction that is disjointed and lacking in coherence.

Extract 1.5

273	T:	what about in Spain if you park your car illegally?
274	L4:	. . . there are two possibilities
275	T:	two [possibilities]
276	L4:	[one] is er I park my car ((1)) and
277	T:	yes . . . if I park . . . my car . . . illegally again Rosa
278	L4:	**(laughter)** if I park my car [illegally]
279	T:	[illegally]
280	L4:	police stat policeman er give me give me
281	T:	GIVES me
282	L4:	gives me? a little small paper if er I can't pay the money
283	T:	it's called a FINE remember a FINE yes?
284	L4:	or if if my car
285	T:	is parked
286	L4:	is parked illegally . . . the policeman take my car and . . . er . . . go to the
287		police station not police station it's a big place where where they have some
288		[cars] they

Task 1.3

Look at extract 1.6 below. Comment on the teacher's error correction strategy. How appropriate is it here where the teacher is trying to elicit student feelings and attitudes? What is the effect of the error correction on the discourse?

Extract 1.6

11	T:	ok does anyone agree with his statement?
12	L:	(2) erm I am agree=
13	T:	=agree be careful with the verb to agree there you as well Ensa that it's WE
14		agree it's not to be agree it's to agREE Ok=
15	L:	[oh I agree]
16	L:	((3))
17	T:	I agree with you but not I AM agree with you the verb is to agree ok so ((3)) to

18		agree with (**writing on board**) is the preposition that follows it I so it's I agree
19		with you I disagree with you … ok em Silvie can you em what were you going
20		to say?
21	L2:	I agree with you because em when when we talk about something em for
22		Example you saw a ((2)) on TV=

In this section, I have described some of the most important features of classroom discourse and illustrated them using data extracts. These features were teacher's control of the discourse, speech modification, elicitation and repair. I have tried to show how different strategies are more or less appropriate according to the particular pedagogic goal of the moment and the teacher's understanding of local context.

In the following section, I present a summary of the work on spoken interaction in classrooms, whereby all interaction can be described and analysed according to a three-part exchange structure.

The IRF exchange structure

One of the most important features of all classroom discourse is that it follows a fairly typical and predictable structure, comprising three parts: a teacher Initiation, a student Response, and a teacher Feedback, commonly known as **IRF**, or **IRE**, Initiation, Response, Evaluation. IRE is preferred by some writers and practitioners to reflect the fact that, most of the time, teachers' feedback is an evaluation of a student's contribution. Teachers are constantly assessing the correctness of an utterance and giving feedback to learners.

This three-part structure was first put forward by Sinclair and Coulthard in 1975 and is known as the IRF exchange structure. The work of Sinclair and Coulthard has had a huge impact on our understandings of the ways in which teachers and learners communicate and has led to many advances in the field. IRF is also known as a **recitation script** or **tryadic structure** (see the glossary).

Look at the example below:

Extract 1.7

1	Teacher:	So, can you read question two, Junya.	I
2	Junya:	[Reading from book] Where was Sabina when this happened?	R
3	Teacher:	Right, yes, where was Sabina.	F
4		In Unit 10, where was she?	I

| 5 | Junya: | Er, go out . . . | **R** |
| 6 | Teacher: | She went out, yes. | **F** |

(Walsh 2001)

In this extract, which is typical of all teacher–learner interaction and occurs very frequently in classrooms all around the world, we can see how the teacher opens the exchange and marks a new phase of activity with the discourse marker 'so'. This opening remark, or initiation (**I**), leads to the question in line 1, which prompts the student response [**R**] in line 2. In line 3, we see how the teacher offers feedback (**F**) to what the learner has said ('Right, yes'). Feedback is an important feature of the three-part exchange since it allows learners to see whether their response has been accepted or not. Frequently, feedback entails some kind of evaluation, such as *good, right, ok*.

In line 3, the cycle begins again, with the next initiation ('where was Sabina?'), which is then clarified in line 4 ('in unit 10, where was she?'). In 5, we see the learner's grammatically incorrect response ('er go out'), followed in 6 by the teacher's feedback and correction. This second IRF sequence follows very logically from the first and was probably followed by a third. Based on this very brief extract, we can make a number of observations about IRF, the most commonly occurring discourse structure in any classroom:

- It enables us to understand the special nature of classroom interaction.

- It enables us to understand why teachers talk so much more than learners: for every utterance made by a learner (**R**), teachers typically make two (**I, F**).

- It allows us to see how, if overused, classroom interaction can become very mechanical, even monotonous. Teachers need to be aware of this.

While the IRF sequence is both commonly found and appropriate at certain times, there are other types of exchange that are more desirable/useful to learning. We'll come back to this point later.

Sinclair and Coulthard's original work took place in L1 primary classes. Based on recordings of teachers and pupils interacting in class, they produced a hierarchical model for understanding classroom discourse. They found that there were three basic kinds of exchange:

1 question-and-answer sequences;

2 pupils responding to teachers' directions;

3 pupils listening to the teacher giving information.

While it is true to say that conversations outside the classroom frequently have a three-part structure, speakers do not usually evaluate one another's performances. Just imagine how your friends or family members would feel if you were to 'evaluate' their remarks all the time!

Here's an example of a typical 'real-world' exchange:

Extract 1.8

1	A:	What's the last day of the month?	**I**
2	B:	Friday.	**R**
3	A:	Friday. We'll invoice you on Friday.	**F/I**
4	B:	That would be brilliant.	**R**
5	A:	And fax it over to you.	**I**
6	B:	Er, well I'll come and get it.	**R**
7	A:	Okay.	**F**

In extract 1.8, a business encounter, the interaction is opened by A in line 1 with a question (an initiation). B's response in line 2 is then confirmed by A in line 3 (feedback), followed by a second initiation by A ('we'll invoice you on Friday'). Note how this second initiation is not a question, but still requires some kind of a response, which B gives in line 4. Note too how, in everyday communication, the feedback move is optional. B's response in line 4 is followed by another initiation by A in line 5. (Although, it is also true to say that feedback does not always occur in classrooms, it is far more prevalent than in everyday exchanges outside the classroom. That is, most responses by learners receive some kind of feedback from the teacher.) Going back to extract 1.8, we see how the exchange concludes with a third tryadic exchange in lines 5–7 comprising an initiation by A (line 5), a response by B (line 6) and feedback by A (line 7). In everyday settings then, even the most simple, ordinary encounter such as a question and response often has three parts to it and not two as people often think. It is also interesting to note that in the world outside the classroom, responses and follow-ups are not usually reactions to test questions (speaker A is not testing speaker B on what day it is, unlike the teacher, above, who was testing the learners' understanding), but show that the speakers have understood one another, and are satisfied with the way the interaction is progressing (*Friday / that would be brilliant / okay*).

For language teachers, understanding the discourse of the classroom itself is crucial, for we teach discourse *through* discourse with our learners. This is another way of saying that in many parts of the world, the main exposure to discourse in English that learners will have is in the classroom itself, via the teacher. A number of studies have compared the discourse of the classroom with 'real' communication (e.g. Nunan 1987). But as van Lier says (1988: 267), 'the classroom is part of the real world, just as much as the airport, the interviewing room, the chemical laboratory, the beach and so on.'

From this brief introduction to the exchange structure of classrooms, we can make a number of important observations:

- All classroom discourse is goal-oriented. The responsibility for establishing goals and 'setting the agenda' lies largely with the teacher. Pedagogic goals and the language used to achieve them are very closely related, even intertwined.

- The prime responsibility for what is said in the classroom lies with the teacher. Teachers control the discourse through the special power and authority they have, but also through their control of the discourse. They control who may speak and when, for how long and on what topic. They control turn-taking through the use of IRF; not only do they initiate a response, they offer an evaluation – further evidence of control.

- Learners take their cues from the teacher and rarely initiate a response. Their role, one which they are socialised into from a very early age, is to answer questions, respond to prompts and so on.

- The IRF sequence enables us to understand interaction in the classroom, and comprehend its special nature. An awareness of IRF enables us to consider how we might vary interaction more and introduce alternative types of sequence (see Chapter 8).

- An understanding of the IRF sequence enables us to model spoken language in the world outside the classroom, suggesting ways of constructing dialogues for teaching, role-plays for practicing conversation, etc.

Challenges for teachers and learners

From what we now know about classroom discourse, what are the challenges that lie ahead for both teachers and learners? In this brief overview, I posit a number of directions for future developments and then return to these in subsequent chapters.

One of the most striking and noteworthy observations about classroom discourse and language teaching is how little time is actually spent making language teachers aware of its importance. Most teacher education programmes, either pre- or in-service pay very little attention to classroom interaction. Typically, teacher education programmes offer some kind of subject-based preparation and training in classroom methodology; a model comprising two strands which is used all over the world. I would advocate a 'third strand' on teacher education programmes that deals specifically with interaction in the classroom. The aim is to sensitise language teachers to the centrality of interaction to teaching and learning and provide them with the means of acquiring close understandings of their local contexts. I suggest that classroom processes will only improve once teachers have the means of understanding local context and are able to improve it. Classroom interaction lies at the heart of this.

A second and related challenge for teachers is the need to acquire what I am calling Classroom Interactional Competence (CIC). Although this is given a fuller treatment in Chapter 8, it is worth introducing it briefly here. When we analyse classroom transcripts, it is immediately obvious that levels of interactional competence vary hugely from one context and from one teacher to another. Some teachers, at some points in time, are very adept at managing interaction in such a way that learning and learning opportunities are maximised. Others use interactional strategies that 'get in the way' and that impede opportunities for learning (Walsh 2002). Examples have been presented throughout this chapter in the various data extracts we have studied.

I define CIC as 'teachers' and learners' ability to use interaction as a tool for mediating and assisting learning' (Walsh 2006: 130). The assumption is that by first understanding and then extending CIC, there will be greater opportunities for learning: enhanced CIC results in more learning-oriented interactions. Teachers demonstrate CIC in a number of ways. For example, ensuring that language use and pedagogic goals are aligned is an important characteristic of CIC. As we have seen in some of the extracts presented here, teachers' use of language and their goals must work together. Other features include the use of extended wait time: allowing a reasonable time to elapse after asking a question and not interrupting students all the time; extending learner responses by careful management of the interaction and paraphrasing a learner's utterance, for example. Similarly, teachers need to be able to help learners as and when needed by scaffolding a contribution, offering a key piece of vocabulary or introducing a new phrase as and when needed, for example. Achieving CIC will only happen if teachers are able to understand interactional processes and make changes to the ways in which they manage classroom interaction.

Other challenges facing teachers in the future is the need to gain a fuller understanding of the relationship between classroom methodologies and classroom interaction. This will be dealt with more fully in Chapter 2, but suffice to say here that a closer understanding of how interactional features manifest themselves in, for example, task-based learning, can only be of benefit to teachers and learners alike. How, for example, does task-type affect interaction and what is the consequence for learning? How might more effective management of classroom interaction result in a more engaged, more dialogic type of learning? And what do we know of the importance of interaction during feedback following a task? This, according to many researchers is the most important part of the task-based cycle and the one most likely to lead to learning. There is much work to do in this area.

From a learner's perspective, a number of challenges lie ahead. Perhaps the biggest and most difficult one is the need to change the interactional behaviours of learners so that they play a more equal role in classroom discourse. When we consider the ways in which learners are socialised into certain types of classroom behaviour, this is a huge challenge. In most content-based subjects, learners answer questions, respond to cues, follow the teacher's initiative, avoid interrupting and so on. And yet, in a language classroom, a very different set of interactional traits is needed if learners are to play a more equal part in the discourse. In language classrooms, we need learners to both ask and answer questions, to interrupt where appropriate, to take the initiative, seize the floor, hold a turn and so on. By following learnt behaviours that are the product of many years of being socialised into classroom rituals and practices, we may be facilitating the kind of 'smooth' discourse profile that prevails at the moment. But are we helping to create interactions that result in learning? I suggest that we need to encourage interactions that have a more 'jagged' profile in which learners play a more central role in co-constructing meanings and in ensuring that there are opportunities for negotiation, clarification and the like. A jagged classroom interaction profile has more of the features that would be found in naturally occurring interactions such as everyday conversation, business encounters and the like. While not denying that the language classroom is a social context in its own right, many of its features are determined by the fact that control of the communication lies with the teacher. In other contexts, roles are much more equal, resulting in different interactional features. Turns are longer, for example, and there are more frequent topic changes. Overlaps and interruptions are more common, as are pauses. I am suggesting that it is in this kind of interaction that learners have the opportunity to acquire the kinds of linguistic and interactional resources that will help them develop as learners. Teachers, while still playing a more central role, would need a far more sophisticated understanding of classroom discourse in order to be able to manage the interaction. We'll return to these ideas in Chapter 8.

Summary

In this chapter, I have provided a brief sketch of some of the main features of L2 classroom discourse, presented under four main themes:

control of patterns of communication, teachers' modified language, elicitation and repair. These themes, or features of classroom discourse, have been chosen because they are representative of the kinds of interaction that typically occur in second language (and other) classrooms. One of the most commonly found structures – the IRF exchange – was then introduced and exemplified. This 'tryadic discourse', first postulated by Sinclair and Coulthard in 1975, is still by far the most commonly occurring discourse structure to be found in classrooms all over the world. Finally, we considered some of the challenges facing both teachers and learners in language classrooms. In Chapter 2, we build on some of these themes by looking at the relationship between classroom discourse and teaching.

Note

1   IRF is explained in the next section. It means teacher initiation, learner response, teacher feedback and is the basic unit of discourse in any classroom.

2 Classroom discourse and teaching

Introduction

In this chapter, we look at the relationship between classroom inter-action and teaching. The basic argument is that teachers can do much to improve their professional practice and enhance learning by studying their own interactions with students, a theme to which we shall return later in the book (see Chapters 6, 7 and 8). The starting point here is to consider how classroom contexts are created through interaction and to then identify how teachers might gain a closer understanding of specific features of the interaction. We then look at the place of interaction in one specific teaching methodology, task-based language teaching (TBLT), before looking at the ways in which teachers' use of linguistic and interactional resources can result in enhanced teaching. In the final section of the chapter, we look at ways in which a focus on classroom interaction can result in teacher development.

Classrooms as contexts

The word *context* has many different meanings and associations. A quick search on the internet produces these:

1 The part of a text or statement that surrounds a particular word or passage and determines its meaning.

2 The circumstances in which an event occurs; a setting.

3 The parts of a piece of writing, speech, etc., that precede and follow a word or passage and contribute to its full meaning. Example: 'It is unfair to quote out of context.'

4 The conditions and circumstances that are relevant to an event, fact, etc.

(www.thefreedictionary.com/context)

From these definitions, we can see that the word *context* can be used to describe both the background against which an event took place and the language used in that event. Of course, there are many, many ways of looking at context, but seeing contexts as a set of circumstances accomplished through language will suit our purposes here. Classrooms are unique social contexts in their own right. As we saw in Chapter 1, classrooms can be characterised and described by looking at a range of interactional features such as teacher elicitation strategies, learner responses and teacher evaluations. Any of the features identified in Chapter 1 mark the discourse as being typical of a classroom. Most of us reading a transcript of a lesson would be able to identify it as a piece of classroom discourse, and make specific comments on what was happening in the discourse.

On the one hand, then, we can say that classrooms are easy to identify and characterise as sites of social interaction. They have interactional features that are easy to recognise and they follow certain routines and procedures that set them apart from other social contexts such as business meetings or dinner parties. And we are able to talk about classroom contexts in different settings. For example, we know that by studying transcripts, we can say with some certainty whether the interactions took place in a primary or secondary classroom, an L1 or L2 context, a lecture theatre, online, and so on. The reason that we are able to do this is that the interaction reveals 'what is really happening' in a classroom and enables us to make assumptions about teaching and learning. So when we talk about the context of a lesson, we can point to things like the age and level of the learners, whether it's a foreign or second language setting, who the teacher is, what materials are being used, the amount of freedom the teacher has to follow her own agenda, and so on. This is context at one level, and it certainly provides us with useful information that may inform practice or aid decisions concerning planning materials, writing a curriculum, selecting assessment procedures and so on.

However, what we are interested in here is a different view of context, one that is much more fine-grained and that helps us understand the moment-by-moment decisions made by teachers 'online', as they teach. Here, then, we are concerned to identify features of the interaction that give a lesson or a teaching session its unique shape, or 'architecture' (Heritage 1997). Only by looking in some detail at the interactions that take place, I suggest, can we gain the kind of up close and emic or insider understandings needed to inform good practice. It is by looking at the 'interactional architecture' (c.f. Seedhouse 2004) of a class, that we, as teachers, get some sense of what is happening and, more importantly, why it is happening.

Detailed examinations of classroom discourse reveal how inter-actants collectively co-construct meanings, how errors arise and are repaired, how turns begin, end and are passed or seized. We can identify specific features of the discourse that help us understand how teaching and learning are accomplished. Features like direct error correction, wait-time, teacher echo, display questions and so on provide vital clues as to the ways in which 'space for learning' is either opened up or closed down. This kind of analysis can help us answer questions such as:

- To what extent do teachers include or exclude learners from the interaction?
- How are opportunities for learning created?
- Who holds the floor and for how long?
- What types of question are asked and how are they answered?
- How appropriate is the language to pedagogic goals?

Which types of discourse promote student engagement and dialogue?

Perhaps more importantly, a fine-grained and detailed analysis of micro-contexts offers us unique insights into what is being taught, how and what learners are learning. By looking at the moment-by-moment management of turns and topics we can see, in the interaction, what is being learnt, what is not being learnt, what is the relationship between what teachers teach and what learners learn. Our endeavour is not simply to describe classroom interaction, it is to develop new understandings and improve the ways in which we teach.

In this chapter, we turn our attention to the ways in which an understanding of classroom discourse can help us enhance our understanding of teaching. We will look at how these understandings can be enhanced in terms of whole methodologies (such as task-based language teaching), in relation to the teaching of specific skills (such as speaking or writing), and in response to specific strategies (such as increasing wait-time, reducing teacher echo). Our focus is the moment-by-moment interactions that collectively constitute a lesson, through which contexts are co-constructed and in which meanings are established. We begin with a consideration of what classroom discourse can reveal about task-based language teaching.

Task-based language teaching

One of the most prevalent teaching methodologies to be found throughout the world today is task-based language teaching (TBLT). TBLT is derived from Communicative Language Teaching (CLT), in particular the work of Hymes (1971) and Wilkins (1976). It aims to bring 'real-world' contexts into the classroom, and it emphasises the use of language for completing tasks rather than as a focus for study.

Language is essentially incidental to task completion – the main focus for learners should be the task. According to Willis (2001: 175), TBLT sees language as 'the driving force in language learning'.

One of the reasons for the popularity of TBLT is that interaction is now widely regarded as being central to language acquisition because it is through interaction that learners modify and develop their language system – with or without teacher intervention. By completing a task with others, especially oral communicative tasks, learners are able to identify gaps in their own knowledge, notice connections between different linguistic features, find ways of saying something even when they do not have the most appropriate language, and so on. Essentially, task completion puts learners in the kind of context in which they might find themselves outside the classroom and obliges them to communicate using whatever linguistic resources they have at their disposal.

Clearly, different tasks place different linguistic and cognitive demands on learners, so teachers need to be able to predict what kind of interaction a particular task will produce and what linguistic and inter-actional resources learners will need to complete a task. Similarly, certain tasks will generate more discussion and more interaction than others.

Consider task 2.1 below:

Task 2.1

Look at the following two communicative activities, A and B. For each, make a note of the kind of language that would be needed to complete the task, and comment on levels of enjoyment and involvement that each task might generate. Which task would you prefer and why? What is the main difference between these tasks?

A
'Girls and boys perform better and achieve greater success when they attend single sex schools.' To what extent do you agree or disagree with this statement? Discuss in groups.

B
You have just crashed in a light aircraft on a remote, desert island. You are one of three survivors. You must decide which of the following items to use to help you stay alive. You may only choose five. Discuss in groups and come up with a list and reasons for your choices:

- parachute;

- knife;

- box of matches;

- map;

- axe;

- bottle of whisky;

- ball of string;

- explosives;

- torch;

- magnifying glass.

According to Jane Willis (1996), one of the principal architects of TBLT, there are three phases to this approach:

- pre-task;

- task;

- language focus.

Each phase will require different levels of involvement from both teacher and students, different roles and different types of interaction. Essentially, each task will pass through a number of stages, summarised below:

Pre-task
- **Lead-in**. This will normally entail some kind of context setting where the task and material are introduced. Here, learners' previous understanding of the topic, language or situation are activated (c.f. schemata setting). The lead-in typically begins outside the material.

- **Set-up**. The task must be 'set', normally involving a clear instruction and organisation of learning. How are students to work: in pairs, groups, alone? Do they have some *rehearsal time*? How will instructions be checked? Do students need a time limit?

Task
- **Run the task**. What is role of the teacher here? How to monitor the task and make sure that learners are 'on task'. How to deal with student problems and offer support and guidance without being too intrusive? How to maximise learners' interactional space?

- **Close the task**. How to bring the class back together in plenary? How to deal with early or late finishers?

Language focus

- **Feedback**. How is feedback to be managed given that this is one of the most important stages of TBLT in terms of learning? How are learner contributions to be handled and supported or scaffolded? How to ensure that learner contributions are maximised, and optimised?

- **Post-task**. How to make the *outcome* of one task the *focus* of the next? How to 'build' through the material?

Under TBLT, then, we can see that different types of interaction are more or less appropriate according to which phase we're at. If, for example, the teacher's goal is to set up a task, there will be minimal learner involvement and teachers will simply 'hold the floor' and normally give some kind of instruction that locates teaching in time and space. While the aim of TBLT is to give learners greater opportunities to play an active role in the learning process, it is both unrealistic and inappropriate to discuss teacher talk in 'quantitative terms' as so often happens. Teacher evaluations of their own interaction often refers to the number of questions asked ('I ask too many questions'), learner involvement ('they are a very passive class') or simply the amount of talk ('I talk too much and my students say nothing'). As we have seen, there are times when a lot of teacher talk is entirely appropriate and necessary (setting up a task, for example), while there are others when a much more 'careful' and restricted type of teacher talk is what is needed (during the 'in-task' phase of TBLT, for example). In the next section, we consider how teachers might make more or less use of language in order to enhance the teaching (and learning) process.

Task 2.2

For each of the following extracts, and using the notes above, say what stage of TBLT we are at, comment on the main focus of the interaction and evaluate how effective the interaction is.

Extract 2.1

T: this morning we're going to be reading about and talking about er music and pop stars and famous people Last Christmas we did a quiz do you remember and it was a picture quiz and some of the pictures were people from your countries. Erm let me see could you work with Ben and could you three guys work together (T organises groups). If you recognise any of those people who they are and what you know about them and then what kind of lifestyle do you think these people have.

Extract 2.2

253	L3:	Ahhhh nah the one thing that happens when a person dies ((2)) my mother used to
254		work with old people and when they died . . . the last thing that went out was the
255		hearing ((4)) about this person =
256	T:	=ahaaa
257	L3:	so I mean even if you are unconscious or on drugs or something I mean it's probably
258		still perhaps can hear what's happened (2)
259	L2:	but it gets ((2))=
260	T:	=aha (2)
261	LL:	/but it gets/there are ((2))/=
262	L3:	=I mean you have seen so many operation ((3)) and so you can imagine and when
263		you are hearing the sounds of what happens I think you can get a pretty clear picture
264		of what's really going on there=
265	L:	=yeah=
266	L:	=and and . . .
267	L1:	but eh and eh I don't know about other people but eh ((6)) I always have feeling
268		somebody watching watch watches me=
269	L4:	=yeah=
270	L1:	=somebody just follow me either a man or a woman I don't know if it's a man I feel
271		really exciting if it's a woman ((4)) I don't know why like I'm trying to do things better
272		like I'm eh . . . look like this . . . you feel! it . . . I don't know=

Extract 2.3

66	T:	=yes it's the result of INtensive farming they call it (**writes on board**) which is er (2) yeah and
67		this is for MAXimum profit from erm meat so as a result the animals suffer they have very

68		BAD conditions and very small erm they're given food to really to make them big and fat and
69		usually it's unnatural and as you said they HAVE to give them a lot of antibiotics because the
70		conditions in which they're kept erm they have far more disease than they would normally
71		have so they give them steroids to make them stronger and of course this is now being
72		passed through to the HAMburger that you eat is contaminated with er=
73	L:	=sorry how do you spell anti- anti-biotics?
74	T:	anti-biotics? anti-biotics yes? erm anti-biotics?
75	L:	how to spell it?
76	T:	oh how do you spell it right (**writes on board**) there's er I think I read a very shocking report
77		recently that nearly all for example chickens and beef now pigs all all these that are reared
78		with intensive farming they're ALL given anti-biotics as a matter of course and of course the
79		public don't hear this until quite a long time after we've been eating it and this this is what
80		makes me angry quite a scandal really . . . sometimes when I listen to these reports I think oh
81		perhaps I should be vegetarian and sometimes er you wonder about the meat=
82	L4:	=how the people who offer food on the street how can you ((2))
83	T:	=er you can't er check that they're=
83	L4:	=no no I mean what the name?

Interaction and teaching

In this section, I present one extract of data (extract 2.4) as a means of showing how teachers can create opportunities for learning through their use of language and interactional resources (see Walsh 2002 for a full version of this discussion). In the extract, the teacher facilitates maximum learner involvement by constructing a micro-context in which learners are maximally involved and in which learning opportunities are clearly created. It is not my intention here to evaluate the instructional skills of the teachers, merely to make the point that much can be done to improve teaching when we pay close attention to the way in which language is used.

In the extract that follows, there is clear evidence that the teacher, by controlled use of language and by matching pedagogic and linguistic goals, facilitates and promotes reformulation and clarification, leading to greater involvement and precision of language on the part of the learners.

Extract 2.4

In this extract with six pre-intermediate adult learners from Brazil, Japan, Korea and Russia, the teacher's stated aim is to provide oral fluency practice using material from Harrap's *Intermediate Communication Games*.

480	L4:	the good news is my sister who live in Korea send eh . . .
481	T:	SENT=
482	L4:	=sent sent credit card to me=
483	T:	=ooh very good news . . .
484	L4:	but bad news [is]
485	T:	[the bad] news is . . .
486	L4:	I don't know password . . .
487	LL:	/password/password/ (2)
488	L1:	pin number=
489	T:	=pin number . . .
490	L4:	what?=
491	T:	=pin number pin number=
492	LL:	=/ahh pin number/pen number/=
493	T:	=pin PIN not pen pin=
494	LL:	=/pin/pin number/p-i-n/=
495	L1:	=I always forgot my pin number
496	L:	=ah pin number=
497	T:	=I don't know my pin number
498	L5:	((2)) she can phone you on mobile phone=
499	T:	=she can . . .
500	L5:	she can say [you]
501	T:	[she can] . . .
502	L5:	she can tell your pin number . . .
503	T:	yeah she can [tell you your pin number]
504	L5:	[she can tell you] this pin number by phone . . .
505	L4:	but I I can't eh ring her because eh because eh the time eh=
506	T:	=the time difference?=
507	L4:	=time difference=
508	L5:	=you can count your time for example look what what's the difference time with your
509		country how many hours? (3)

510	L:	eight hours=
511	L5:	=eight hours ok you can phone early in the morning it will be evening in your
512		country=
513	L4:	=if I go to home if ((5)) if I call her Korea it's eh [midnight]
514	L:	[midnight] . . .
515	L5:	ok you can phone in the morning ((3))=
516	L4:	=yeah at [eight]
517	L5:	[at eight] o'clock at nine o'clock you can call=
518	L6:	=in Japan same=
519	T:	=it's the same eight hours?=
520	L6:	=yeah=
521	L4:	=I'm very busy=
522	L5:	=what you are busy it's eh just reason you [((5))]]
523	L4:	[((4))]=
524	T:	=for god's sake give him a break (**laughter**)

In the 44 lines of text that make up this extract, there are several specific features of the teacher's use of language that facilitate learner involvement and create opportunities for learning:

Direct error correction

Maximum economy is used when correcting errors and the teacher opts for a very open and direct approach to error correction, as preferred by learners (Seedhouse 1997). This is far less time-consuming and intrusive than the more 'sensitive' (and therefore time-consuming) error correction strategies preferred by many teachers. Errors are corrected quickly and directly (in 481, 485, 489, 493) and the discourse is allowed to flow with minimal interruption by the teacher. While not suggesting that all error correction should be direct and minimalist, there is a certain logic in keeping error correction to a minimum in oral fluency practice activities in order to reduce interruption and 'maintain the flow'. The teacher in extract 2.4 succeeds very well in achieving this and the discourse is allowed to proceed with minimum interruption.

Content feedback

Many of the features of this extract mirror a naturally occurring conversation and the teacher quite appropriately provides personal reactions to comments made by learners: reacting to a comment made (in 483) and making use of humour (in 524). Given that one of the teacher's stated aims is 'to provide oral fluency practice', her use of conversational language is appropriate to her pedagogic purpose; language use and pedagogic purpose coincide. The teacher's use of language strongly resembles utterances found in the 'real world' and reinforces the aim of promoting oral fluency. Appropriate use of conversational language creates an atmosphere that is conducive to learning and is likely to promote learner involvement. Feedback on the message rather than its form is also more conducive to genuine communication and is more appropriate in the setting outlined here.

Checking for confirmation

Teachers who constantly seek clarification, check for confirmation and who do not always accept the first contribution a student offers are more likely to maximise learning potential than those who do not (Musumeci 1996). In the previous extract, the sole instance of the teacher checking for confirmation (line 519) does serve to maintain the flow and keep channels open. Here, a genuine question by the teacher not only facilitates a more interactive exchange, it ensures that learners are working together and that misunderstandings are minimised.

Extended wait-time

One of the most striking features of the extract is its turn-taking structure. As the discourse progresses, the teacher takes more and more of a 'back-seat' and 'hands over' to the learners. In lines 507–523, learners successfully manage the turn-taking and topic management themselves with no intervention by the teacher. Extended *wait-time*, the time allowed by teachers to answer a question (see, for example, Nunan 1991) not only increases the number of learner responses, it frequently results in more complex answers and leads to an increase in learner/learner interaction. Again, this teacher confirms the importance of maintaining harmony between language use and pedagogic aim; the teacher's use of language, consciously or subconsciously, is very much in tune with her specific aim at this stage of the lesson.

Scaffolding

(See turns 489, 491, 497, 503.) Communication breakdown is a very common feature of L2 classrooms. Often it occurs because learners do not know a particular word or phrase or do not possess the appropriate communicative strategies. To pre-empt breakdown, it is the role of the teacher to intervene and feed in the missing language. Timing and sensitivity to learner needs are of utmost importance and many teachers intervene too often or too early. Scaffolding (Bruner 1990; Lantolf and Thorne 2006) involves more than simply error correction. It is a skill similar to the one possessed by many parents when helping their young children struggling to find the right word at a given moment. It requires the ability to listen actively and make economical use of language. The examples in this extract illustrate this important practice very well: latched modelling (in 489 and 491), where the teacher quickly models the language needed at the end of a previous turn; alternative phrasing (in 497), where she offers a different way of saying something; prompting (in 503).

Of a total of forty-two turns (thirty made by learners, twelve by the teacher), ten teacher contributions succeed (whether intentionally or not) in engaging learners and in promoting longer, more complex turns. Throughout much of the extract, there is clear evidence that the teacher's language use and pedagogic purpose are at one; that the teacher's stated goal of promoting oral fluency is consistent with her use of language. Her verbal behaviour allows learners to play a full and active role in the discourse, producing more complete, more natural responses. Instead of 'smoothing over' the discourse and 'filling in the gaps' by pre-empting learner responses, the teacher only intervenes as and when necessary, giving language support, correcting errors or adding a personal comment of her own.

As far as the learner contributions are concerned, it is evident from this extract that learners and teacher are actively engaged in constructing a piece of discourse which, in many respects, resembles a conversation; an observation that again coincides with the teacher's pedagogic goal and reaffirms the need for teachers to be 'in tune' with their aims and use of language as the lesson unfolds. Throughout this piece, learners self-select (508–516), overlap (511/512, 514/515) and latch (where one turn immediately follows another, as in turns 494/495, 507/508, 509/510); these are all features that are common to naturally occurring conversation and add further weight to the coincidence of language use and pedagogic purpose.

What becomes apparent from this extract is that we cannot talk about the second language classroom context (singular); rather, we need to talk about contexts (plural), in which teachers and learners jointly construct the discourse. In extract 2.4, the discourse is constantly shifting according to the changing agenda of the lesson and according to different participation structures. Successful teaching entails using linguistic and interactional resources that are 'fit for purpose', that enable pedagogic goals and language use to coincide and that take account of the changing nature of the discourse. Under this view of context, a quantitative view of teacher talking time (TTT) is, to a large extent, redundant. What is more important is the *appropriacy* of language used in relation to the 'context of the moment' and task in hand.

Classroom discourse and teacher development

One of the most useful ways to help teachers develop and improve their professional practices is to place classroom discourse at the centre of the process. By helping teachers understand interactional processes more fully and by getting teachers to study their own use of language and its effects on learning, it is possible to greatly enhance microscopic understandings of classroom processes, thereby improving the quality of both teaching and learning.

A number of calls have been made over the years for teachers to discover for themselves what kinds of interaction foster learning and what the role of the teacher is in creating and managing that interaction:

> The challenge set before teachers is to recognise both the obvious in their classrooms and the not so obvious within themselves and their students, to understand how both of these dimensions shape the dynamics of classroom communication, and to equip their second language students with the competencies they need to get the most out of their second language experiences.
>
> (Johnson 1995: 169)

> For teachers to implement pedagogical intentions effectively [. . .] it is important [for them] to develop an understanding of the interactional organisation of the L2 classroom.
>
> (Seedhouse 1997: 574)

> [. . .] the challenge for teachers of ESL students [is] to find out more about the types of interaction that occur in their classrooms, and to also reflect on teaching practice and curriculum implementation which have the potential to facilitate second language development in the classroom context.
>
> (Glew 1998: 5)

Most of the studies on classroom interaction are descriptive rather than pedagogic in nature (Thompson 1997: 99), concerned to further understanding of the process of second language acquisition in the formal context. While these studies have certainly increased understanding of the ways in which languages are learnt in the classroom setting, they are less accessible to the very people they are intended to influence: language teachers.

In the remainder of this chapter, we consider how language teachers might improve their professional practices by focusing on classroom discourse. In the discussion that follows, we evaluate how teachers' use of their own classroom recordings can improve key aspects of their performance. The discussion addresses four key areas for teacher development that can be addressed by looking at classroom discourse data:

1 Improving questioning strategies.

2 Making the discourse more communicative.

3 Improving interactive decision-making.

4 Dealing with reticence.

Improving questioning strategies

In Chapter 1, we saw how questioning occupies much of a language teacher's time. It is one of the most important strategies used in the classroom to elicit response from learners. It is also, arguably, one of the most difficult skills to master, even for the most experienced teacher. In 1990, Keith Richards designed a 'mini-course' that set out to improve teachers' questioning skills through the use of film, self-evaluation and micro-teaching. The quantitative results, summarised below, showed a marked improvement in questioning strategies.

Questioning technique	Before training (frequency)	After training (frequency)
Thought-provoking questions	37.3%	52.0%
Prompting questions	8.5%	13.9%
Repetition of teacher questions	13.7%	4.7%
Teacher answering own questions	4.6%	0.7%

This study clearly underlines the fact that teachers can be trained to ask more appropriate (indeed, fewer) questions and hints at the positive results – in terms of learner involvement – that such strategies can bring. The results summarised by Richards indicate quite clearly a change in the teachers' questioning strategies and the increased potential for learner involvement. Awareness raising, using data from teachers' own lessons, can have far-reaching effects on what students learn and increase opportunities for meaningful participation.

In another study focusing on improving teachers' use of questions, Thompson (1997) highlights the need for language teaching professionals to ask appropriate questions and emphasises the complexity attached to good questioning. In this project, Thompson set out to help trainee teachers on an initial teacher education programme to categorise question types as a way of helping them identify options in their teaching. In other words, there was a concern to ensure that choice of question reflected pedagogic goals. A three-way classification of questions was devised, enabling questions to be analysed according to:

(a) Form. Essentially, this is a grammatical categorisation: whether the questions are closed or open, or, more traditionally, *yes/no* or *wh-*. The distinction is important since closed questions are easier to answer than open ones; asking a closed question may facilitate involvement in the form of a short answer, which can then be followed with an open *wh-* question to extend the learner's contribution.

(b) Content. The focus of the question may relate to personal facts, outside facts or opinions. While the value of 'personalising' questions cannot be denied, since it often results in increased learner investment in the discourse, Thompson argues that 'personalisation does not necessarily mean that real communication is taking place' (1997: 101).

(c) Purpose. The distinction here is between questions that are for display and questions that are for communication. The distinction between referential and display questions has been stated elsewhere (see Chapter 1). According to Thompson, the distinction between display and referential questions is over-stated, the real issue being the extent to which teachers *behave* as if they know the answer to a question; genuine communication can be facilitated when teachers act as if they do not know the answer to a question or deliberately ask questions (about learners' culture or professional background) to which they do not know the answer.

Task 2.3

Comment on the questions used in the extract below. How effective are the strategies used by this teacher? What evidence is there that she is successful in handling questions?

28   T: Have you any idea what country life would have been like?
29   L: Scary.
30   T: Why would it be scary?
31   L: Because it would be dark and there would be no cars or anything.
32   L: There'd be no lights
33   T: But what's it like in the country now?
34   L: It would have been hard work. There would have been big tractors like till do the crops out of the ground.
35   T: Exactly.

The main value of the framework lies in its potential to make practitioners think about their choice of question in relation to what they are doing in the classroom and, more importantly, about their role in the interaction; a realisation, for example, that student contributions do not always have to be evaluated (Thompson 1997: 105). Arguably, the framework has even greater potential for raising awareness when used in conjunction with teacher-generated data such as audio recordings and/or lesson transcripts as against the reading texts employed in the original study.

Making the discourse more communicative

For many years now, researchers and practitioners have been interested in comparing the communication that takes place in classrooms with that of the 'outside' or 'real' world. One of the main reasons for this is the kind of concern expressed here by David Nunan more than twenty years ago (1987: 144), 'in communicative classrooms, interactions may [. . .] not be very communicative after all'. The lack of *genuine* communication in the contemporary second language classroom, has been criticised more overtly by other researchers such as Legutke and Thomas (1991: 8–9): '[. . .] very little is actually communicated in the L2 classroom. The way it is structured does not seem to stimulate the wish of learners to say something, nor does it tap into what they might have to say.'

In a 2008 study, Scott Thornbury had teachers use their own lesson transcripts as a means of raising awareness of the importance of classroom interaction with small groups of trainee teachers. Trainees were asked to record, transcribe and analyse one segment of a lesson, identifying those features of their talk that were felt to be more or less communicative and commenting on them in a written evaluation. From their self-evaluations, the following features of communicative classroom talk were identified:

- Referential questions, which require greater effort and depth of processing on the part of the teacher, one possible reason for language teachers' preference for display questions over referential questions.

- Content feedback, where the focus is on meaning, rather than language form. This is quite rare in many second language classrooms. Most of the feedback from teachers to students is form-focused and deals with language-related issues.

- Wait-time. This is the amount of time a teacher waits after asking a question before getting a response. Typically, it is very short, even less than a second. Thornbury found that even slight increases in wait-time result in an increase in the quantity and quality of learner contributions and an increase in the number of learner questions.

- Student-initiated talk. Requests for clarification and confirmation checks point to ownership of the discourse and suggest that learning, through negotiated meaning, is taking place. When learners are seeking clarification, asking questions or checking their own understanding, they are more likely to be engaged with the learning process.

The main conclusions from Thornbury's study are that teachers can be sensitised to making their classrooms more communicative through a more appropriate use of language and interactional resources. He also commented on the fact that getting students to work in groups and pairs is not in itself 'communicative' and that learners need to be helped and guided if they are to really engage with L2 classroom discourse. Later in this book, we'll see how teachers can foster student-centredness while performing a central role in managing the interactions that take place. Simply 'handing over' to learners will not, I suggest, in itself result in a student-centred, communicative classroom.

In a second study aimed at helping teachers make more communicative use of their language, Richard Cullen argues that there is a need to analyse teachers' use of language from a *qualitative* rather than *quantitative* perspective. 'Good' teacher talk does not necessarily mean 'little' teacher talk; rather, effective teacher talk 'facilitates learning and promotes communicative interaction' (1998: 179). Very often, teachers are concerned to reduce the amount of teacher talk in their classes, while, at the same time, increasing the amount of learner talk. A quantitative approach to classroom talk is less helpful than a more qualitative one in which talk is evaluated according to its purpose in a lesson at a particular moment (see, for example, Seedhouse 2004; Walsh 2006).

In the 1998 study, Cullen suggests that the communicativeness of classroom discourse should be judged in accordance with what constitutes 'communicative' in that context, as opposed to what is communicative in other social contexts. Models of communication that constantly compare the second language classroom with the 'real world' are unrealistic and may be unattainable for many teachers; put simply, the classroom has to be treated as a context in its own right. Any attempt to judge the communicativeness of teacher (or learner) talk should be made in relation to what is meant by 'communicative' in that context.

Four features of communicative teacher talk are identified – referential questions, content feedback, speech modifications, negotiation of meaning – in addition to features of non-communicative teacher talk that include excessive use of display questions, form-focused feedback, teacher echo, sequences of IRF discourse chains. Any analysis of the communicative value of teacher talk should take account not only of its ability to foster meaningful communication among learners, but also of the extent to which it coincides with the teacher's pedagogic purpose. For example, the communicativeness of an instruction would be measured in terms of how well that instruction was carried out or the extent to which it permitted negotiation of meaning or clarification by learners.

According to Cullen, there are three advantages to this approach. First, the categories of teacher talk are based on what goes on in the classroom, not what goes on in a another social context. Second, any evaluation of the communicativeness of teacher talk is based on 'what it takes to be communicative in the context of the classroom itself' (see above). Third, a model of communicative language teaching recognising the importance of pedagogic functions is more likely to be achieved by practising teachers than one that constantly compares the L2 classroom with the outside world. By getting teachers to look at the pedagogic value of their talk, the extent to which communication and pedagogic purpose coincide, a far more realistic, and for many practitioners, a far more easily attainable, model of classroom communication can be constructed. The communicativeness of classroom discourse has to be related to its context: the second language classroom; only then can accurate and fair measures of its 'worth' be made (Cullen 1998: 186).

Enhanced interactive decision-making

One of the key characteristics of effective teaching is good decision-making. Put simply, good teachers make good interactive decisions; decisions that are appropriate to the moment, that engage learners, that seek out opportunities to teach, that facilitate learning and learning opportunity.

Look at the extract on p. 42 in which a teacher working with a group of intermediate adult learners is getting the class to describe funny experiences from their school days. The extract begins with an open question in 1, followed by a request for clarification in 2. Following the clarification in 3, the learner gives a response in 4 that is corrected and extended by the teacher in 5. His request for more information ('what happened, what made it funny'?) results in an extended learner response (6), which is clarified by the teacher in 8 and re-articulated by L1 in 9. The teacher paraphrases this contribution in 10 and this receives confirmation from L1 in 11.

What is interesting in this extract is the way in which the teacher constantly clarifies, extends and summarises for the class. He does not simply accept the first L1 contribution in 4, but asks for more details. This process requires the teacher to make decisions that are interactive, which enable learners to sustain a turn and allow the rest of the class to follow the discourse. At any point in this interaction, the teacher could have simply closed down the learner's contribution and moved on to another student. He chose not to and succeeded in engaging this learner in an extended piece of spoken interaction.

Extract 2.5

1	T:	what was the funniest thing that happened to you at school (1) Tang?
2	L1:	funniest thing?
3	T:	the funniest
4	L1:	the funniest thing I think out of school was go to picnic
5	T:	go on a picnic? So what happened what made it funny?
6	L1:	go to picnic we made playing or talking with the teacher more closely because in the school
7		we have a line you know he the teacher and me the student=
8	T:	=so you say there was a gap or a wall between the teacher and the students so when you=
9	L1:	if you go out of the school you went together with more **(gestures 'closer' with hands)**=
10	T:	=so you had a closer relationship [outside the school]
11	L1:	[yeah yeah]

Here's what the same teacher said about this extract:

Basically he's explaining that on a picnic there wasn't this gap that there is in a classroom – psychological gap – that's what I'm drawing out of him. There's a lot of scaffolding being done by me in this monitoring, besides it being managerial, there's a lot of scaffolding because I want to get it flowing, I want to encourage them, keep it moving as it were. I'm clarifying to the class what he's saying because I know in an extended turn – a broken turn – and it's not exactly fluent and it's not articulate – I try to re-interpret for the benefit of the class so that they're all coming with me at the same time and they all understand the point being made by him.

The teacher's comments suggest quite clearly that his interactive decisions are both conscious and appropriate for this stage of the interaction. He shows great awareness here of both this learner's needs and the needs of the class as a whole. He also makes very good use of an appropriate metalanguage to discuss what he perceives to be happening in the data (scaffolding, clarifying, extended turn, re-interpret for the class, etc.). From these two extracts, we can see the importance of developing interactive decision-making strategies in order to promote learner engagement and to create opportunities for learning.

In a 1996 study, Kathy Bailey addressed teachers' decision-making and looked at the ways in which teachers' interactive decisions cause them to depart from their lesson plan. Her concern was to develop understandings of the decisions teachers took to depart from their lesson plans. Essentially, the concern was to understand the ways in which teachers move away from 'ritualistic' routines and practices while teaching and adopt alternative practices at given moments in a lesson. Participating teachers were simply asked to view lesson extracts where they had departed from their lesson plan and justify the interactional decisions taken. From their interview comments, Bailey established the following six principles of interactive decision-making:

1 Serve the common good. Where several learners are perceived by the teacher as having the same problem (raised by one student's question), there can be some justification for dealing with the problem (linguistic or otherwise) at length, resulting in a departure from what was planned.

2 Teach to the moment. Lessons may be abandoned completely or partially when a "window of opportunity" (page 28) results in the teaching of something pertinent to the moment. (Here, the lesson-plan was dropped completely in response to a question about the American electoral college system.)

3 Further the lesson. Decisions pertaining to the organisation of learning may result in changes to what was originally planned. For example, a planned group-work activity may be rejected in favour of completing the task individually.

4 Accommodate learning styles. Preferences by learners about the way 'things get done' in the classroom may result in departures from what was planned.

5 Promote students' involvement. Learners may be encouraged to develop a contribution that is felt to be particularly valid or relevant to a specific 'teaching moment'.

6 Distribute the wealth: ensuring fair and even turn-taking by encouraging more reticent learners and 'reining in' the more vocal ones.

Much of the work done on initial and in-service teacher education programmes focuses on the relationship between what was planned and what happened in reality, or what teachers believe and what they do in reality (Li and Walsh, forthcoming). Typically, teachers gain credit for teaching to the plan and are criticised for deviating from what was planned. Bailey's study offers a very helpful alternative approach and focuses on the decisions made while teaching. As I call it, 'online decision-making' – pedagogic decisions made while teaching – is at least as important as the decisions made before teaching or while planning a lesson. Some may even say that online decision-making, and the need for effective interactive decisions, are more important than what goes on during planning. Good teaching is based on far more than 'planfulness' (Leinhardt and Greeno 1986: 76). As Bailey demonstrates quite clearly, skilled teaching is about the interactive choices that are made online, about the decisions that are taken in the fast flow of the lesson. Perhaps more importantly, good interactive decision-making can be *acquired* by sensitising teachers to the alternatives open to them, using the kinds of reflective practices described by Bailey (ibid.).

Dealing with reticence

For many language teachers around the world, dealing with reticent students is a very common problem and a dominant feature of classroom life. Much learner discourse in larger classes is characterised by single-word responses, whispered replies to teacher prompts, or silence (see, for example, Lee and Ng 2009). Typically, there is very little evidence of learner-initiated clarification requests, learner questions or extended learner turns. Teacher talk may account for 80 per cent or more of the spoken interaction (c.f. Tsui 1998), with silence and frequently repeated teacher questions predominant features of the discourse. Many readers will identify very closely with this kind of context.

Under such conditions, with minimal participation, it is unlikely that much is being learnt at all. If learners are not engaged in the discourse and participating actively, they have little opportunity to try out (and later learn) new language, test their own hypotheses or develop strategies for dealing with unknown language. For many teachers, coping with silence is a major concern, often resulting in teachers answering their own questions, a predominance of teacher echo, an acceptance of one-word responses and a sense of frustration and even failure.

In order to address this issue, Amy Tsui set up a study in 1996 in Hong Kong in which teachers were required to make one video- or audio-recording of a lesson, identify one problem in their classes, devise strategies to overcome the problem, try them out and then evaluate the whole process in a later lesson. The problem of learner reticence manifested itself in a number of ways according to teacher perceptions. These include: a lack of self-confidence and willingness to take risks; a fear of mistakes and derision; a fear (on the part of teachers) of silence; an uneven distribution of turns, with teacher bids going mainly to the brighter learners; incomprehensible input – teachers' contributions were too vague or too difficult to understand. The practitioners in the study reported a number of strategies used to overcome reticence in the language classroom:

- **Lengthening wait-time**. Silence was considered to be a waste of time because, as one teacher commented, 'time is too precious'. Earlier studies confirm that teachers do not allow sufficient wait-time owing to a need to cover the syllabus and a fear that silence results in boredom and a loss of pace in the lesson (White and Lightbown 1984: 236). Similar reasons were given by teachers in the 1996 study. However, Tsui also reports that while silence is 'not necessarily a bad thing', excessive wait-time can increase learner anxiety.

- **Improving questioning strategies**. Tsui notes that one of the strategies identified by the teachers in the study was to improve their questioning strategies by asking more referential questions and fewer display questions. While an increase in referential questions did not necessarily result in longer or better learner responses, allowing planning time to answer those questions did; some teachers commented on the value of getting students to write down their answers before verbalising them.

- **Accepting a variety of answers**. Allowing a variety of responses and emphasising that there was no one 'right' answer was found to be of some value in initiating learner responses, with one teacher allowing learners three choices after each question: answer, ask for help or ask for more time.

- **Making use of group work and peer support**. Interaction in the 'safety' of a group before open class feedback was found to be effective as a means of getting students to speak out since it allowed rehearsal in a low risk, high gain situation.

- **Providing content feedback**. Content feedback was found to be effective since learners knew that their errors would not be corrected. Content feedback entails giving feedback on the message itself rather than the words used to express the message.

In conclusion, Tsui suggests that a greater awareness of effective anxiety-reducing strategies is needed if language learning is to be made a more productive and enjoyable experience. Implicit in her remarks is the suggestion that teachers need to be sensitised to strategies that are effective in reducing anxiety, perhaps by reflecting on classroom-recordings and having opportunities to discuss them.

To conclude this section and using some of the main themes reviewed here, what do we now know about the role of classroom discourse in improving teaching and learning? What are the main ways in which an understanding of classroom discourse can be used in second language teacher development?

The first thing to note is that any attempt to help teachers understand classroom discourse is motivated, in the first instance, by a desire to enhance learning. While the very term 'teacher talk' immediately conjures up images of teacher-centredness, most of the studies reviewed here are instigated by a concern for the learners. The use of appropriate questioning strategies is designed to increase learner involvement, as is the concern to help teachers make more interactive decisions – decisions that were exclusively guided by the learners. Similarly, Tsui's study (1996) was motivated by learner reticence. Essentially then, learners are central to and instrumental in the process of enhancing teachers' awareness of language use in the L2 classroom.

A second theme that emerges from the discussion in this section is the importance to teacher development of teacher-generated data. Reflective practices are more easily accomplished when teachers analyse their own data, using recordings from their own lessons. Perhaps more importantly, we need to find ways of helping teachers analyse and interpret data without having to transcribe everything. This is something we return to in Chapter 6. For now, suffice it to say that second language teacher development would benefit hugely from having teachers collect, analyse and interpret data from their own classes.

A third theme that emerges is the need to acquire an emic (insider) perspective on classroom discourse and interactional processes. This perspective is one that assumes that the use of teachers' voices, actions and stories is more conducive to gaining a true understanding of interactional processes in the L2 classroom than the imposed perspective of the researcher. An insider perspective is also easier to obtain when teacher-participants are encouraged to verbalise their experiences in some way. For example, in the studies reviewed in this section, Bailey uses stimulated recall to initiate dialogues with participating teachers; Tsui makes use of post-teaching interviews, while Thornbury prefers a form of written self-evaluation. Each procedure has its own merits and can be adapted according to local conditions. Further, we can see that the complexities of classroom interaction in the L2 context can best be understood when data are collected using a variety of instruments: a multi-mode method. Apart from enhancing reliability and validity, multi-mode methods of data collection ensure that 'all the angles are covered', that the setting is viewed from more than one position. From a teacher development perspective, this means that any approach to helping teachers understand classroom discourse should use more than one method: for example, classroom recording with interview, lesson observation plus focus group, etc. True understandings of the complexities of classroom interaction can only be gained when we have as accurate a picture as possible of what is really happening – this entails using more than one type of data.

Summary

In this chapter, we have made a case for putting interaction at the centre of effective teaching, using the argument that interaction lies at the heart of effective classroom practice. By studying their own interactions with students, either recorded or recorded and transcribed, I suggest that teachers can do much to improve their professional practice and enhance learning and learning opportunity. From an understanding that contexts are not static and fixed, but dynamic and fluid, we considered how teachers and learners co-create micro-contexts through their interactions. It is in these micro-contexts that learning occurs. The challenge for L2 teachers is to gain microscopic understandings of their interactions with learners. By studying the specific interactional strategies they use, teachers can promote more active, engaged and dialogic learning environments. By placing classroom interaction at the centre of their professional development, language teachers are more likely, I suggest, to create micro-contexts in which learning opportunities abound. In order to achieve this, I would argue that teachers need to be equipped with appropriate tools to study their own contexts. This is something to which we'll return throughout this book.

3 Classroom discourse and learning

Introduction

In Chapters 1 and 2, we established that L2 classrooms are as much a social context as any other 'real world' context, such as a travel agent's, a dentist's, an airport check-in counter. Rather than comparing the L2 classroom to the 'real world' (which exists outside the classroom), we should acknowledge that the L2 classroom is as much a part of the real world as any other context. The point was made in Chapter 2 that any language lesson should actually be seen as a series of micro-contexts, which are jointly constructed by teachers and students through their interactions. In all classroom contexts, linguistic and interactional resources are the conduit through which opinions, feelings, emotions, concerns are expressed and through which the 'institutional business' (i.e. language learning) gets done.

Our focus now shifts to an examination of the relationship between interaction and learning, opening with a discussion of what we mean by learning in an L2 classroom context. We consider why interaction is regarded by many researchers and practitioners as lying at the heart of learning and look at ways of uncovering the relationship between interaction and learning. Much of the work that has been done to explain the relationship between interaction and learning has considered interaction from either a broadly cognitive position, in which interaction somehow influences our ability to think and process new knowledge, or from a more social perspective, in which learning is viewed as a social process in which interaction plays a central role. It is important to note that under both views of learning, interaction plays a key and pivotal role.

Our discussion opens by considering the complex relationship between language learning and interaction.

Language learning and interaction

Any discussion on learning a language in a formal context (a classroom), as opposed to acquiring a language in an informal context (outside the classroom), must begin with some definition of what is meant by learning. We have all been language learners at some time in our lives, many of us still are. Yet, what do we understand by learning a second language? What does it mean 'to know' a language?

Personal reflection

Take a few minutes to think of your experiences as a language learner. What does learning mean for you? Make a list, or write your own definition. How have your ideas about learning changed over time?

For most of us, learning means 'acquiring', 'getting', 'having', 'possessing' new skills or new knowledge. As learners, we say things like 'I can't talk about what I did yet, I haven't learnt the past tense'. Eventually, once we 'have' the past tense, we are able to talk about and describe past experiences. We often regard learning a language as acquiring an ever-expanding repertoire of new skills and knowledge. First, we 'get' the simple present tense, then we move on to the simple past, present perfect and so on. We acquire one 'building block' (such as 'going to' future) before we move on to the next. In many parts of the world, languages are taught like this, in much the same way that content-based subjects such as maths, history and science are taught. We even talk about 'delivering' lectures, suggesting that knowledge and skills can somehow be packaged and then offered to learners.

While it is easy to understand why this view of learning prevails, it may be useful to consider an alternative. Rather than seeing learning as 'having', we can also consider learning as 'doing' (see Larsen-Freeman 2010). Under this view, learning is regarded as a process, an activity, something we take part in, perform. Learning is regarded as a dynamic, constantly shifting process in which participants collectively construct meanings. Learning is not something we have or own, it is something that we participate in – it entails encounters with others. Learning is regarded much more as a social rather than a cognitive process. Our actions, activities and interactions with others all work together to determine what it is that we learn. Learning entails completing a task, taking part in an activity, talking, discussing, debating and arguing with others. It is this view of learning, as a complex and dynamic process, which lies at the heart of contemporary teaching methodologies such as TBLT (see Chapter 2).

It is not my suggestion here that learning is *either* having *or* doing; it is almost certainly both (see Sfard 1998). What I am suggesting, however, is that an understanding of learning in a formal, classroom context must pay close attention to the 'doing' dimension since this is something we can study, analyse and evaluate. We cannot look inside the heads of our students and see what they are learning. We *can* look at what they say, how they interact, how they use the L2 and so on; this is where we can really begin to uncover some of the finer nuances of learning as a process. Under this view of learning, studying interaction, quite simply, is the same thing as studying learning (c.f. Ellis 2000; Pekarek Doehler 2010).

Task 3.1

For extract 3.1 below, comment on what seems to be 'happening'. What do you think the teacher is trying to achieve here and what is being learnt? How did you decide?

Extract 3.1

187	T:	=what do we call I'm going to try and get the class to tell you what this word
188		is that you're looking for . . . er we talk about military **(claps hands)** . . . military what?
189	L:	((1))=
190	T:	=like fight=
191	L:	=kill=
192	T:	=no not [kill]
193	L:	[action] action=
194	T:	=no ((2)) military?=
195	LL:	=power=
196	T:	=power think of another word military?
197	LL:	((3))force=
198	T:	=so she believes in a FORCE for?
199	L:	that guide our lives=
200	T:	=that guides our lives=

To summarise our discussion so far, we have established that:

- classrooms are social contexts just like any other context involving human interaction;

- any lesson is made up of a series of micro contexts that are established through the interactions that take place between participants;

- it is through interaction that micro-contexts are created;

- learning is as much about what students do as what they have;

- interaction lies at the heart of learning.

Interaction, from what we have said so far, is clearly very important and something that we need to study. Why is this so? Why is interaction seen as being so central to language learning? How can teachers and learners gain a closer understanding of the *interactional architecture* (Seedhouse 2004) of their classes? What impact might such an understanding have on learning efficacy? In the discussion that follows, three reasons are presented for the centrality of interaction to learning.

According to van Lier (1996: 5), 'interaction is the most important element in the curriculum', a position that coincides with that of Ellis (2000: 209; original emphasis), 'learning arises not *through* interaction, but *in* interaction'. As such, interaction needs to be understood if we are to promote learning. The discussion above supports both of these claims: if we want to understand learning, we should begin by looking at the interactions that take place in our classes. Further, there is now increasing evidence to suggest that learner–learner interaction does not have the impact on language learning that was once suggested (see, for example, Foster 1998; Rampton 1999). This position suggests that the teacher now has an important role to play in creating and managing interaction that is 'acquisition rich' (Ellis 2000). The point is that even in the most student-centred class, the teacher is instrumental to managing the interaction (Johnson 1995); there is, then, a need to help teachers acquire 'microscopic understandings' (van Lier 2000) of the interactional organisation of the L2 classroom.

A second reason for studying interaction is that it allows practitioners to make good interactive decisions. 'Good teaching' is as much about the decisions teachers take while they teach as it is about the planning that goes on before teaching (see Chapter 2). Good, effective interactive decisions are the ones that influence learning, which create space for learning (Walsh *et al.* 2010), which support learning rather than impede it. Making appropriate choices in the interaction is not something that can be easily mastered without some understanding of the relationship between interaction and learning: a realisation, for example, that asking yes/no questions all the time severely restricts learners' opportunity to offer extended turns and become engaged in the interaction. Or that extended use of teacher echo (constant repetitions) restricts the space that learners may have to interact.

Third, I suggest that if teachers are to enhance their understanding of the interactional organisation of the L2 classroom, then the obvious starting place is their own classes. For most teachers, professional development entails improving the learning experience of their students. In order to do this, I would argue, teachers should focus on the interactions taking place in their own classes. For this to happen, there is a need for more appropriate tools for investigating classroom discourse, although a starting point for teacher development is for teachers to simply record their classes and spend some time analysing the interactions that took place. More will be said about this in

Chapters 7 and 8. In the next section, the discussion offers an overview of learning as a cognitive activity.

Learning as a cognitive activity

This section offers a necessarily brief overview of some of the more important hypotheses that have attempted to explain the complex relationship between interaction and learning. Three main hypotheses are presented, all placing interaction at the centre of learning: Krashen's Input Hypothesis (1985), Long's Interaction Hypothesis (1983, 1996), Swain's Output Hypothesis (1985, 2005).

Personal reflection

What is the relationship between the language used in the classroom and the language learners acquire? Is there a direct, one-to-one relationship? What can teachers do to maximise learning (i.e. acquisition) opportunities?

These questions have been around for some time now and there is still little agreement. Some researchers, for example, Cazden 1986, argue that there is no direct relationship between the language used in a language classroom and the language learnt; others, like Allwright, suggest quite the opposite: 'the processes of classroom interaction determine what language learning opportunities become available to be learned from' (1984: 156).

According to Ellis (1990), it is helpful to distinguish between *interaction* and *formal instruction* when assessing the role of classroom communication in the process of SLA. Interaction is regarded as the process by which samples of the target language are made available to learners, while formal instruction is defined as the way in which the teacher intervenes directly and provides samples of 'specific linguistic features for learning' (1990: 93). For many teachers, providing samples of language equates to modelling: the input that teachers provide and that learners typically acquire in some form. According to Krashen (1985), all input must be comprehensible if learning is to occur. His input hypothesis is based on the assumption that learning will only occur when the input learners receive – often in the form of a teacher's modelling – is at or slightly higher than the language level of the learners. For modelling to be effective, it is clear that learners must be exposed to an appropriate pronunciation, with correct word stress, intonation and so on. Although the precise nature of a teacher's input is still not fully understood, it is clear that teachers do need to be sufficiently aware of their use of language to both promote interaction and to allow language acquisition to occur. Language that is too complex or too simple will fail to engage learners in a level of activity that is at or slightly beyond their level of competence. Language that is too 'dense', 'wordy', or 'idiosyncratic' will have a similar effect.

And yet, despite the claims of Krashen, it is quite clear that managing interaction entails far more than modifying input for learners. Simplified input will not in itself result in SLA; comprehensible input is 'an insufficient condition for second language acquisition to occur' (Glew 1998: 1). Indeed, it is quite feasible that over-simplification may have a counter effect on acquisition since negotiation will become redundant (Musumeci 1996). Quality interaction, interaction that is 'acquisition rich' (Ellis 1998: 145) has to be initiated, managed and sustained by teachers through careful and knowing management of the turn-taking sequences that occur in face-to-face communication. Put differently, teachers and learners need to gain a comprehensive understanding of the interactive processes that facilitate learning. Interaction does not simply happen, nor is it a function of the teaching methodology; interaction, in an acquisition rich classroom, is both instigated and sustained by the teacher.

To illustrate this point, look at the ways in which interaction is managed in extract 3.2 below. This teacher is working with a small group of eight pre-intermediate adult learners in a multilingual context. In the discourse, it is apparent that she uses a number of different strategies to manage the interaction and ensure that the group is kept together. In 285, for example, she acts as a model, correcting an error and modelling the correct form, a task that is done quickly and unobtrusively (indicated by the latched turns, marked =) in order not to disrupt the flow of the interaction. In 287, she acts as 'support', reinforcing L3's contribution and making it available to the rest of the class by writing it on the board. Finally, in turns 289, 291 and 293, her role is to inform, to act as a source of linguistic input in response to the learner's prompt in 288. This skilful management of the discourse, entailing the adoption of different roles, ensures that the class 'stays together', that learners are able to follow the lesson and that learning opportunities are maximised.

Extract 3.2

284	L3:	[the good] news is he boughted the new car=
285	T:	=he bought a new car=
286	L3:	=a new car a new car but bad news is (2) he crashed it crashed crashed it his car=
287	T:	=he crashed it yes the good news is (**writes on board**) he bought a new car the bad news is he crashed it=
288	L3:	=so if I want to say accident how to say?=

289 T: =he HAD an accident=
290 L3:   =he had an accident=
291 T: =he had an accident or he crashed his car he crashed
            his car=
292 L3:   =what what is formal? (2)
293 T: ahh . . . about the same really he had an accident more
            formal maybe . . .
294 L3:   he had an accident (2)

Following on from the work of Krashen, Long proposed a slightly different perspective on the role of interaction in learning. Long's interaction hypothesis (1983, 1996) argued that learning occurs when students are negotiating meaning. Negotiation of meaning (also 'negotiation for meaning') was regarded by Long as being central to second language acquisition. It is also the principle on which CLT (communicative language teaching) is based. Essentially, learners negotiate meaning when they are seeking or offering clarification and confirmation. It is through this constant process of negotiating meaning that second language learning occurs, according to Long, that is.

Long's interaction hypothesis has received considerable scrutiny over the years and has been found to be more or less in evidence according to the different studies that have taken place. Early studies (see, for example, Doughty and Pica 1986; Gass and Varonis 1985) found that meanings are only negotiated when participants are all non-native speakers of varying proficiencies and with different L1s. They also found that the extent to which negotiation of meaning is determined is largely dependent on who has access to the information: a learner seeking information is more likely to negotiate meaning than a learner holding it, for example. One of the main criticisms of Long's hypothesis is that the work was conducted under 'laboratory conditions'; learners were taken out of their regular classes and asked to perform certain tasks. When we consider the extent to which negotiation for meaning occurs in 'normal' classes, we find that it is considerably less than was first claimed (see Foster 1998).

According to Long (1983, 1996), SLA is promoted when, through communication breakdown, learners have to negotiate for meaning. By asking for clarification and confirming comprehension – key features of Long's interaction hypothesis – it is argued that acquisition occurs. Of course, in any conversation, meanings are negotiated and it can be claimed that, to a large extent, the classroom is no different. The 'social process of negotiation of meaning' (Pica 1997: 60) has been of considerable interest to researchers for many years. Negotiation enables learners to provide each other with comprehensible input, to give and gain feedback on contributions and to modify and restructure utterances so that meanings are made clear.

In his more recent version of the interaction hypothesis, Long highlights the centrality of the more competent interlocutor in making input comprehensible, in enhancing learner attention, and in encouraging learner output. In Long's own words (1996: 451–452):

[. . .] negotiation for meaning, and especially negotiation work that triggers interactional adjustments by the NS or more competent interlocutor, facilitates acquisition because it connects input, internal learner capacities, particularly selective attention, and output in productive ways.

There is clearly considerable emphasis here on the role of the teacher, the more 'competent interlocutor', who is crucial to ensuring that input is comprehensible and that learner output is 'shaped' in some way so that it is 'productive'. There seems to be a suggestion too in the above citation that there is a need to reconsider the interaction that occurs between teacher and learners, a departure from an earlier version of the interaction hypothesis (Long: 1983), which also addressed learner–learner interaction.

The teacher in extract 3.3 below is working with a group of multilingual, advanced adult learners. He is preparing to introduce a reading comprehension task on poltergeists and precedes the reading with an open class discussion on 'out of body' experiences. It is clear that the students in the extract have a high level of English and are able to express themselves quite well, even when discussing complex topics. Confusion arises in 146, however (indicated ((2)), as the student is unable to recall the word 'smoke'. The teacher's clarification request in 147 highlights the need for greater precision on the part of L1; his request for clarification draws attention to the fact that there is a problem that needs to be repaired. He interjects again in 151 and his prompt eventually leads to another student offering the word *smoke* in 155. Essentially, then, turns 146 to 158 entail negotiation for meaning and arguably contribute to the extended and complex turn produced by L1 at the end of the extract in 160. The teacher plays a vital role in the discourse, highlighting the problem in the first instance, offering support in the form of scaffolded input and finally guiding the learner – with the help of a classmate – to her intended meaning.

Extract 3.3

144   L1:   [I believe] in soul no I don't believe in heaven certainly not I believe that the universe eh we have place where the souls are together and eh I remember ((5))we were in sauna it was my grandmother

145   T: yes=

146 L1: =and something went wrong there and eh ... the the
           ((2)) couldn't go through the chimney
147 T: which couldn't? ... the the steam or ... no?=
148 L1: =not steam eh blow? blow? not blow ... eh something
           from their fire they have eh=
149 T: =yeah=
150 L1: =a blow ... not blow=
151 T: =a fire?=
152 L1: =when you make a fire=
153 T: =yes=
154 L1: =and eh what is=
155 L: =smoke?=
156 L1: =smoke smoke yes=
157 T: =uh huh=
158 L1: =smoke wouldn't go through the chimney and the sauna
           was erm warmed up?=
159 T: =yes=
160 L1: =warming up and it all stays in this room and the
           room was full of this smoke and ((4)) and somebody
           eh I don't know eh probably a priest but I remember
           erm how I saw my body on the floor lying down like
           I was sleeping and my grandmother was pulling me
           to the cold shower and then suddenly I like eh again
           was con conscious?=
161 T: =yes=

We have already acknowledged that much of Long's work is
based on studies that were conducted outside the classroom, under
'laboratory conditions'. When we look at negotiated meaning in
the classroom, a different picture emerges, with many learners
negotiating only at word level, by repeating utterances, by remaining
silent, or by avoiding negotiation by 'pretending' to have understood (see, for example, Tsui 1996; Foster 1998). In a 1996 study,
Musumeci found very little or no negotiation; indeed, quite the reverse
(1996: 314):

[...] teachers [...] speak more, more often, control the topic of
conversation, rarely ask questions for which they do not have
answers, and appear to understand absolutely everything the
students say, sometimes before they even say it!

The overall conclusion in Musumeci's (1996) study – that there was
little or no evidence of sustained negotiation – is significant to the
current context; learners' ability to formulate, re-formulate, clarify and

seek clarification are important indicators not only that language acquisition has taken (or is taking) place but also that something is being understood and eventually learnt. By 'filling in the gaps', teachers may facilitate a coherent and flowing discourse, but they may also deny learners opportunities to get to grips with target language forms and identify potential problems in understanding. The present situation indicates that negotiation is barely occurring at all in many L2 classrooms; significant changes in attitudes, expectations and the verbal behaviour of both teachers and learners are necessary if language acquisition and learning potential are to be optimised.

In terms of classroom communication, if negotiation for meaning is to occupy a more central role in the learning process, there is a need for a major shift in the ways in which understandings are accomplished. This will entail greater emphasis on negotiated understanding, more requests – by teachers and learners alike – for clarification, less acceptance by teachers of the 'first response' given by learners. In short, discourse that may be less 'easy on the ear', but through which learning opportunities are maximised and where problems and shortfalls (in language acquisition) are more transparent.

Extract 3.4 offers an example of classroom discourse that is 'less easy on the ear', but that allows identification of problems and deficiencies in students' language. Here, a group of advanced learners is recalling memories of supernatural experiences. L1 is recalling an incident from her childhood when she passed out in a sauna. Confusion arises in 174: the teacher seeks clarification, asking L1 if the 'person' watching from above had a body. This is misunderstood in 175 as the student thinks the teacher is alluding to her real body in the sauna and continues recalling the experience in 177. The teacher persists with requests for clarification in 178 and 180 and eventually gets the response he was looking for in 181. While this whole extract lasted less than one minute, it serves to illustrate a number of valuable strategies, each of which, in some way, contributes to SLA. First, there is a need on the part of teachers to really listen to a learner's response and evaluate its communicative potential. That is, is there a message and is it unambiguous? Second, teachers would be well-advised not to always accept a learner's first contribution. Here, for example, it would have been quite common practice for the teacher to have accepted L1's contribution in 175 and there would have been no further negotiation for meaning. Third, teachers should be prepared to persevere until they are satisfied that the intended meaning has been conveyed. Furthermore, one reason these strategies are valuable, not only from a SLA perspective, is that this is what learners will encounter outside the classroom in their day-to-day dealings with native-speakers.

Extract 3.4

172　T:　　=and did you see colours? was it like a colour [((2))]
173　L1:　[it was] white it was white because I thought it was
　　　　　　　smoke like it was like somebody smoking white and
　　　　　　　green and [but]
174　T:　　[you you] saw from above did you see did you have a
　　　　　　　body?=
175　L1:　=I have body it was naked of course eh no [I did have
　　　　　　　body]
176　T:　　[no I didn't mean]
177　L1:　I I (**student wolf whistles**) no I mean I watched me like
　　　　　　　I was somewhere in the corner of the ceiling ((3)) and
　　　　　　　I watched my body on the floor and my friend was
　　　　　　　lying down . . .
178　T:　　Sure but but the YOU that was watching?=
179　L1:　=yes I was watching all these=
180　T:　　=but did this you have a body? . . .
181　L1:　no I don't and I remember my grandmother was
　　　　　　　shouting please please come in come back like and
　　　　　　　my I remember my body was holding down and my
　　　　　　　grandmother was trying to rise me up?=
182　T:　　=yes=

Furthering the work of both Krashen and Long, Swain (1985, 2005) proposed the output hypothesis as an alternative way of looking at the role of interaction in L2 acquisition. Under this view, language acquisition through interaction will only occur when learners have an opportunity to speak; our focus should therefore be more on learner output and less on the interaction or input which they receive. Bygate (1988) reinforces the notion that speaking may be more important than comprehensible input:

> It is only when the learner is being required to piece together his own utterances that he is being obliged to work out – and hence learn – his own plans of verbal action, all the while evaluating his output in the light of his meaning intention.

According to Swain (1985: 248–249), output is important because it forces the learner to develop precise, coherent and appropriate linguistic resources, 'pushed language use', and because it requires the learner to pay close attention to syntax and test hypotheses. The concept of 'pushed output' is central to this position; opportunities to interact in a classroom, in themselves, may not be adequate. Through the teacher's negotiation of meaning, learners are helped to refine their contributions so that they can be understood (see extract 3.4). In other words, learners have to pay attention not only to the form of an utterance, but also to its function and degree of appropriacy at a given point in an exchange.

In her most recent version of the output hypothesis, Swain (2005) maintains that output enhances fluency and promotes 'noticing' by allowing learners to identify gaps between what they want to say and what they are able to say. Her position is that much can be learned about classroom communication by looking at the dialogues that unfold between teachers and learners and between learners and learners. Adopting a more social view of learning, Swain stresses the dialogic nature of language learning, arguing that an understanding of learning processes can be enhanced by understanding dialogues more fully.

The kind of noticing Swain describes (see also Schmidt 1993) is exemplified below in extract 3.5, in which a group of upper-intermediate learners is preparing for a listening activity from *New First Certificate Masterclass* on the topic of lying. Here, the give and take of the dialogue is more conducive to gaining an understanding of what is actually *happening* than the isolated utterances of teacher or learners. In addition, the extract highlights the need for learners (or teachers) to identify gaps in their interlanguage. When the teacher's prompt in 99 receives no immediate response, she is able to feed in the missing vocabulary, *white lie*, in 101. By considering classroom discourse as a form of dialogue, understandings about teaching and learning processes can be greatly enhanced, and gaps in learners' interlanguage identified.

Extract 3.5

94	T:	=like for example what kind of situation might have been necessary (4)
95	L:	when you don't want to explain what you have done and you don't want to have troubles
96	T:	(2) right=
97	L:	=to say nothing [and]
98	L:	[when you] want to be polite[(((1))]]
99	T:	[when] you want to be polite yes if you want to be polite or if you don't want to hurt somebody's feelings sometimes what do we call . . . we saw it last week a little lie it's not serious=
100	L:	=oh yes . . .
101	T:	=white lie good a little white lie so that may be to protect somebody or to . . .
102	LL:	=/white lie/=

Interactive classrooms, where learners are engaged in task-based learning, certainly promote learner independence. Yet there are frequently problems with tasks that have little or no teacher supervision: students may not take the task seriously, make extensive use of L1, withdraw from the task, dominate the discussion, or perform poorly. Under these conditions, there is certainly a strong argument that the teacher must play a more prominent role in the ensuing dialogue.

An example of the way in which a teacher might play a more prominent role without totally dominating the discourse is offered in extract 3.6 below. Note how learner 3 holds the floor and controls the topic of discussion. Apart from requests for clarification and confirmation checks on the part of the teacher and other learners (in 39, 41, 45, 47), L3 has control of the topic and is able to produce relatively long, coherent turns, culminating in the final, extended turn in 50. This student succeeds in communicating her message – aided, perhaps, by the fact that she has complete control of the topic. Arguably, the opportunities for practice and for maximising SLA are as great – if not greater – in this type of open-class discussion, where the teacher plays a scaffolding role, than in more 'private' pair- and group-work activities.

Extract 3.6

36	L3:	=I see . . . in my city . . . one woman she has a baby =
37	T:	=yes=
38	L3:	=and she didn't have any money for that and she stole erm a tin of milk=
39	T:	=a tin of=
40	L3:	=of milk=
41	T:	=milk=
42	L3:	=milk for the children=
43	T:	=yes
44	L:	((2))
45	T:	she went to prison?
46	L3:	she went to prison but at the same time time . . . how do you say . . . the ((6))?
47	T:	=sorry could you [repeat]?
48	LL:	[prefect]
49	T:	=the prefect [yes] the prefect
50	L3:	[yes] he stole the money the city but no no problems no problems but erm everybody knows he stole the money and erm he's got the money one day later he says tells the I don't want ((1)) I don't want to go on as a prefect (unintelligible)

The research that has been conducted on social interaction in the formal, L2 context indicates a need among language teachers to develop a less prominent, yet still influential, position (see, for example, Walsh 2003). From this new position, rather than 'taking a back seat' or 'handing over' to learners, teachers would be empowered to facilitate, monitor and evaluate student contributions, while paying closer attention to the ways in which their (teachers') language contributes to the language learning process. From this position, constant refinements can be made to the quantity, quality and function of teacher input in relation to desired learning outcomes.

This necessarily brief overview of some of the main theories that have been proposed in order to explain the complex relationship between interaction and language learning both underline its importance and highlight an overall lack of agreement about its precise function. It does seem clear that interaction contributes in some way to language learning, but we still do not really know precisely how. Ellis (1990) posits three roles for classroom interaction:

1 Strong: interaction in some way determines SLA.

2 Weak: interaction facilitates SLA.

3 Zero: interaction is not necessary for learning to take place.

Task 3.2   (TC)

What do *you* think? Look at the extract below and consider the role of interaction in L2 learning. To what extent do you think that learning opportunities are created here? Do you think, based on what you have read so far, that there is a relatively strong or a rather weak relationship between interaction and learning?

273	T:	what about in Spain if you park your car illegally?
274	L4:	. . . there are two possibilities
275	T:	two [possibilities]
276	L4:	[one] is er I park my car ((1)) and
277	T:	yes . . . if I park . . . my car . . . illegally again Rosa
278	L4:	**(laughter)** if I park my car [illegally]
279	T:	[illegally]
280	L4:	police stat policeman er give me give me
281	T:	GIVES me
282	L4:	gives me? a little small paper if er I can't pay the money

```
283    T:     it's called a FINE remember a FINE yes?
284    L4:    or if if my car
285    T:     is parked
286    L4:    is parked illegally . . . the policeman take my car and
              . . . er . . . go to the police station not police station
              it's a big place where where they have some [cars]
              they
```

In this section, the discussion has centred on the role of interaction in learning by considering three hypotheses: input, interaction and output. The position taken is that while interaction is central to the L2 teaching/learning process, the interactive processes that make up classroom discourse is at present not adequately understood by either teachers or learners. The discussion now turns to a view of learning as a social, rather than a cognitive, process.

Learning as a social process

In the last fifteen or twenty years, there have been a number of significant developments to challenge traditional and long-standing views of both the nature of language and the nature of learning. Perhaps the starting point for these developments was the seminal paper by Firth and Wagner (1997 and revisited in 2007), which challenged existing conceptualisations of learning. The Firth and Wagner paper argues that learning should be seen as a social process and that language should be viewed as a complex, dynamic system that is locally managed by interactants in response to emerging communicative needs. Under this view, learning can be traced in the moment-by-moment co-construction of meanings and by using conversation analysis (CA). The relatively new, emergent field known as CA-for-SLA quite clearly views learning as participation (see above) and maintains that we can measure and track learning through the interactions that take place (Markee 2008).

This said, social views of learning have actually existed for much longer. Socio-cultural theories of learning emphasise its *social* nature; learners interact with the 'expert' adult teacher 'in a context of social interactions leading to understanding' (Röhler and Cantlon 1996: 2). Learning, under this perspective, entails dialogue, discussion and debate as learners collectively and actively construct their own understandings through interactions with others who may be more experienced. This view of learning owes its origins to the influential work of the Russian philosopher Lev Vygotsky (1978), whose theories have been applied to language learning contexts by researchers such as Lantolf (2000) and Lantolf and Thorne (2006).

By emphasising the social, dynamic and collaborative dimensions of learning, proponents of socio-cultural theories of learning stress its 'transactional' nature: learning occurs in the first instance through interaction with others, who are more experienced and in a position to guide and support the actions of the novice. During this part of the process, language is used as a 'symbolic tool' to clarify and make sense of new knowledge, with learners relying heavily on discussions with the 'expert knower'. As new ideas and knowledge are internalised, learners use language to comment on what they have learnt; spoken interactions are used to both transmit and clarify new information and then to reflect on and rationalise what has been learnt.

Learning and the Zone of Proximal Development (ZPD)

According to Lantolf (2000: 17), the ZPD should be regarded as 'a metaphor for observing and understanding how mediated means are appropriated and internalised'. Lantolf goes on to offer his own definition of the ZPD: 'The collaborative construction of opportunities [. . .] for individuals to develop their mental abilities' (ibid.).

A number of key terms emerge from the work of Vygotsky and Lantolf, including 'collaboration', 'construction', 'opportunities' and 'development'. Other writers use a similar terminology: van Lier (2000: 252), for example, refers to opportunities for learning as 'affordances', while Swain and Lapkin (1998: 320) talk about 'occasions for learning'. Ohta (2001: 9) talks about learners' '. . .level of potential development as determined through language produced collaboratively with a teacher or peer'. As a construct in the present context, the value of the ZPD lies in its potential for enabling consideration of the 'give and take' in the teaching/learning process. The 'collaborative construction' of opportunities for learning is examined through the ways in which teachers and learners collectively construct meaning in L2 classroom interaction.

In extract 3.7 on p. 64, for example, a group of upper-intermediate students are discussing ways of regulating lives. The extract has been selected to illustrate the importance of collaborative meaning-making and the need to allow interactional space so that teachers and learners can create opportunities for language acquisition. Note that this is a very different stance to the one that has been advocated under CLT methodologies; simply 'handing over' to learners and getting them to perform in pairs and groups will not, under socio-cultural theory, contribute much to language learning. Instead, the teacher plays a focal role, guiding, clarifying, supporting and shaping contributions so that learners have opportunities to reflect on and learn from the unfolding interaction. Here, for example, in 398, 400, 402, the teacher paraphrases and summarises L1's previous contributions as a means of offering support and enabling other students to follow the dialogue. While the dialogue is mainly between the teacher and L1, this strategy of summarising and checking and negotiating is important if all class members are to understand and contribute to the discussion. The rapid turn-taking in the extract (indicated by =) identifies it as being almost conversational in nature, with one big difference: the teacher participates in the dialogue but, more importantly, ensures that messages are understood and refined for the other listeners, the other students.

Extract 3.7

398	T:	=so it's eh . . . I . . . from a sceptical point of view what you have is a way of regulating your life =
399	L1:	=yes=
400	T:	=and eh giving you direction =
401	L1:	=yeah=
402	T:	=and goals and meaning [and]
403	L4:	[so] do you think ((6)) ?. . .
404	L1:	no I think that eh for example that my argument is that if I take alcohol I'm culpable I get sick=
405	T:	=everybody does=
406	L1:	=but I think for me it's like a sign stop doing this=
407	T:	=me too ((3))=
408	L1:	=or take take ((2)) for yourself and you won't feel sick you'll be like high?=
409	T:	=yes=
410	L1:	like yes ((4)) . . .
411	T:	so it's good for you as far as being good?=
412	L1:	[yes I think so]

A key concept under this view of learning is that of 'scaffolding', used to refer to the linguistic support given by a tutor to a learner (Bruner 1990). Central to the notion are the important polar concepts of challenge and support. Learners are led to an understanding of a task by, on the one hand, a teacher's provision of appropriate amounts of challenge to maintain interest and involvement, and, on the other, support to ensure understanding. Support typically involves segmentation and ritualisation so that learners have, in the first instance, limited choice in how they go about a task that is broken down into manageable component parts (Bruner, 1990: 29). Once a task has been mastered, scaffolds are removed and the learner is left to reflect and comment on the task.

Clearly, the amount of scaffolded support given will depend very much on the perceived evaluation by the 'expert' of what is needed by the 'novice'. In a classroom context, where so much is happening at once, such fine judgments can be difficult to make. Deciding to intervene or withdraw in the moment by moment construction of classroom interaction requires great sensitivity and awareness on the part of the teacher and inevitably teachers do not 'get it right' every time.

Consider how the word *toe* is scaffolded in the extract below (in 261). A group of pre-intermediate learners is working with oral fluency practice materials, but is unable to complete one task because they do not know the word *toe*. The teacher's demonstration (in 259), modelling (in 261), reinforcement (in 263 and 265), and definition (in 267) all serve to ensure that this piece of vocabulary is introduced, used and remembered by learners.

Extract 3.8

259	T:	=he dislocated his shoulder I don't think he did I think he did this come here come here come here I think he did this **(teacher stands on student's foot)**
260	L:	AEERGH thank you my ((2)) **(laughter)**
261	T:	the bad news is he what did he do? what did he do? he (4) to step on someone's toe . . .
262	L2:	to step on someone's =
263	T:	=toe=
264	L2:	=toe? this one up toe yes?=
265	T:	**(writes on board)** he asked her to dance the bad news is he stepped on her toes . . .
266	L2:	this one toes=
267	T:	=toes like fingers but on your feet=
268	L2:	=ah (3)

There are a number of reasons why a social approach to learning is attractive. In the first instance, the emphasis on the importance of social interaction is in tune with what is currently considered to be 'good practice' in ELT methodology: an emphasis on discovery-based learning through problem-solving; the use of task-based instruction that emphasises 'learning by doing' (see Chapter 2); the centrality of pair- and group-work not only to maximising interaction, but increasingly to co-operative learning (Ng and Lee 1996) are all important features of the contemporary EFL classroom. According to van Lier (1996), social development can only become language acquisition when the *quality* of the interaction is maximised. Collaboration with the teacher, less able learners, more able learners and the individual's own resources can facilitate interaction that is both meaningful and productive.

Arguably, the quality of that interaction is very much dependent on the teacher's ability to manage complex interactional processes and 'correctly' interpret the learning environment.

Second, the process of 'scaffolded instruction' (Bruner 1983, 1990), involves learners in taking risks; learning support is gradually withdrawn as learners become more independent, solving problems for themselves and gradually acquiring new knowledge and skills about the L2 through a process of 'dialogic inquiry' (Wells 1999). Central to the process is the support system offered by the tutor, the extent to which scaffolds are left in place or withdrawn, the amount of scaffolding given and the extent to which learners are made aware of its value (Donato 1994).

Finally, under socio-cultural theories of learning, dialogue is crucial in helping learners acquire new knowledge. For this to happen, learners need interactional space and support to express their ideas or thoughts. Opportunities for learning (i.e. language acquisition) are maximised when new concepts and language can be both understood and verbalised. However, the centrality of speech to learning has another, more significant dimension in that consciousness, considered by Vygotsky as being central to learning, is developed through social interaction. Learners become more *aware*, through participation in social activity, of themselves as learners.

This section has presented a necessarily brief overview of the contribution of socio-cultural theories of learning to an understanding of second language acquisition in the formal context. The relevance of Vygotskyan theories of learning stems from the importance attached to the social, interpersonal dimension of learning, from the acknowledgement that development can be assisted or 'scaffolded' and from the mediating force of dialogue.

Summary

This chapter has reviewed a sample of the literature on class-based second language acquisition. Starting with an explanation of the relationship between learning and interaction, the discussion then presented a critical review of the place of interactionist theories of second language acquisition. In the final part of the chapter, a second strand to the theoretical framework for language learning was presented in the shape of socio-cultural theories of education and learning.

The main message of the chapter is that interaction in the second language classroom is fundamental to language acquisition; that at present, the interactional processes are only partially understood; that, if interaction is to promote meaningful learning, it has to be mediated; that the prime responsibility for creating interaction-centred learning opportunities lies with the teacher.

4   Approaches to studying classroom discourse

Introduction

This is the first of three chapters that consider different approaches to studying interaction in the L2 classroom. Any attempt to understand classrooms must begin with description, as Kumaravadivelu observes:

> What actually happens there [in the classroom] largely determines the degree to which desired learning outcomes are realised. The task of systematically observing, analyzing and understanding classroom aims and events therefore becomes central to any serious educational enterprise.
>
> (Kumaravadivelu 1999: 454)

Essentially, any understanding of the 'interactional architecture' (Seedhouse 2004) of the second language classroom requires selection and mastery of particular tools – it is these tools that are presented here. In the sections that follow, a critique is presented of the principal approaches that have been used to investigate classroom interaction: interaction analysis, discourse analysis, and conversation analysis. Chapter 5 presents alternative approaches to studying classroom discourse, while Chapter 6 offers a framework that can be used by researchers and practitioners to evaluate classroom interaction.

Any attempt to capture what really happens in classrooms usually means making a recording, either audio or video, and then transcribing that recording, either fully or partially. Before considering the principal approaches that may be used to analyse classroom discourse, I will discuss the issues involved in recording and transcribing classroom data.

Recording and transcribing classroom interaction

Classrooms are highly complex places where there is so much going on at any one point in time that it would be very difficult to capture everything. Multiple interactions are the norm and multi-party talk underpins every action, every activity, every moment. Not only are there technical problems associated with *recording* what actually happens, there are, more importantly, enormous issues associated

---

Personal reflection

Think of a recent class that you either taught or participated in as a student. What can you remember about that class? What problems would you have in recollecting 'what happened' in that class?

What are the main difficulties associated with 'recording' classroom interaction? How would you deal with some of those difficulties?

---

with *transcribing* spoken discourse as written text. In this section, I briefly outline some of the difficulties associated with recording and representing spoken interaction in classrooms.

Recording

The first decision that must be made is how to record classroom interaction. Basically, there are four choices:

1 audio-recordings;

2 video-recordings;

3 observation;

4 narrative.

Audio recordings are, in many ways, the easiest means of capturing spoken interaction in classrooms. Modern technology makes it very easy to record the interaction, using digital recorders positioned carefully around the room. More elaborate techniques might entail the use of lapel microphones or multi-directional microphones that are more sensitive and may result in higher quality recordings. The main difficulty associated with audio-recordings is the presence of background 'noise' – a constant presence that can make deciphering very difficult. This can be overcome, to some extent, by ensuring that recording devices are positioned in such a way that if something is not clear on one recorder, it can be picked up on another one.

Video-recordings are a relatively straightforward means of recording interaction in the classroom and have the added advantage of providing a visual representation of what happened. To get the best recordings, two cameras are usually needed: one at the front of the classroom pointing to the back, one at the back pointing to the front. In this way, it is possible to record all the interaction taking place, especially if video cameras are supplemented by the use of digital recorders positioned around the room. This system normally means that it is possible to capture all actions and spoken interactions. The main disadvantage with the use of video is that it can be quite intrusive and result in unusual or unexpected behaviour by students or teachers. The other issue is how to transcribe gestures, body movements, actions, etc. in the written representation of a lesson.

Observation is quick and easy to organise but may have other difficulties. Observers may have to be trained in the use of an observation schedule (see 'interaction analysis' below), and may not be able to record every detail of the interaction. Observers may also be prone to bias and record what they think they saw rather than what actually happened. It is unlikely that two observers would record what they saw in exactly the same way; there are then issues around the reliability of the data and the extent to which the observation is a faithful record of the class. One way of making observation more objective is to use 'focused observation', whereby the observer focuses on one detail in the interaction such as teacher's use of questions, oral feedback, learner involvement, etc. This approach has the advantage of allowing the observer to focus on only one element in the interaction and ignore everything else.

A narrative approach to recording classroom observation entails the use of an observer who writes a descriptive account of the lesson as a narrative. The 'story' that is told of a particular lesson is then used to make changes to practice or to investigate particular phenomena in the interaction. Obviously, the main problem associated with this approach is the difficulty of writing down every detail of what occurs in a classroom. Even the best observers are sure to miss key moments and cannot capture everything.

Whichever approach to recording is adopted, there are a number of principles that should be followed:

- Ethical considerations. Written permission must be obtained from all participants before any recording can begin. In the case of young children, this may also involve getting the permission of parents. In some contexts, the faces of students must not be visible in order to protect their identity. Participants must be told what the recording will be used for, how it will be used and how their anonymity will be ensured. They must have the option of being able to opt in or out of the recording and to leave at any time (see BERA guidelines on research ethics by visiting: www.bera.ac.uk/ethics-and-educational-research-2/).

- How much data? Depending on what the recordings are to be used for, it is worth considering how much data will be needed. This will depend both on the purpose of the recording and on the way it is to be transcribed. It may, for example, be perfectly feasible to use only a few hours of recording if the recordings are transcribed in great detail (see below, transcription).

- Sound quality. For audio and video-recordings, steps need to be taken to ensure that the best quality recordings are made. There is nothing more frustrating than working with recordings where only part of the interaction can be heard. Things to think about include: the choice of room, the use of carpet and curtains to help reduce 'echo', positioning of equipment, number of recorders, selective recording where only some of the participants are included, and so on.

- The role of the observer. The relation of the observer to the participants needs to be given some thought: should they be known or an 'outsider'? In cases where the observer is also another teacher, how might this affect the group dynamics? Where should the observer sit and what part should they play in the lesson? What is the potential for bias, or lack of objectivity?

Once recordings have been made, the next step is transcription.

Transcription

The main concern of transcription is to 'represent reality' as accurately and faithfully as possible. There has been much discussion and debate on this over past decades and there is still only partial agreement as to the extent to which a written transcript can accurately represent a spoken encounter. In the same way that photography sets out to provide a visual record of 'reality', a transcript offers a written record of a spoken interaction. As we shall see, this is not without its problems. Even photography has changed in the way it represents reality: compare the photographs of thirty years ago with modern, digitally enhanced photographs that provide a sharper, more detailed representation of the same image. The same comparison may be said of transcripts: a transcript may offer a rather bland summary of an encounter or a highly detailed description that attempts to record every detail.

Initial attempts to problematise transcription focused largely on the technical side of representing in writing a spoken text. Clearly, there are huge technical difficulties associated with actually hearing what was said, eliminating background noise, including all the finer nuances of spoken language, representing all of this in a written form. There are technical difficulties too at the level of representation: do we opt for broad or narrow transcripts, for example? A broad transcript captures the essence of what was said, the words themselves or even their intended meaning, but ignores the fine details such as a stressed syllable, a pause, a rising intonation, overlapping speech. These technical difficulties remain as much a problem for transcribers as they have always done.

However, and more importantly, there are factors to consider that go beyond the purely technical side of transcription. Methodological decisions made at the time a transcript is produced will greatly influence our understandings of a particular discourse encounter such as a second language class. The precise relationship between the interaction that took place and the words and symbols used to represent it is crucial and complex. That relationship involves the transcriber making key decisions such as:

- Do I include all pauses and how do I represent them?

- How do I record particular gestures, facial expressions, body movements, etc. – or do I simply ignore them?

- What is the 'correct' way to record emphatic speech? Do I even need to record it?

- Do I organise the written text by turn at talk, as conversation analysts do, or by linguistic utterance, showing breath groups and intonation?

- Should intonation be included – if so how do I record it?

- Do I need to transcribe everything – or even anything?

The list goes on. The point I am making here is that important decisions are taken at the time a transcript is produced: these decisions will influence understandings of reality, our ability to interpret the data and our potential to make changes to practice – if that is our intention.

By way of illustration, I am going to take two transcripts of the same event and show how each offers a different interpretation of that event. Both transcripts are taken from Bucholtz (2007) and relate to a research project on nerdy American teenagers, conducted in 1998. The transcripts below relate to an interview that the author conducted with one teenager.

Extract 4.1

Fred: We're always the nerds. We like it. We're glad to be the nerds and the squares. We don't drink, we don't do any drugs, we just get naturally high, we do insane funny things. And we're smart. We get good grades.

In the first extract, the main details of the original interview have been retained. As we read the extract, we get a good sense of Fred's feelings of being a nerd, what this means, why they like it and so on. From an interviewer's perspective, it seems to offer sufficient detail of the interview, without burdening the reader with 'unnecessary' detail.

Essentially, extract 4.1 is a summary of the interview and is highly typical of the kind of data used as 'evidence' in qualitative research reporting interviews. While it certainly captures the essence of that encounter, it omits all the detail of the interaction.

In contrast, consider extract 4.2 below, which offers a micro-analytic rendition of the same event. Here, we see how the main ideas represented in 4.1 were co-constructed by both speakers. Rather than a triumphant boast about being a nerd, which is the impression given in 4.1, the actual interaction demonstrates that the interviewer (Mary) actually did quite a lot of work to elicit Fred's intended meaning. The details of this transcript reveal particular features that indicate that this interaction was a joint enterprise and that meanings were established together:

- Overlapping speech (in lines 1–2, 8–9, 16–17, etc., indicated [ ]).

- Acknowledgement tokens (in lines 22 and 27) that demonstrate understanding by Mary.

- Pausing (in lines 20, 33 and 38) that may indicate interactional trouble or pausing for thought.

- Latched turns (marked =) in lines 12–13, 30–31, 34–35), indicating rapid speech or interruptions.

The overall impression we get as readers when we read extract 4.2 is that, rather than being boastful and triumphant, Fred is 'feeling her way' in the discourse, expressing herself with some difficulty and perhaps embarrassment. Mary, by contrast, prompts, guides and helps the interlocutor to say what she really means – the hallmark of a good interviewer.

Extract 4.2

```
1     Mary:  [So ]
2     Fred:  [We're al]ways the nerds.
3            We like it.
4     Mary:  You@'re the nerds?
5     Fred:  We're <creaky> {glad} to be the ner:ds,
6            a@nd the squa:res and,
7     Mary:  Is that what
8     Fred:  [we don't– ]
9     Mary:  [you say ] you are?
10    Fred:  <[i?]> Well,
11           we don't exactly s:–
```

12		We don't always say it,=
13		=I say it. n@
14	Mary:	@@[@!]
15	Fred:	[But-]
16	Mary:	@ You're [[prou:d.]]
17	Fred:	[[you]] know,
18	Mary:	[@@]
19	Fred:	[we don't–]
20		We just don't (0.5) drink,
21		we d [on't (.) <rapid> {d]o
22	Mary:	[Mm.]
23	Fred:	any drugs,}
24		we don't–
25		we just,
26		<smiling voice quality> {get ↑naturally high},
27	Mary:	A[ha:.]
28	Fred:	[@:]
29	Mary:	[[So that makes you nerds?]]
30	Fred:	[[We just do insane]] funny things.=
31		=I don't know,
32		maybe.
33		(0.6)
34	Mary:	So:=
35	Fred:	=And we're smart.
36		We get <[e?]>-
37		good grades.
38		(1.3) Mostly.

As Bucholtz herself says (2007: 788):

It is obvious that my original transcript was not merely woefully inadequate, but dangerously inaccurate in its representation of the interaction. Fred's comments are not the product of an autonomous, triumphant voice of nerd pride but are rather the result of considerable co-construction (and obstruction) by me as the researcher.

This illustration, I hope, serves to demonstrate the importance of the decisions that are made at the transcription stage in terms of level of detail and faithfulness of the written representation of the spoken interaction. Consider how essential it is, then, in a classroom context, to try to both capture and represent the interaction and to make a case for the level of detail included in the transcript.

In the next section, I present the first of three approaches to analyzing spoken interaction.

Task 4.1

Whatever approach to transcription you adopt, you will need to use some kind of transcription system. Consider the one below. How appropriate is this for transcribing classroom discourse? Are any of these features unnecessary? Would you include any other features not mentioned here?

(Adapted from van Lier 1988; Johnson 1995)

Transcription system

T:	-	teacher
L:	-	learner (not identified)
L1, L2, etc.:	-	identified learner
LL:	-	several learners at once or the whole class
S3, S4	-	Student 3, 4, etc.
/ok/ok/ok/	-	overlapping or simultaneous utterances by more than one learner
[do you understand?]		
[I see]	-	overlap between teacher and learner
=	-	turn continues, or one turn follows another without any pause
. . .	-	pause of one second or less marked by three periods
(4)	-	silence; length given in seconds
?	-	rising intonation – question or other
!	-	emphatic speech: falling intonation
((4))	-	unintelligible 4 seconds a stretch of unintelligible speech with the length given in seconds
Paul, Peter, Mary	-	capitals are only used for proper nouns
T organises groups	-	editor's comments (in bold type)

Interaction analysis approaches

For many years, especially in the 1960s and 1970s, interaction analysis (IA) was the most popular and widely used means of analysing classroom interaction. According to researchers and practitioners at that time, one of the most reliable, quantitative approaches to analysing interaction was through the use of observation instruments, or *coding systems*, to record what the observer thinks is happening at any given moment. From these recordings and the ensuing statistical treatment, classroom profiles can be established, which, it is argued, provide an objective and 'scientific' analysis of the interaction. According to Brown and Rodgers

(2002), over 200 different observation instruments now exist, while Chaudron (1988) calculated that there were approximately twenty-six systems available for analysing interaction in the L2 classroom.

The observation schedules used in IA have a number of features in common:

- They use some system of ticking boxes, making marks, recording what the observer sees, often at regular time intervals.

- They are considered reliable, enabling ease of comparison between observers and generalisability of results (but see 'limitations' on page 77).

- They make assumptions about the ways in which classroom discourse progresses, often in a linear fashion that can be easily recorded.

- They are used extensively in teacher training, particularly for developing competencies and raising awareness.

A review of the many different instruments that are now available is beyond the scope of this chapter. Following Wallace (1998), in the brief summary that follows, observation instruments are divided according to whether they are *system-based* or *ad hoc*.

System-based approaches

By 'system' is meant that the instrument has a number of fixed categories that have been pre-determined by extensive trialling in different classroom contexts. There are several advantages to using a fixed system: the system is ready-made – there is no need to design one from scratch; because the system is well-known, there is no need for validation; any system may be used in real-time or following a recording; comparisons between one system and another are possible.

A brief summary of some of the better known schedules is now presented, beginning with one of the earliest systems put forward by Bellack *et al.* in 1966. Based on the interaction of fifteen teachers and 345 students, the instrument importantly identified a number of pedagogical moves that could be categorised into common teaching cycles. For example, the moves *structure, solicit, respond* and *react* frequently occur together:

Extract 4.3

T:	We're going to look today at ways to improve your writing	**STRUCTURE**
T:	Would you like to tell me one of the mistakes that you made?	**SOLICIT**

| S: | The type of the verb | **RESPOND** |
| T: | The verb, it means there's a problem with the verb | **REACT** |

(Walsh 2001)

Bellack *et al.*'s three-part exchange: *solicit, respond, react* – or as it is now more commonly described: *initiation, response, feedback* (IR(F)) – is, even today, regarded as the very fabric of classroom interaction by most practitioners (see Chapter 1). As such, it represents a significant contribution to our understanding of the processes of classroom interaction and reveals much about the ways in which teachers and students communicate. Some researchers and practitioners argue that an IR(F) exchange structure may indicate an overly teacher-centred classroom, although this criticism has been countered by others. Kasper (2001), for example, argues that learners can be more actively involved in teacher-fronted classroom interaction when teachers offer more participation rights in the conversation. Her work suggests ways in which teachers can facilitate learner involvement in the interaction.

The work of Bellack *et al.* was further advanced by Flanders (1970), whose FIAC system (Flanders Interaction Analysis Categories) assigned classroom interaction to various categories of teacher and student talk:

Teacher talk

1 Accepts feelings.

2 Praises or encourages.

3 Accepts or uses ideas of pupils.

4 Asks questions.

5 Lectures.

6 Gives direction.

7 Criticises or uses authority.

Pupil talk

8 Pupil talk: response.

9 Pupil talk: initiation.

Silence

10 Period of silence or confusion.

Although this instrument does attempt to offer a finer grained classification of classroom discourse, the categories are still rather broad and it is questionable whether the instrument could adequately account for the complex interactional organisation of the contemporary classroom – content or second language – where teacher and learner roles are, arguably, more equal and where student–student interaction is commonplace. Again, this instrument also works on the assumption that all classroom interaction progresses in a 'neat and tidy' manner – this is clearly not the case.

In later years, instruments became more complex and included more and more categories designed to capture the complexities of classroom interaction. The COLT system (Communicative Orientation to Language Teaching), for example, was proposed by Allen *et al.* in 1984 and comprised seventy-three categories. The main aim of COLT was to enable the observer to make a connection between teaching methodology and language use. The instrument is directly linked to communicative methodology and considers how instructional differences impact on learning outcomes. It was devised in two parts. Part A focuses on classroom organisation, tasks, materials and levels of learner involvement, while Part B analyses learner and teacher verbal interaction, considering such things as evidence of an information gap, the existence of sustained speech, the quantity of display versus referential questions. The COLT instrument is certainly one of the most sophisticated devised to date *vis-a-vis* L2 classrooms and makes use of a considerable range of both qualitative and quantitative modes of analysis. A revised version of COLT was presented in 1995 by Spada and Frohlich.

While the most recent version of this instrument is certainly more sophisticated and attempts to capture many of the features of classroom interaction, it has its limitations, as the authors recognise:

> If one is interested in undertaking a detailed discourse analysis of the conversational interactions between teachers and students, another method of coding and analyzing classroom data would be more appropriate.
>
> (Spada and Frohlich 1995: 10)

From this necessarily brief overview of three of the main instruments used in system-based approaches to IA, it is fair to say that the approach has a number of serious limitations:

- Patterns of interaction have to be matched to the categories provided; the results are, therefore, pre-determined. How do observers deal with events or interactions that do not 'fit' the categories?

- Coding systems emphasise the observer's interpretation of events, often at the exclusion of that of the participants. The perspective is therefore *etic (*from the outside), rather than *emic* (from the inside).

- No allowance is made for overlap; the categories for observation are discrete and there is an underlying assumption that classroom discourse proceeds in a sequential manner (T -> Ss -> T -> Ss and so on). In fact, this is simply not the case: overlaps, interruptions, back-channels, false starts, repetitions, hesitations are as common in language classrooms as they are in naturally occurring conversation (Edwards and Westgate 1994).

- Observers may fail to agree on what they see: two observers may 'see' the same class in different ways and produce two different accounts of the same interactions. This may have serious consequences for validity and reliability.

- Coding systems fail to take adequate account of context. All varieties of interaction are evaluated in the same way and from the same perspective (Seedhouse 1996).

Task 4.2

Go back to the description of FIAC on page 76. Use the ten categories given in this instrument to analyse the extract below. What problems did you encounter? In what ways might this instrument be suitable or unsuitable for L2 classrooms?

11	T:	ok does anyone agree with his statement?
12	L:	(2) erm I am agree with=
13	T:	=agree be careful with the verb to agree there you as well Ensa that it's we! agree it's not to
14		be agree it's to agree! Ok=
15	L:	[oh I agree]
15	L:	((3))
16	T:	I agree with you but not I AM agree with you the verb is to agree ok so ((3)) to agree with
17		**(writing on board)** is the preposition that follows it I so it's I agree with you I disagree with
18		you . . . ok em Silvie can you em what were you going to say?
19	L2:	I agree with you because em when when we talk about something em for example you
20		saw a ((2)) on TV=

As we have seen, it is unlikely that highly structured observation instruments, such as the ones outlined in this section, can adequately account for the complexities of most classrooms. In order to explain the features of a particular context, it seems likely that less structured, yet tailor-made instruments are more suitable. While still following a broadly IA approach, these *ad hoc* observation instruments (Wallace 1998) are more sensitive to context and are normally designed with a specific goal in mind. As such, they offer descriptions that are likely to be both more accurate and more realistic.

'Ad hoc' approaches

In contrast to system-based interaction analysis, *ad hoc* approaches offer the construction of a more flexible instrument, which may, for example, be based on a specific classroom problem or area of interest. The instrument may be designed as part of an action research project in which practitioners wish to answer a particular question such as: how can I improve the quality of the feedback I give my students? Alternatively, the instrument might be designed through consultation with either teachers or students working in a specific context.

Consider the following example, an extract from Walsh 2006 (see Chapter 6):

F. Seeking clarification   1. Teacher asks a student to clarify something the student has said.

2. Student asks teacher to clarify something the teacher has said.

This instrument was used to help teachers gain closer understandings of their teacher talk. This is one category, from a total of fourteen used in the original, focusing on the ways in which teachers seek clarification (see Appendix A for the original).

Now look at the extract below and the commentary that follows. In what ways does this instrument help us, as observers, to gain closer understandings of the interaction?

Extract 4.4

```
121   T:      =yes so tell me again what you mean by that?=
122   L::     =the first is the introduction the second eh in this case
              we have the ((3)) who you are to eh
123           introduce yourself a few words about yourself and where
              you live and what I do [and]
124           T: [so ] . . . yes?=
125   L:      =and then it's the problem what happened . . .
```

126	T:	yes=
127	L:	=and you need to explain it and why you are writing because probably you did something like
128		you gave the information to the police but it didn't happen . . .
129	T:	right=
130	L:	=which is why it's ((2))=
131	T:	=so can I ask you why did you write it in your head as you said?=
132	L:	=I don't know it's like a rule=
133	T:	=right so it's like a rule what do you mean? . . .

In this extract, we can see several examples of the teacher seeking clarification (in 121, 124, 131 and 133). Throughout the extract, the teacher's prompts stimulate the learner to offer an explanation: 'it's like a rule' (line 132). Although the actual explanation is not forthcoming, even by the end of the extract, arguably, the teacher's requests for clarification do serve the purpose of 'pushing' this learner to say more and offer an explanation. The teacher's use of backchannels or acknowledgement tokens ('yes' in line 126 and 'right' in line 129) also tell the student that she has been understood, that she still has the floor and that she should continue with her explanation.

The main advantage of this approach to IA is that it allows us, as observers, to focus on specific details in the interaction that we can then describe and attempt to explain. The whole process is much more from the inside looking out and less from the outside looking in. In other words, an *ad hoc* system is more likely to promote understanding and generate explanations than the system-based approaches discussed above. The fact that the instruments are designed in relation to a particular question or problem within a specific context makes the whole research process more meaningful and realistic. Perhaps most important of all is the fact that we are more likely to have confidence in the data.

We can summarise the main advantages of *ad hoc* approaches to interaction analysis as follows:

- *Ad hoc* approaches to classroom observation give participants ownership of the research design process and greater insights into the issues under investigation.

- By focusing on the detail of the interaction, such approaches allow practitioners to access and understand complex phenomena that might otherwise take years of class experience to acquire.

- *Ad hoc* systems enable observers to focus on the microcosms of interactions that might so easily be missed by the 'broad brush' descriptions provided by systems-based approaches.

Having given a brief critique of interaction analysis, I now turn to discourse analysis approaches to analysing classroom interaction.

Discourse analysis approaches

Discourse analysis is the study of spoken or written texts. Its focus is on words and utterances above the level of sentence and its main aim is to look at the ways in which words and phrases function in context. For example, the frequently used *'Could you turn to page 36?'* might be interpreted as a request under DA. Other utterances may be less easy to classify. The phrase 'the window's open', when uttered in a classroom, might function as a request (please close it), an explanation (that's why it's so cold), a drill (everyone repeat), a definition (as a way of showing the meaning of *open*). According to Seedhouse (2004: 56), 'the overwhelming majority of previous approaches to L2 classroom interaction have implicitly or explicitly adopted what is fundamentally a discourse analysis approach.'

Perhaps the earliest and most well-known proponents of DA are Sinclair and Coulthard (1975) who, following a structural-functional linguistic route to analysis, compiled a list of twenty-two speech acts representing the verbal behaviours of both teachers and students participating in primary classroom communication. The outcome is the development of a descriptive system incorporating a discourse hierarchy:

- LESSON

- TRANSACTION

- EXCHANGE

- MOVE

- ACT

Act is therefore the smallest discourse unit, while lesson is the largest; acts are described in terms of their discourse function, as in the two examples of speech acts below, *evaluation* and *cue*:

Extract 4.5

Act	Function	Realisation
Evaluation	evaluates	*right so it's like a rule* what do you mean?
Cue	evokes bid	yes *so tell me again* what you mean by that

Perhaps the most important contribution of Sinclair and Coulthard to our understandings of classroom discourse is their realisation that most classroom discourse follows an IR(F) structure. For every move made by a student, teachers typically make two, as in:

I	T:	what's the past tense of go?
F	S:	went
F/E	T:	went, excellent.

Thus, we can say that most teaching exchanges follow an IRF structure, made up of three moves, with each move containing one or more speech acts. Not only does this help to confirm the fact that teachers do speak much more than students in most classrooms, it also demonstrates how teachers often control the discourse. (For a full discussion of the IRF exchange, please see Chapter 2.)

The main difficulty associated with allocating utterances to functions is that any utterance can perform a range of functions (see the above example). In a multi-party setting such as a classroom, where there are so many things going on at the same time, deciding on a linguistic function may be extremely problematic. According to Stubbs (1983), it is almost impossible to say precisely what function is being performed by a teacher (or learner) at any point in a lesson. As with most functional analyses, inside or outside a classroom, an utterance can have any number of functions depending on crucial contextual clues such as who said it, to whom, how they said it, why they said it and so on. Classification of classroom discourse in purely structural-functional terms is consequently problematic. Levinson (1983) takes up the same argument, stressing the fact that any one utterance can perform a multitude of functions, especially in a classroom setting where interaction patterns are so complex. The consequence of this is that there is no way, under speech act theory, to account for gestures or behavioural traits.

Task 4.3

Look at the extract below and analyse it according to language functions. What difficulties did you encounter in deciding on the function of each utterance? How well does IRF account for the overall structure of this interaction?

Extract 4.6

1	L:	no that's bad news=
2	L:	=so it's good news (**laughter**)
3	LL:	/bad news/ ok / no no that's good news/ . . .
4	L2:	bad news . . .
5	L:	no that's bad news=
6	L3:	=ah good good news (2)
7	L1:	no no that's wrong you have to do bad news . . .
8	L2:	yes it's a bad news because [you]
9	L:	[no but that's] good news=
10	T:	=that's good news G N good news . . .

One of the main limitations of the Sinclair and Coulthard system is that it was derived from data recorded in 'traditional' primary school classrooms during the 1960s. In this context, and by the authors' own admission, it was possible to identify very clear status and power relations between teachers and learners. Consequently, the ensuing discourse had a very clear structure that was largely dominated by question and answer routines. In the contemporary L2 classroom, where there is, arguably, far more equality and partnership in the teaching–learning process, it is doubtful whether the framework could adequately describe the structure of classroom communication.

As Wu (1998: 529–530) says:

the cumulative effect of teacher–student interaction cannot be accounted for within the [Sinclair and Coulthard 1975] framework. It is clear that such hierarchical categorisation, though shedding some light on the mechanism of teacher–student verbal exchanges, is not enough to demonstrate its entire dynamic process.

To summarise this section, we can say that DA approaches are both descriptive and prescriptive and attempt to categorise naturally occurring patterns of interaction and account for them by reference to a discourse hierarchy. The starting point is structural-functional linguistics: classroom data are analysed according to their structural patterning and function. For example, the interrogative structure *'What time does this lesson end?'* could be interpreted as a request for information, an admonishment, a prompt or cue. Any attempt to analyse classroom data using a DA approach, therefore, involves some simplification and reduction. Matching utterances to categories may be problematic owing to the issues of multi-functionality and the absence of a direct relationship between form and function. In general,

DA approaches fail to take account of the more subtle forces at work such as role relations, context and sociolinguistic norms that have to be obeyed. In short, a DA treatment fails to adequately account for the dynamic nature of classroom interaction and the fact that it is socially constructed by its participants. By the same token, DA approaches do not adequately account for the range of contexts in operation in a lesson and for the link between pedagogic purpose and language use.

In the final section of this chapter, a critique is presented of a more naturalistic approach to classroom discourse: conversation analysis.

Conversation analysis approaches

The origins of conversation analysis (CA) come from an interest in the function of language as a means for social interaction (Sacks, Schegloff and Jefferson 1974). CA is based on the premise that social contexts are not static but are constantly being formed by the participants through their use of language and the ways in which turn-taking, openings and closures, sequencing of acts, and so on are locally managed. Interaction is examined in relation to meaning and context; the way in which actions are sequenced is central to the process.

In the words of Heritage:

> In fact, CA embodies a theory which argues that sequences of actions are a major part of what we mean by context, that the meaning of an action is heavily shaped by the sequence of previous actions from which it emerges, and that social context is a dynamically created thing that is expressed in and through the sequential organisation of interaction.
>
> (1997: 162)

According to this view, interaction is *context-shaped* and *context-renewing*; that is, one contribution is dependent on a previous one and subsequent contributions create a new context for later actions. Under this microscopic view of context, one person's contribution is inextricably linked to that of another person. Order in spoken discourse is established through sequential organisation: the way in which one utterance is connected to another.

To see how this works in a classroom, consider extract 4.7 below. In the extract, every turn is uniquely linked to the previous and following ones and there is a clear sense that this represents a coherent piece of discourse that could have only occurred in a classroom context. Turns 187–199 make up a piece of spoken text that is coherent and logical because of the ways in which one turn is interdependent on another. The whole extract is a good example of a piece of discourse that is co-constructed by participants and that is shaped by a goal-oriented activity: here, eliciting the word *force*.

Extract 4.7

187	T:	=what do we call I'm going to try and get the class to tell you what this word
188		is that you're looking for . . . er we talk about military (**claps hands**) . . . military what?
189	L:	((1))=
190	T:	=like fight=
191	L:	=kill=
192	T:	=no not [kill]
193	L:	[action] action=
194	T:	=no ((2)) military?=
195	LL:	=power=
196	T:	=power think of another word military?
197	LL:	((3))force=
198	T:	=so she believes in a FORCE for?
199	L:	that guide our lives=
200	T:	=that guides our lives=

Although the origins of CA lie in ordinary spoken interaction, its relevance to institutional discourse – such as a classroom – cannot be ignored. Here, the goals and actions of participants are closely linked to, and to some extent constrained by, the institutional business. In a language classroom, for example, most interactions are related to the enterprise of learning a second language; turn and topic management, sequential organisation and choice of lexis are all determined by that enterprise and by the roles of interactants. Essentially, an institutional discourse CA methodology takes as its starting point the centrality of talk to many work tasks: quite simply, the majority of work-related tasks are completed through what is essentially conversation, or 'talk-in-interaction' (Drew and Heritage 1992: 3). In many work contexts, we find an expert and non-specialist: doctor–patient, counsellor–client, teacher–student. The interactions that take place in these contexts are largely shaped by the roles performed by the interactants and by the business of the moment. It comes as no surprise therefore that teachers typically ask questions and students (usually) answer them. What CA can do is to uncover something of the detail of these interactions by looking at the ways in which contexts are co-created in relation to the goal-oriented activity in which they are engaged (Heritage 1997: 163). All institutions have an overriding goal or purpose that constrains both the actions and interactional contributions of the participants according to the business in hand, giving each institution a unique interactional 'fingerprint' (Heritage and Greatbatch 1991: 95–6). Thus, the interactional patterning (or 'fingerprint') that is typical of, for example, a travel agent's will be different from that of a dentist's, or newsagent's.

Personal reflection

What interactional features make up the *fingerprint* of an L2 classroom? Examples include questions and responses to questions.

   How many others can you think of? How do these features compare to those found in other social contexts, such as meetings, chat shows, job interviews?

While the discourse of L2 classrooms does not and should not be interpreted as fully resembling a conversation, there are some strong parallels. Essentially, what takes place in an L2 classroom between teachers and learners and learners and their peers can be described as 'conversation'. It is, for the most part, two-way; it entails turn-taking, turn-passing, turn-ceding and turn-seizing; it makes use of topic switches and contains many of the features of 'ordinary' conversation such as false starts, hesitations, errors, silence, back channelling and so on.

In the words of Edwards and Westgate (1994: 116):

> The point is not that classroom talk 'should' resemble conversation, since most of the time for practical purposes it cannot, but that institutionalised talk [. . .] shows a heightened use of procedures which have their 'base' in ordinary conversation and are more clearly understood through comparison with it.

The relevance of a CA approach to the L2 classroom context is not difficult to perceive. CA attempts to account for the practices at work that enable participants in a conversation to make sense of the interaction and contribute to it. There are clear parallels: classroom talk is made up of many participants, and there have to be smooth transitions and clearly defined expectations if meanings are to be made explicit. Possibly the most significant role of CA is to **interpret** from the data rather than **impose** pre-determined structural or functional categories.

For many researchers and practitioners working with classroom data, CA offers a way of answering questions that are related to teaching and learning. Rather than studying features of the interaction *per se* – what ten Have (2007) calls 'pure' CA – the research interest may be more closely linked to educational practices. This 'applied' form of CA may be used to provide insights that may inform the actions of practitioners. For example, a CA analysis may reveal how teachers create opportunities for learning in the interaction, or, indeed, restrict them. As Richards (2006: 5) points out, CA can perform an 'enabling rather than an enacting role' in providing insights for professional practice. Applied CA will seek to 'translate' the resulting descriptions into terms relating to substantive issues in the relevant field, such as ways of improving classroom practices.

The main features of a CA approach to analysing L2 classroom interaction are summarised:

- The aim of CA is to account for the structural organisation of the interaction as determined by the participants. There should be no attempt to 'fit' the data to preconceived categories.

- The approach is strictly empirical. CA forces the researcher to focus on the interaction patterns emerging *from* the data, rather than relying on any preconceived notions which language practitioners may bring *to* the data (Seedhouse 2004).

- The observer is seen as a 'member' of the interaction, trying to view the experience through the eyes of the participants. The aim is to offer an emic (insider) perspective.

- Context is dynamic and mutually constructed by the participants. Contexts are therefore constantly changing as a lesson progresses and according to local demands and constraints.

- Talk is seen, in an institutional setting, as being goal-oriented: participants are striving towards some overall objective related to the institution. In a language classroom, for example, the discourse is influenced by the fact that all participants are focusing on some pre-determined aim [SM1]– learning a second language.

- The analysis of the data is *multi-layered*. CA approaches emphasise both context and the sequentiality of utterances. Because no one utterance is categorised in isolation and because contributions are examined in sequence, a CA methodology is much better-equipped to interpret and account for the multi-layered structure of classroom interaction.

An example may help to make some of these ideas clearer. Extract 4.8 below is taken from a class of adult learners who are preparing to read a text on euthanasia. The teacher's stated pedagogic goal for this segment of the lesson was to improve oral fluency and there follows a discussion on ways of prolonging life. In the extract, by looking at longer extracts of data and using a CA approach, a number of observations can be made.

In the extract, we can see that turn-taking between teacher and students is fairly even – indeed, students have more interactional space than the teacher, who only intervenes as and when necessary (in 115, 117 and 119). Turns follow one another quickly and there is little pausing, as indicated by (=), showing latching: one turn follows another without any pause. This may be significant since silence and pausing are often signs of interactional trouble; there is, then, a sense that the discourse flows freely and that participants have equal status and rights. Participants make frequent use of acknowledgement tokens such as *ugh* (line 111), *yeah* (113), *oh* (117), which serve the important function of 'oiling the wheels of the interaction' (McCarthy 2003) and letting everyone know that they have been understood. There is no repair at all in this extract, and although errors do occur, they do not impede communication at all and are simply ignored. There is evidence too that meanings are being negotiated (in 109–110, 112–113, 114–115, 116–117) – an indicator that something is being communicated.

Extract 4.8

109	T:	[no ok alright] . . . so Jan you want to live forever?=
110	L3:	=yeah if money can afford it I will freeze body =
111	L:	=ugh . . .
112	L1:	what are you going to do? . . . frozen frozen you body?=
113	L3:	=yeah=
114	L1:	=cryonics? . . .
115	T:	=yeah it's cry cry cryo[genics]
116	L1:	[cryonics] cryogenics . . . no cryonics=
117	T:	=oh is it? ok=
118	L1:	=I think so I don't know . . .
119	T:	let me check it it might be in this one . . . **(looks in dictionary)**

Even at a very basic level and focusing on a limited amount of data (11 turns in extract 4.8), our understanding of 'what happened' can be greatly enhanced under a CA methodology. Rather than allocating utterances to preconceived categories, there is an attempt to 'let the data speak for themselves', indicating how understandings are derived in the goal-oriented activity of the moment. Minute adjustments in the discourse can often be explained in relation to the moment-by-moment co-construction of meaning as participants attend to some pre-conceived agenda.

However, it cannot be denied that CA approaches do have a number of limitations. These include:

- Selectivity. Some researchers criticise CA for being over selective. Snatches of discourse and their ensuing commentaries may appear to have been selected randomly with no attempt to evaluate their significance to the discourse as a whole. Any selection of data may appear contrived or idealised in order to illustrate a particular point with little attempt to relate them to the exchange as a whole.

- Inability to generalise. A more serious criticism of CA approaches is their inability to generalise findings because they focus on one specific and very narrow context. While this may be true of many qualitative research tools, it is particularly applicable to a CA methodology owing to the centrality of context. That is not to say that context-specific data are not valid or worthwhile; merely that they cannot be extended to other contexts. This objection is countered, however, if we acknowledge that the aim of classroom-specific research is not so much to generalise as to promote understanding and facilitate replication to another context. Class-based, ethnomethodological research sets out to report trends, patterns and tendencies rather than absolutes; 'studies of classroom interaction will clearly be extremely complex and tentative, and one must take care not to draw hasty conclusions from superficially identifiable interactional tokens' (van Lier 1996: 143).

Summary

This chapter has provided a critical overview of some of the better-known approaches to investigating L2 classroom interaction. Starting with an account of the main issues that must be addressed when recording and transcribing classroom interaction, I presented a critique of the more traditional, and arguably more static, interaction and discourse analysis traditions. In the final section conversation analysis was offered as a potentially more powerful, though not unproblematic, approach to recording classroom discourse.

In the next chapter, the focus shifts to alternative approaches to analysing classroom discourse.

5 Alternative approaches to studying classroom discourse

Introduction

Chapter 4 focused on some of the better-known approaches to analysing classroom discourse in the form of interaction analysis, discourse analysis and conversation analysis. In this chapter, we consider other approaches that can be used to collect and analyse classroom data and evaluate their relative merits or shortcomings. By the end of this chapter you should have a pretty good idea about how to choose an appropriate approach for analysing spoken interaction in the classroom. In the next chapter, I introduce a framework for evaluating classroom interaction that can be used to help teachers improve their classroom practices.

Personal reflection

Make a note of some of the difficulties we have discussed in analysing classroom discourse. Based on what you now know, which approaches to studying interaction seem appropriate to your context? How would you go about studying interaction in one of your classes and how might you deal with some of the problems you have listed?

Corpus linguistics

A corpus is a collection of texts that is stored electronically on a computer or other form of electronic storage. These texts can be from written sources such as books, magazines, junk mail, letters, advertisements, business documents, literature, academic papers, emails and internet pages. A corpus can also be a collection of spoken texts, such as conversations, phone calls, speeches, TV chat shows, classrooms and so on. A corpus, therefore, is a collection of real language that people use in all types of situation. Because this language can be stored easily on a computer, it can be searched quickly and easily using special software. This makes it very suitable for research into how language is really used. Corpus linguistics is the study of language in use, using specialised software to carry out searches.

Using a corpus is not unlike using an internet search engine. It is essentially a large database that you can use to find every occurrence of a word or phrase. Just like an internet search, the 'hits' that result from your search will, in a matter of seconds, pop up on your screen.

For instance, if we ask a corpus to find examples of the word *exactly*, within seconds, the search software will give us a list that looks like this:

train for a job and a lot of love. [p] This is **exactly** what the YMCA has and will continue to
full adjustable in order to support book sat **exactly** the right angle and weighed cords hold the
a free planning service and will work out **exactly** the amount of panelling you need to buy for
starters, there's only one joke - which isn't **exactly** original in the first place. It's the one
wrong, that they're without fault. They're not **exactly** lying but they're certainly not telling the
We opted for Shaker furniture, as it had **exactly** the clean lines we were looking for. A four-
if Moscow had not operated in every instance **exactly** as Washington might have wished. He did not
but Brand suddenly realised it summed up **exactly** his interest in Ella's death. [p] As he
and the other two little girls were treated **exactly** alike. [o] We would be taken into the
close to the Celestial North Pole, but not **exactly** central. With the passage of centuries, the
I don't remember." But someone told you." Not **exactly**. I just did know it was needful. I couldn't
the ancient Britons, as I call them: they are **exactly** what that Roman (Suetonius or Agricola,
[p] Cos what happened all these girls did **exactly** the same thing. I was made quite clear that
There is no doubt they (the robbers) knew **exactly** what they were looking for." He described
had liked it. Oh yes, I soothed, it was fun. `**Exactly**!" she beamed. `A fun read, a woman's book,
illustrious predecessors is play her part with **exactly** the right weight so that she appeals to
and arrange another abduction [p]. That was **exactly** what happened to Pam Green, whose two sons
TV Week [/h] [b] Ivan Waterman [/b] [p] WHAT **exactly** has Mariella Frostrup got? A funny surname?
to that word `fun again. Whatever it means **exactly**, manufacturers clearly feel that when it
And he finds out Ernesto is missing. That's **exactly** the way it happened. Now, everybody tells me
see?" [p] I get you," Stan said. `I understand **exactly** what you mean." And he waited with a child's
in the baby boom year of 1947, Dewaere was **exactly** thirty-five years old when he died, a fact
crisis? What is the climax of the story? Why, **exactly**, does Sammy quit his job? Does anything lead

Source: www.collins.co.uk/Corpus/CorpusSearch.aspx

These are called *concordance* lines. Concordance lines essentially tell us how a word is used with other words, how it combines to create particular meanings, which words it normally associates with and so on. Essentially, concordance lines give us a lot of very useful information about a particular word or words.

Task 5.1

Go to the Collins Bank of English website at www.collins.co.uk/
Corpus/CorpusSearch.aspx . Use this free software to perform the
following operations for *not really*.

1 Under the corpus concordance sampler, type in not+really in the
'type in your query' box. Now tick the 'British transcribed speech'
box.

2 Click 'show concs' (concordances). You'll get a list of concordance
lines for *not really*.

3 Read through the concordance lines. What observations about
not really can you make? How might you use this with a group
of learners?

4 Consider how this approach could be used with a corpus of
classroom discourse. What might it reveal?

Apart from giving us concordance lines, corpus software can also
tell us how many times a word occurs in the whole corpus. However,
if this information is to be reliable and useful to us as teachers,
materials designers, or researchers, it has to come from a well-designed
corpus. When we construct a corpus, we must do so in a principled
way to ensure that it is representative, just as we would do if we were
conducting a survey using questionnaires, for example. So if we were
to build a corpus of classroom discourse, we'd need to think about
some or all of the following:

Example of a type of corpus	Possible design considerations
Corpus of classroom interactions	• What language levels? • How many nationalities? • How many age groups? • What range of teachers: experienced, novice, native speaker, non-native speaker? • How many classes? • What types of classes?

Apart from the representativeness of a corpus, the other key
consideration we need to make is its size. Until quite recently, it was

assumed that the bigger a corpus the better it is. Some of the largest corpora that are currently available contain over one billion words! Such mega-corpora are usually held by English-language publishers who make them available to their authors for materials design. Large corpora are also used in making dictionaries. Here are some examples of large publisher corpora:

- Collins, under the COBUILD project, has a corpus of 450 million words of contemporary written and spoken English. Fifty-six million words of this is available online as part of *Wordbanks Online English*.

  Source: www.collins.co.uk/Corpus/
  CorpusSearch.aspx

- Cambridge University Press has a corpus of one billion words which it makes available to its authors.

  Source: www.cambridge.org/elt/corpus/cic.htm

- Longman has a written corpus of 100 million words, 5 million words of American spoken English and 10 million words of student writing.

  Source: www.longman.com/dictionaries/corpus/
  (O'Keeffe *et al.* 2007)

As a rule of thumb, a 'large' corpus means more than 5 million words and 'small' usually means fewer than 5 million words. One of the interesting developments in corpus linguistics in recent years, and which is of relevance here, is that it is now becoming increasingly common for researchers to use much smaller corpora of around 50,000–100,000 words. The reason for this is that these smaller corpora are usually highly context-specific and applied to address a particular problem. It is not difficult, for example, to see how a small corpus of around 50,000 words of university small group talk could be usefully applied to look at the ways in which local and international students interact in seminars. Here, a small corpus has been used to address a 'real world problem' in a very useful and illuminating way. The reason this approach works is that all the data are recorded in a single, homogeneous context and used in response to a particular question or problem. The corpus is not simply descriptive, but pro-active in relation to a particular issue.

The argument I am making then is that corpus linguistics, in the present context, should focus more on what a corpus can *do* than what a corpus *is*. (For definitions, the reader is referred to Biber *et al.* 1998; Sinclair 1997). Corpus linguistics (CL), at least here, should be viewed as a *methodological tool* that will help us investigate classroom discourse. The range of tools that CL provides us with is discussed briefly below, but essentially, CL will help us to automatically find what we are looking for. CL will count frequencies and find key words and it will allow us to find patterns that we could not otherwise find, but it will not explain the dynamics of these interactions in the context of the recordings.

Increasingly, CL is being applied to contexts and domains outside of the study of language itself where the *use* of language is the focus of empirical study in a given context. Such contexts include courtrooms and forensic linguistics (Cotterill 2010), the workplace (Koester 2006), the classroom and educational contexts (O'Keeffe and Farr 2003; Walsh and O'Keeffe 2007), political discourse (Ädel 2010), advertising and the media (O'Keeffe 2006), among other areas. In all of these cases, CL is used as a tool and another approach is drawn on as a framework; these include CA, discourse analysis and pragmatics (see below).

CL has at its disposal a range of techniques that can be used for the study of language, all of which can be used to study classroom discourse. These include:

Concordancing

As we saw in the example above, concordancing is a core tool in corpus linguistics and it simply means using corpus software to find every occurrence of a particular word or phrase. The search word or phrase is often referred to as the *node* and concordance lines are usually presented with the node word/phrase in the centre of the line with seven or eight words presented at either side. These are known as Key-Word-In-Context displays (or 'KWIC' concordances). Concordance lines challenge us to read in an entirely new way, vertically, or even from the centre outwards in both directions. They are usually scanned vertically at first glance, that is, looked at up or down the central pattern, along the line of the node word or phrase. Here are some sample lines from a concordance of the word *way* using the Limerick Corpus of Irish English (LCIE) taken from O'Keeffe *et al.* 2007:

Ireland is no different in a **way** then em what they were
of you anyhow? Now in a **way** 'What Dreams may come' it's
in college in fact it's a **way** of life and you find this
he present things in such a **way** that he would persuade
of life is to live in such a **way** that when you die your soul
he obviously lived a certain **way** of live and they wanted to
to deal with in a different **way** they couldn't deal with it
stadium that's the easiest **way** to describe it. There is a
find this the most effective **way**. Ok now today em you have as

there is no evidence either **way**. You can't have evidence
from the top and works his **way** down. The theologian will
so it speaks and works its **way** up. The theologian starts

Our concordance analysis of this extract reveals the following:

- *Way* frequently co-occurs with the preposition *in* (*in a way, in no way*, etc.).

- It is often used to form fixed or semi-fixed phrases (*in a way, on the way, a way of life, in such a way*, etc.).

- *Way* is frequently followed by another preposition (to, down, up, etc.).

- It occurs more frequently in the middle of a clause than at the beginning or end.

And so on. There are many other observations we could make and just think how valuable this approach is when we use a larger extract, restrict our search to three words either side of the node, or expand it to seven words either side of the node. Concordance line analysis is very productive in terms of looking at language patterning such as idiomatic usages or collocation (for a detailed illustration, see O'Keeffe *et al.* 2007).

Word frequency counts or word lists

Another common corpus technique that software can perform is the extremely rapid calculation of word frequency lists (or word lists) for any batch of texts. By running a word frequency list on a corpus, you get a rank ordering of all the words in order of frequency. This function facilitates enquiry across different corpora, different language varieties and different contexts of use. Below, for example, are the first ten words from three very different spoken corpora:

- Service encounters: a sub-corpus of the Limerick Corpus of Irish English (LCIE) comprising shop encounters (8,500 words).

- Friends chatting: a sub-corpus of LCIE, consisting of female friends chatting (40,000 words).

- Academic English: The Limerick-Belfast Corpus of Academic Spoken English (LIBEL CASE, one million words of Academic English).

Even from the first ten most frequent words, we can see differing patterns of use (any of these words can then be concordanced to look at how they are functioning in the texts):

	A	B	C
1	You	I	the
2	Of	And	And
3	Is	The	Of
4	Thanks	To	You
5	It	Was	To
6	I	You	A
7	Please	It	That
8	The	Like	In
9	Yeah	That	It
10	Now	He	is

Source: Walsh and O'Keeffe 2007.

From this very brief extract, we can make the following observations:

- The shop (column A) and casual conversation (column B) results show markers of interactivity typical of spoken English such as *I, you, yeah* (as a response token), *like, please, and thanks* (see Carter and McCarthy 2006).

- The first ten words of the academic corpus (C) lack the interactive markers found in first two columns. The academic corpus has more of the features of a written text such as a high frequency of articles, *a* and *the*, use of the preposition *of*, use of *that*.

Again, there are many other observations that we could make from this data. The point is that CL allows us to make important and reliable observations from our data very quickly.

Key word analysis

This function allows us to identify the key words in one or more texts. Key words, as detailed by Scott (2008), are those whose frequency is unusually high in comparison with some norm. Key words are not usually the most frequent words in a text (or collection of texts), rather they are the more 'unusually frequent' (ibid). Software compares two pre-existing word lists and one of these is assumed to be a large word list that will act as a reference file or benchmark corpus. The other is the word list based on the text(s) that you want to study. The larger corpus will provide background data for reference comparison. For example, we saw above that *the* is the most frequent word in the LIBEL corpus of spoken academic English (see above). Scott (2008) notes the key word facility provides a useful way of characterising a text or a genre and has potential applications in the areas of forensic linguistics, stylistics, content analysis and text retrieval. In the context of language teaching, it can be used by teachers and materials writers to create word lists, for example in Languages for Specific Purposes programmes (e.g. English for Pilots).

Cluster analysis

The analysis of how language systematically clusters into combinations of words or *chunks* (e.g. *I mean, this that and the other,* etc.) can give insights into how we describe the vocabulary of a language (Wray 2000, 2002; McCarthy and Carter 2002). As O'Keeffe *et al.* (2007) note, the way in which words cluster together into chunks has implications for what we teach in our vocabulary lessons and how learners approach the task of acquiring vocabulary and developing fluency. As a corpus technique, the process of generating chunks or cluster lists is similar to making single word frequency lists. Instead of asking the computer to rank all of the single words in the corpus in order of frequency, we can ask it to look for word combinations, for example two-, three-, four-, five-, or six-word combinations. For example, using *Wordsmith Tools,* here are the twelve most frequent three-word combinations from the LIBEL corpus:

1 A lot of

2 And so on

3 I don't know

4 At the moment

5 In other words

6 A number of

7 A couple of

8 A little bit

9 A bit of

10 As I said

11 First of all

12 As well as
      (Walsh and O'Keeffe 2007)

What is interesting from this cluster analysis from a classroom discourse perspective, is the frequency of words and phrases that are used to 'point' in the discourse and to locate learning in time and place.

Phrases like *as I said, first of all, in other words* perform an important signposting function and enable learners to find their way through the discourse or 'navigate' their way in the interaction (Breen 1998). If teachers do not signpost for their learners and highlight the direction the discourse is going, it is a little like reading a newspaper without punctuation; we very quickly get lost and confused. Effective teachers use discourse markers naturally and almost without thinking.

Task 5.2

In the following extract, all the signpost words (discourse markers) have been removed (marked XXXX in the text). Add in what you consider to be the most suitable word or phrase. What functions are these signpost words performing and why are they important here?

> T: XXXX we're going to be reading about and talking about
> er music and pop stars and famous people Last XXXX
> we did a quiz XXXX and it was a picture quiz and some
> of the pictures were people from your countries. XXXX let
> me see could you work with Ben and could you three guys
> work together (**T organises groups**). If you recognise any
> of those people who they are and what you know about
> them and then what kind of lifestyle do you think these
> people have. XXXX you can begin when you're ready.

In this section, I have outlined the main benefits of a CL approach to the study of classroom discourse and highlighted its main advantages in terms of speed and accessibility of data and reliability of findings. In the next section, I consider how CL might combine with other approaches, especially CA (Conversation Analysis).

Combined approaches

While CL offers a very useful means of analysing relatively large corpora of spoken interactions, its focus is largely on individual and collections of words. The perspective on the interaction that CL offers is a distant one that portrays general trends and patterns rather than a detailed, 'up-close' view of the interaction. To use Batstone's (1994) analogy of the view from an aeroplane as it comes into land, CL offers us a view from around 10,000 metres. At this height, we can see the landscape below and make out lakes, rivers and mountains. But we cannot make out the detail. Our CL analysis allows us to make generalisations about word frequencies and collocations, but it does not permit us to get close to the interaction and to see how interlocutors really communicate. To do this, we need to drop down to around 200 metres.

At this height, we can see much more detail. We can see cars and roads, we can make out the car park at the airport, we can even see people. In order to get this level of detail, we need another approach to our analysis. To do this, we need to combine CL with another approach since CL is unable to account for some of the features of spoken interaction that occur at the higher levels of utterance and turn. In order to conduct a detailed analysis at this level of the discourse, I propose that CL can usefully be combined with conversation analysis (CA), an established and respected approach to providing detailed, micro-analytic descriptions of spoken interaction. This combined approach, using both CL and CA (henceforth, CLCA) cumulatively gives a more 'up-close' description of spoken interactions in an educational setting than that offered by using either one on its own. From the analysis, we can gain powerful insights into the ways in which interactants establish understandings and observe how words, utterances and text combine in the co-construction of meaning.

As I have shown previously, the current trend in corpus-based approaches to the study of discourse is towards smaller, more specialised and context-specific corpora. Arguably, such corpora lend themselves to multiple layers of analysis and provide opportunities for combining different methodologies. Previously, when it was 'fashionable' to only construct large corpora, the main focus was on lexical patterning rather then discourse context because 'large corpora were lexically rich but contextually poor' (Walsh *et al.* 2010). That is, when researchers look at a lexical item in a 100 million word corpus, they are detached from its context. However, when researchers record, transcribe, annotate and build a small, contextualised spoken corpus, a different landscape of the possibilities opens up in areas beyond lexis to areas of use (especially issues of pragmatics, interaction and discourse).

In what ways might it be desirable and useful to combine CL with CA? As we have seen in Chapter 4, CA is essentially concerned with turn-taking and explores all the associated features – such as topic, turn management, turn preference, sequential organisation, repair – in micro detail. At first sight, it might appear that CL and CA have very little in common. CL deals with large texts and pays little attention to context, whereas CA looks at the microscopic details of shorter texts that are highly contextualised. CA uses a qualitative analysis, CL's is quantitative. The main focus of CL is lexis: single words, combinations of words, word clusters. CA, on the other hand, is more interested in turns: sequential organisations, sequencing, shifts and so on.

This said, in fact, both CA and CL have a number of features that link them:

- Both use a corpus of empirical data.
- Both refer to baseline comparisons with other types of interactions (canonical sequential order in the case of CA, reference corpora in CL).
- CA offers an emic, close-up perspective, CL complements by providing a bigger picture.
- Both start from the data and work outwards to construct context (from turn order in CA, from patterns in CL).
- Both attach importance to lexis in creation of meanings (though this is downplayed in CA).
- Word patterns (CL) often lead to consistent turn patterns (CA).

How might a combined CLCA approach be used in the study of classroom discourse? The following example may help to illustrate this. In a study on small group teaching in Irish universities, Walsh *et al.* (2011) used a combined CLCA approach in order to provide 'thick' descriptions of spoken interaction. The authors argue that this combined approach enables features of spoken discourse to be described at both micro (word) and macro (text) levels. A CLCA methodology reveals the relationships between interaction patterns and lexical chunks. By looking at sequences of turns alongside, for example, discourse markers, new levels of understanding can be reached, the authors claimed. As the authors themselves say:

> This approach to analysis provides powerful insights into the ways in which interactants establish understandings in educational settings and, in particular, highlights the inter-dependency of words, utterances and text in the co-construction of meaning.
>
> (Walsh *et al.* 2011)

The following extract from the same study illustrates some of the merits of a combined CLCA approach.

Extract 5.1

```
1   T:    how are you getting on with your other ahh module (.)
2         ahh the the the filming one
3   S3:   we're filming a scene at the moment we're editing and
4         it's crazy
```

```
5    T:    yeah you see it is crazy isn't it (.) this week now
6          is going to be unbelievable
7    S3:   it's just music and we're just putting it together
8          you see now (.) you know you've all the footage but
9          you're there trying
10   S?:   ( )
11   S3:   we have so much footage and it's just like you some
12         people have to accept that some of it
13   S?:   ( )
14   T:    yeah well it's like essays isn't it (.) I mean you
15         can't write from the middle you know=
16   S4:   =that was my idea so we can't lose that and you're
17         like going=
18   T:    =who who's the director?
19   S3:   I wish I was the director
20   S2:   in our in my group John C is
21   T:    okay yeah you see that's the thing like you know I
22         mean like really it does all come down to the
23         director and the people should respect that
24         immediately you know (.) that doesn't happen that
25         often (.) you know what I mean it can get the roles
26         can get dispersed
```

(Walsh *et al.* 2011)

This extract is taken from a module on 'film studies'. One of the striking features that emerged from the quantitative analysis (CL) of the corpus were the high frequencies of *you know* and *you see* (highlighted in extract 5.1). These discourse markers are used frequently in classrooms in order to create 'shared space' where learning can occur. According to Carter and McCarthy (2006), *you see* usually marks new information while *you know* generally marks shared information. In this study, there were significant differences in the frequencies of *you know* and *you see* when compared with a corpus of everyday talk:

The interesting point here is that in the corpus of higher education discourse, we find an exceptional number of *you knows* (marking shared information) but we find more or less the same amount of *you sees* (marking new information). The priority to build on and appeal to shared knowledge and 'shared space' is central to both the pedagogic and interactional process. In extract 5.1, the same result is borne out. There are a large number of occurrences of both *you see* and *you know*, but it is evident that *you know* is used much more frequently in order to establish common ground, create shared space, demonstrate empathy between tutor and students, and create a sense that 'we're all in this together; I'm here to help you'.

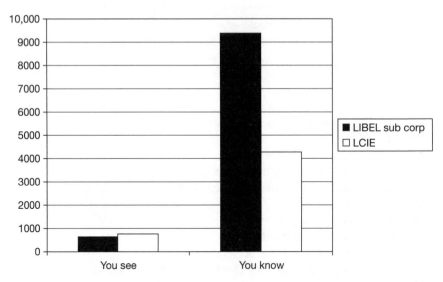

Figure 5.1 Comparison of 'you see' and 'you know' in LIBEL sub corpus and LCIE (normalised results)

From this linguistic analysis of the extract (using CL), we now turn to an analysis of the interaction (using CA). Our analysis of the interaction in extract 5.1 reveals the following:

- Turns are evenly distributed and fairly symmetrical: it is not immediately obvious who the tutor is.

- Students manage the turn-taking independently of the tutor in a way that is similar to casual conversation.

- In response to the teacher's opening turn, one student (S3) produces an account of a group's experiences of making a film, including an assessment of the situation ('it's crazy'), to which the tutor offers a preferred (agreeing) response with the discourse marker 'yeah' and the repetition of the assessment, before building on this to project what experiences will be like in the future.

In lines 11 and 12, S3 indicates that 'some people' may have problems in accepting that material has to be cut, and in line 19, seems to be expressing frustration either about the existing director, or the lack of a director's role in the group.

Throughout this extract, tutors take students' experiences and feelings and build on them, thus orienting to a pedagogic goal of reinforcing appropriate behaviours and identities in the context of professional practice. Throughout, the tutor plays a more or less equal role, listening attentively, as indicated by the use of acknowledgement tokens (in lines 5, 14 and 21).

A lot of pragmatic work takes place in lines 21–26, where *okay* marks a switch in orientation, and the tutor switches roles from empathic listener to tutor. Here, there is a lot of interactional work in order to change footing (Goffman 1981): *okay yeah you see that's the thing like you know I mean like really*. His stance after this preface is that of teacher again, giving instruction and passing on new knowledge. The interactional work is apparently needed in order to change from equal interactant to tutor, to move from a position of role symmetry to one of role asymmetry.

In the preceding analysis and discussion, I have tried to demonstrate that CL and CA can be usefully combined in any study of classroom discourse. Not only are they mutually beneficial, they actually offer each other synergies and enable a deeper, richer level of analysis. The approach is iterative: it requires a switch from CL to CA, back to CL and then on to further CA. One approach informs the other, provides direction and enables closer analysis. For example, the frequency counts of *you know* and *you see* alone do not provide the whole picture. Looking at how they actually operate in a piece of interaction gives a much fuller 'flavour' of the relationship between linguistic forms and interactional features. More importantly, this combined analysis gives real insights into how people communicate in an educational setting. Had this study used CL on its own, it would have achieved interesting lists of high frequency items but it would not have brought us anywhere near the depth of understanding offered by a CA framework. Similarly, if the data had been viewed from a purely CA perspective, the analysis would have identified some interesting interactional features but overlooked the high frequencies of certain items and ignored how specific lexical features operate in the interaction.

In the next section, the discussion turns to variable approaches to analysing classroom interaction, which focus on promoting detailed understandings of micro-contexts in a bid to understand the complex relationship between language, interaction and learning.

Variable approaches

As teachers, we spend a lot of time talking about and even promoting context. For example, for some time now language teachers have been encouraged to always make sure that new language is presented 'in context' rather than 'in isolation'. We make frequent references to 'real world' contexts, which apparently lie somewhere beyond the classroom and in which language is used for 'real' communication. What's more, we contrast these 'real' contexts with the classroom context, which, by inference, is not real and indeed may be viewed as being in some way inferior to the real world. This is clearly not the case: the language classroom is as much a 'real' social context as any other and should be viewed as such.

According to Drew and Heritage (1992), much of the research on L2 classroom interaction to date has adopted an approach whereby context is viewed as something static, fixed and concrete. The majority of studies have had one of two central goals, attempting to account for either the nature of verbal exchanges, or the relationship between SLA and interaction (Wu 1998). Whatever their focus, most studies have referred to **the** L2 classroom context (singular), implying that there exists such an entity and that it has fixed and describable features that are common to all L2 contexts. One possible explanation for this is the overriding concern of both practitioners and researchers to compare L2 classroom interaction with 'real' communication. By following this line of enquiry, many researchers have failed to acknowledge that the classroom is as much a 'real' context as any other situation in which people come together and interact. As van Lier (1988) says:

> The classroom is in principle and in potential just as communicative or uncommunicative as any other speech setting, no more, no less. Nor should the 'real world' stop at the classroom door; the classroom is part of the real world, just as much as the airport, the interviewing room, the chemical laboratory, the beach and so on.

Task 5.3

Look at the following list of L2 classroom activities. Which ones do you consider to be closer to 'real-world' communication and which ones are more 'artificial'? Place each on the continuum below and then consider how you decided which one went where.

Artificial   *Real*

←——————————————————————————————————————→

1 Planning a composition with a group of students.

2 Doing a role play.

3 Discussing homework with students.

4 Modelling new language.

5 Watching a video and answering comprehension questions.

6 Taking part in a class debate.

More recent work by Van Lier (2000) considers classroom inter-action from a more variable perspective, arguing that the L2 classroom environment is constantly shifting and that we need to focus more on the different interactional processes at work in order to understand that environment. He draws parallels with natural science, where any changes to one species will affect another one. Other writers have proposed that classroom interaction should be investigated from a multi-layered perspective; a perspective where participants play a crucial role in constructing the interaction and under which different varieties of communication prevail as the lesson unfolds according to particular pedagogic purposes (see, for example, Johnson 1995; Lantolf 2000; Seedhouse 2004; Tsui 1998).

The assumptions on which this variable view of context are based are, first, that all L2 classroom discourse is goal-oriented; second, that the prime responsibility for establishing and shaping the interaction lies with the teacher (Johnson 1995); third, that pedagogic purpose and language use are inextricably linked (Cullen 1998). L2 classroom interaction is analysed according to the relationship between pedagogic actions and the language used to achieve those actions. A variable perspective offers, its proponents maintain, a more realistic interpreta-tion of classroom discourse. Specifically, there is the recognition that interaction patterns do and should vary according to the different agendas and social relationships of the participants and according to the linguistic and pedagogic purpose of the teacher. A blanket IR(F) interpretation does not explain the finer variations that make up the different contexts under which classrooms operate. Any analysis of the interaction patterns in operation at a given point in a lesson must take account of the fact that those patterns are dynamic and mutually constructed by the participants, not static and pre-determined. The notion of the single context is invalid and unworkable.

A number of writers have studied classroom interaction using a variable approach. What follows is a brief summary of some of the more recent studies.

van Lier (1988)

Van Lier identifies four types of L2 classroom interaction. The first, which he calls 'less topic-orientation, less activity-orientation', is typical of everyday conversation and therefore the least structured, allowing the most freedom for self-expression. Type 2 (more topic-orientation, less activity-orientation) is typical of the type of interaction that occurs when information is provided in instructions or a lecture. The inter-action is one-way and involves little in the way of an exchange of ideas or opinions. His third type, more topic-orientation, more activity-orientation occurs when information has to be exchanged following specific and pre-determined lines, as in an interview, joke or story. The final category, type 4 (less topic-orientation, more activity-orientation), is typified by substitution drills, pair work and activities that have very specific procedures.

While it is unlikely that van Lier's classification is exhaustive and capable of accounting for all types of interaction, it is certainly representative of the typical patterns that occur. It also makes some attempt to relate language use to activity; rather than proposing a purely functional framework, van Lier's scheme relates classroom activity to type of language used.

Jarvis and Robinson (1997)

This study presents 'a framework for the analysis of verbal interaction between teacher and pupils in primary-level EFL lessons' (1997: 212). Considering the pedagogic functions of language, the researchers identified a *focus-build-summarise* structure to classroom interaction, based on six pedagogic functions, viz: (1) show acceptance of pupils' utterances; (2) model language; (3) give clues; (4) elaborate and build up the discourse; (5) clarify understandings; (6) disconfirm or reject. The researchers examined teachers' strategies for dealing with pupil responses as a means of assessing the extent to which meanings were aligned or formulated. This process, resulting in cognitive change, is based on the Vygotskyan principle of *appropriation* (Vygotsky 1978, 1999), whereby children 'appropriate' new meanings through two-way interaction with a more experienced interlocutor. According to Mercer (1994), appropriation can be compared to a process of paraphrase and recapping within the learner's pedagogic framework. One of the main findings of Jarvis and Robinson's study is that teachers can facilitate or hinder learning opportunities by using language that is or is not pedagogically appropriate.

Kumaravadivelu (1999)

Kumaravadivelu conceptualises a framework for what he terms Critical Classroom Discourse Analysis (CCDA) (1999: 453) aimed at 'understanding what actually transpires in the L2 classroom' (ibid.). The framework reflects the sociolinguistic, socio-cultural and sociopolitical dimensions of classroom discourse. CCDA is socially constructed, politically motivated and historically determined; the L2 classroom is viewed as a constituent of a larger society that includes many forms of power, domination and resistance (472). Understanding the interaction that occurs requires an awareness of the voices, fears, anxieties and cultural backgrounds that result in the commonly found mismatches between 'intentions and interpretations of classroom aims and events' (473).

Understanding classroom interaction, under the perspective advanced by Kumaravadivelu calls for far more than an understanding of the roles of input and acquisition in SLA; far more too than an awareness of conversational conventions manifested in turn-taking routines. Under CCDA, understanding the interaction of the second language classroom requires an awareness of what participants bring to a classroom, in terms of their beliefs, attitudes, knowledge, expectations, conditioning and so on, as well as what actually goes on in the classroom. Howard (2010) terms these external factors (what participants bring) and internal factors (what actually happens). Clearly, any interaction is determined by a complex mix of external and internal factors.

Seedhouse (2004)

Using a CA methodology that focuses on turn-taking and sequence, Seedhouse characterises four classroom contexts out of a total of six he had identified earlier (Seedhouse 1996: 124–131):

(a) Form and accuracy contexts, where the focus is on linguistic form and accuracy and the pedagogic purpose of the teacher is to elicit from learners a string of forms for evaluation. Turn-taking and sequence are tightly controlled by the teacher.

(b) Meaning and fluency contexts, where the teacher's aim is to maximise interaction within the classroom speech community and maximise the learning potential of the classroom context. The main focus is on fluency rather than accuracy and participants are encouraged to express their personal feelings or emotions. Turn-taking and topic management are less tightly structured, there is more freedom for students to self-select and, in general, learners have more interactional space.

(c) Task-oriented contexts, where learners communicate with each other to complete a specific task using largely transactional language.

(d) Procedural context, where the teacher's aim is to 'set something up', instruct or establish a procedure for work in progress. Typically, there is no turn-taking at all and this context is characterised by a single, long teacher turn and silence on the part of the learners.

In an earlier study (1997), Seedhouse looks at the relationship between pedagogy and interaction with regard to repair. How do teachers organise repair? Specifically, what strategies do they use when correcting oral errors and what strategies do learners expect them to use? His finding, 'that teachers perform a great deal of interactional work to avoid performing direct and overt negative evaluation of learner linguistic errors' (1997: 563) indicates not only that teachers tend to avoid overt error correction, but, perhaps more significantly, that their choice of language and pedagogic purpose are in opposition. That is, although the teacher's intention is to correct errors (pedagogic purpose), their choice of language seems to militate against this. While learners accept that error correction is an essential part of the language learning process, teachers seem to shy away from overt correction because they believe it is in some way 'face-threatening' (Brown and Levinson 1987). The stance adopted by teachers is largely influenced by what would constitute an appropriate course of action outside the classroom where overt correction might be considered less acceptable. Yet in the language classroom, adult learners expect and indeed want to be corrected. A teacher's decision to correct errors in a less 'threatening' manner by carefully selecting language that avoids loss of face may actually prevent or hinder repair from occurring.

Perhaps the most notable feature of each of the studies reviewed here is the recognition that the L2 classroom is made up of a series of contexts that are linked to the social, political, cultural and historical beliefs of the participants (see, for example, Kumaravadivelu 1999). Contexts are created by teachers and learners as they engage in face-to-face interaction and according to teachers' pedagogic goals at a given moment. Classroom interaction is therefore socially constructed *by* and *for* the participants, leading some writers to suggest that we should think of learning 'as a process of becoming a member of a certain community [necessitating] the ability to communicate in the language of this community and act according to its particular norms' (Sfard 1998: 6). A variable approach to the study of L2 classroom contexts, by focusing more on participation, enables greater understanding of 'language socialisation' (Lantolf 2000: 156).

A second feature of the studies reviewed here is the emphasis they place on the relationship between language in interaction and learning. An understanding of the relationship between classroom communication and educational goals, the ways in that language use can facilitate or hinder learning (Walsh 2002), has implications for teacher education since it replaces 'broad brush' views of interaction with fine grained paradigms that permit greater understanding of the interactional and learning processes at work. By looking at longer stretches of discourse and by considering the relationship between language use, pedagogic goals and learning opportunities, it is possible to obtain a more complete understanding of 'what is happening' in the discourse.

Third, in the studies reviewed in this section, there is an absence of an agreed metalanguage for describing and accounting for L2 classroom micro-contexts. Seedhouse proposes four 'contexts' (2004: 102); Jarvis and Robinson six 'pedagogic functions' (1997: 212); van

Lier, four 'types of interaction' (1988: 156). This lack of an agreed metalanguage makes the processes of comparison and generalisation practically impossible, as the constructs used have different meanings. Description and understanding of L2 classroom interaction is unlikely to be advanced until an appropriate nomenclature is identified and utilised by teachers and researchers alike. In Chapter 6, I present a framework that offers, at least in part, a solution to this problem.

Summary

The aim of this chapter was to present alternative approaches for studying classroom interaction, beginning with corpus linguistics (CL). The main advantage of CL is that it offers rapid and reliable profiles of classroom discourse and enables us to understand how linguistic features 'work' in specific classroom contexts. For example, I commented on the ways in which discourse markers (such as *you know, you see, right, ok, next*, etc.) perform key functions in classrooms and, when used properly, greatly assist the learning process. CL's main disadvantage is that it largely ignores the finer details of classroom interaction and fails to recognise the ways in which meanings are jointly achieved. A combined CLCA approach was proposed as one way of overcoming such shortcomings, allowing a 'multi-layered' perspective that offers a description of both linguistic and interactional features.

In the final section of this chapter, I presented a brief summary of the work that has been done to promote variable approaches to analysing classroom interaction. Here, there is a recognition that classroom discourse cannot be viewed as being 'all of a oneness', where interactional and linguistic features occur in a more or less fixed and predictable way. Instead, variable approaches recognise that classroom interaction proceeds in line with the pedagogic goals of the moment. Micro-contexts are co-constructed in the interaction as participants work towards clearly defined, and constantly shifting, goals. So, for example, if the teacher's goal is to set up a pair-work task, she may use long teacher turns, frequent pausing, specific discourse markers (such as *first, next, then*), and so on. If, on the other hand, her aim is to elicit student opinions, there may be longer learner turns, more role asymmetry, frequent overlaps, interruptions and false starts – in short, the interaction will resemble more closely a casual conversation.

Recognising that classroom discourse is constantly shifting, that goals are always changing and that language use and pedagogic goals must work together are, I suggest, fundamental to teacher development. One of the most effective means of developing as a teacher is to gain closer understandings of classroom interaction: in Chapter 6, I present a framework that is designed to help teachers improve the quality of the interaction taking place in their classes as the first step towards improving teaching and learning.

6 Enhancing understandings of classroom discourse

Introduction

In the last chapter, I presented an argument for adopting a variable approach to classroom discourse, which emphasises the fact that interaction and pedagogic goals are inextricably linked, that the discourse is constantly changing according to the teacher's agenda, and that teaching and learning can be greatly improved by adopting a variable approach. In this chapter, I present a framework (SETT: self-evaluation of teacher talk) designed in collaboration with L2 teachers and that aims to foster teacher development through classroom interaction. Essentially, my aim is to get teachers to think about classroom interaction as a means of improving both teaching and learning. (For a fuller discussion of this work, see Walsh 2006.)

Since its inception in 2006, SETT has been used in a number of contexts, including: initial teacher education programmes (PGCE) for English and Drama teachers (Walsh and Lowing 2008); INSET courses for experienced teachers; a study evaluating the value of classroom observation in the Middle East (Howard 2010); on CELTA programmes around the world; a primary science classroom; various secondary EFL contexts around the world; two university classroom contexts, and an Irish medium secondary classroom. In short, the framework has been used extensively to promote awareness and understanding of the role of interaction in class-based learning and to help teachers improve their practices.

The SETT framework comprises four classroom micro-contexts (called *modes*) and fourteen interactional features (called *interactures*). Classroom discourse is portrayed as a series of complex and inter-related micro-contexts (modes), where meanings are co-constructed by teachers and learners and where learning occurs through the ensuing talk of teachers and learners. The next two sections offer a summary of the framework, beginning with a description of each mode and then characterising the different interactures.

Personal reflection

Based on what you now know about classroom discourse and your own experience, how would you like to change your own use of language in the classroom? How would you like to improve your teacher talk and improve the quality of the interaction? What steps have you already taken to improve classroom interaction and how effective were they?

The SETT framework: modes

The SETT framework is designed to help teachers both describe the classroom interaction of their lessons and develop an understanding of interactional processes as a way of becoming a 'better' teacher. The starting point, based on the discussion in Chapter 5, is that the single, L2 classroom context does not exist; contexts are locally constructed by participants through and in their interaction in the light of overall institutional goals and immediate pedagogic objectives. The notion of 'the L2 lesson context' is too broad-brushed; 'contexts are locally produced and transformable at any moment' (Drew and Heritage 1992: 19). In short:

- The L2 classroom context is made up of a series of micro-contexts, linked to a range of 'external' factors (c.f. Howard 2010) such as beliefs, attitudes, previous experience and so on.

- Contexts are created in and through the interaction, which is also the way in which meanings are co-constructed (c.f. Lantolf and Thorne 2006).

- The relationship between language use and pedagogic goals requires closer understanding (c.f. Seedhouse 2004).

In other words, it is impossible to separate pedagogy and interaction, which come together through talk: pedagogic goals are manifested in the talk-in-interaction. Using the term *mode* encompasses the interrelatedness of language use and teaching purpose. A mode is defined as 'an L2 classroom microcontext which has a clearly defined pedagogic goal and distinctive interactional features determined largely by a teacher's use of language' (Walsh 2006: 62). The definition is intended to emphasise the idea that interaction and classroom activity are inextricably linked, and to acknowledge that as the focus of a lesson changes, interaction patterns and pedagogic goals change too.

In the 2006 study, Walsh set out to design a framework that could be used by teachers to evaluate and gain closer understandings of the interactions taking place in their classes. The work was conducted in a UK university's English Language Centre and the participants were the tutors and students of that centre. Recordings were made and analysed using an applied conversation analysis methodology (ten Have 2007). To summarise, the following procedures were followed:

- The total size of the corpus is approximately 100,000 words, or twelve hours.

- Data were analysed using an applied CA methodology.

- Participants were then invited to study the transcripts in a series of workshops in which the precise focus of each lesson was discussed in relation to pedagogic goals.

- Interaction patterns were found to vary according to instructional activity; for example, establishing procedures to complete an activity resulted in a very different pattern of interaction to open-class discussion.

- The different patterns manifested themselves in the turn-taking, sequence of turns and topic management. Once a pattern had been identified, the data were analysed for further examples of the same pattern as is the 'norm' under conversation analysis.

(Psathas 1995: 52)

Following this procedure, four patterns, four micro-contexts were identified. These were called *modes*: managerial mode, classroom context mode, skills and systems mode, materials mode.

Each mode is made up of specific interactional features (such as display questions, repair, content feedback) and particular pedagogic goals. The four modes are included as being representative, rather than comprehensive, and can be adapted to suit local contexts. They are based on the analysis of frequently occurring classroom discourse features and are designed to help teachers develop detailed understandings of their own contexts.

Heritage and Greatbatch's (1991) notion of 'fingerprints' is helpful to the present discussion. In that study, the researchers identify a number of socially constructed contexts in different institutional settings that they term 'fingerprints' to differentiate interactional organisations from one workplace to another. Thus, the 'fingerprint' of a doctor's surgery will have a different exchange and participation structure to that of a solicitor's office. Following Heritage and Greatbatch, under SETT, each L2 classroom mode has its own distinctive fingerprint, comprising pedagogic and linguistic features. Thus, the fingerprint of *classroom context* mode is markedly different to that of *managerial* mode; both are different again from *skills and systems* mode.

Table 6.1 L2 Classroom modes

Mode	Pedagogic goals	Interactional features
Managerial	To transmit information To organise the physical learning environment To refer learners to materials To introduce or conclude an activity To change from one mode of learning to another	A single, extended teacher turn that uses explanations and/or instructions The use of transitional markers The use of confirmation checks An absence of learner contributions
Materials	To provide language practice around a piece of material To elicit responses in relation to the material To check and display answers To clarify when necessary To evaluate contributions	Predominance of IRF pattern Extensive use of display questions Form-focused feedback Corrective repair The use of scaffolding
Skills and systems	To enable learners to produce correct forms To enable learners to manipulate the target language To provide corrective feedback To provide learners with practice in sub-skills To display correct answers	The use of direct repair The use of scaffolding Extended teacher turns Display questions Teacher echo Clarification requests Form-focused feedback
Classroom context	To enable learners to express themselves clearly To establish a context To promote oral fluency	Extended learner turns Short teacher turns Minimal repair Content feedback Referential questions Scaffolding Clarification requests

Source: Walsh 2006.

The four modes, together with their interactional features and typical pedagogic goals, are summarised in Table 6.1 above.

In the following sections, a description of each mode, together with examples from the data, is presented. A full account of the transcription conventions used appears in Appendix B. The numbers given in brackets refer either to a whole extract, or a line in an extract; thus, (6.1) refers to the whole extract, while (14) refers to line 14 in the extract.

Managerial mode

Managerial mode accounts for what goes on in the organisation of learning. Its prime pedagogic goal is to organise learning in time and space and to set up or conclude classroom activities. It frequently occurs at the beginning of lessons, as illustrated in extracts 6.1 and 6.2 below, characterised in the first instance by an extended teacher turn of more than one clause and a complete absence of learner turns. In each extract, the focus is on the 'institutional business' of the moment, the core activity of the school, organisation or whatever. In managerial mode, there are frequent repetitions, directives and instructions. At the end of managerial mode, there is typically a handing over to learners and a movement into another mode; in extract 6.1, for example, the words 'so Miguel' act as a transition to another mode, here, skills and systems. Note too the use of discourse markers such as *ok, so, now, right*, etc., which help learners to follow what is being said and give direction to the discourse.

Extract 6.1

1   T: Ok we're going to look today at ways to improve your writing and at ways that can be more effective for you and if you look at the writing which I gave you back you will see that I've marked any little mistakes and eh I've also marked places where I think the writing is good and I haven't corrected your mistakes because the best way in writing is for you to correct your mistakes so what I have done I have put little circles and inside the circles there is something that tells you what kind of mistake it is so Miguel, would you like to tell me one of the mistakes that you made (3)

Extract 6.2

1   T: now could you turn to page ... 59 page 59 at the top of the book (**students find place in book**)

When managerial mode occurs at the beginning of a lesson, the teacher's main concern is to 'locate' the learning temporally and pedagogically (extract 6.1), or spatially (extract 6.2). Once learning has been located, learners are invited to participate: *so Miguel, would you like to tell me one of the mistakes that you made.* Locating learning is an important first step in building a main context; consequently, in many respects, managerial mode functions as a support to the other three modes. We can say that it is an 'enabling' mode (McCarthy and Walsh 2003).

Although it is most commonly found at the beginning of a lesson, managerial mode may occur post-activity or as a link between two stages in a lesson, as indicated in extract 6.3 below, where the teacher's aim is to conclude an activity and move the lesson on. As in the previous extracts, turn-taking is wholly managed by the teacher, learners have no interactional space and the agenda, the pedagogic goal of the moment, is firmly in the hands of the teacher. Once the activity is concluded, the learners are organised into three groups and the lesson moves from one type of learning (pair-work practice) to another (open class checking in groups). Throughout, the teacher's use of language and pedagogic purpose are at one: the language used is appropriate to the pedagogic goal of the moment.

Extract 6.3

5   T: all right okay can you stop then please where you are
           . . . let's take a couple of . . . examples for these and
           . . . put them in the categories er . . . so there are three
           groups all right this one at the front Sylvia's group is A
           just simply A B and you're C (**teacher indicates groups**)
           all right so . . . then B can you give me a word for ways
           of looking (3) so Suzanna . . . yeah

The transition markers *all right, okay, so* signal the end of one part of the lesson and alert learners to the fact that the lesson has moved on, that pedagogic goals have been realigned with a shift in focus to a new activity. These discourse markers are essential for learners to follow the unravelling interaction and 'navigate their way' (Breen 1998) through the classroom discourse. They function like punctuation marks in a written text, or intonation patterns in a spoken text and are crucial to understanding. In cases where discourse markers are not used, the boundaries between modes are difficult to detect and learners may become confused as to what they are expected to do. Most teachers have encountered comments by learners such as: 'What are we supposed to be doing?'; 'Where are we?'; 'What's the task?'. These, and similar questions, testify to the need for signposting and the use of language that is related to the pedagogic goals of the moment.

Task 6.1

Thinking about your own teaching, how does managerial mode manifest itself in your classes? In what ways do you manage learning? What difficulties do you encounter in organising and managing learning and how might you overcome those difficulties?

To summarise, managerial mode is characterised by one, long teacher turn, the use of transition markers and an absence of learner involvement. Its principal pedagogic purpose is the management of learning, including setting up a task, summarising or providing feedback on one particular stage of a lesson.

Materials mode

In this mode, pedagogic goals and language use centre on the materials being used. All interaction typically evolves around a piece of material such as text, tape, worksheet and so on. In most cases, the interaction is tightly controlled and follows the IRF exchange structure. If we look at extract 6.4 below, we see a clear example of materials mode. Here, learners are completing a cloze exercise on sports vocabulary and the teacher directs their contributions; the interactional organisation is almost entirely determined by the materials and managed by the teacher. Teacher and learner turns are mirrored by the material: the teacher elicits responses (in lines 81, 83, 85, 87, 90, 92, 95, 99, 104, 108) and learners respond (in lines 84, 86, 88, 91, 94, 96, 98, etc.). The sequence is 'classic IRF', the most economical way to progress the interaction, with each teacher turn functioning as both an evaluation of a learner's contribution and initiation of another one. There is only one turn (in line 103) that is not determined by pedagogic goals, though it is related; unusually, it is a learner's correction of the teacher's pronunciation. Very little interactional space or choice of topic are afforded since the interaction is organised exclusively around the material. Pedagogically, the focus can be interpreted as providing vocabulary practice around a specific piece of material. Key items of vocabulary are elicited, confirmed and displayed by the teacher through echoes of a previous contribution.

Extract 6.4

81	T:	now . . . see if you can find the words that are suitable in in these phrases
82		**(reading)** in the world cup final of 1994 Brazil Italy 2 3 2 and in a shoot-out . . .
83		what words would you put in there? ((1))
84	L7:	[beat]
85	T:	[what] beat Italy 3 2 yeah in?
86	L7:	in a penalty shoot-out
87	T:	a what?
88	L7:	in a penalty shoot-out
89	T:	in a penalty shoot-out very good in a penalty shoot-out . . . **(reading)** after

90		90 minutes THE?
91	LL:	the goals goals goals (**mispronounced**)
92	T:	[the match] was . . . what?
93	L:	[match]
94	LL:	nil nil
95	T:	nil nil (**reading**) and it remained the same after 30 minutes OF (3)
96	L5:	extra time
97	T:	extra time very good Emerson (**reading**) but then Italy?
98	L5:	lost (2)
99	T:	but then Italy . . . what?
100	L5:	lost=
101	T:	=lost ok 3–2 in the penalty shoot-out after Venessi and Bagio
102		(**mispronounced**) both missed
103	L:	Bagio (**correcting teacher's pronunciation**)
104	T:	Bagio yes Spanish (**reading**) this was the fourth time that Brazil had?
105	LL:	=won=
106	T:	=won . . .
107	LL:	/won won/
108	T:	the World Cup very good (5) and ((2)) what's that word? ((5))

While turn-taking and topic choice in this mode are largely determined by the material, there are varying degrees of association, evidenced in extract 6.5. In this extract, a group of pre-intermediate students is working on fluency practice and while the interaction still stems from the activity they are engaged in (indicated by the 'on-task' comments of the participants), learners are given far more interactional space and manage the turn-taking themselves. The teacher is still involved, but only intervenes when necessary to clarify (10, 16). The IRF sequence no longer prevails and there is apparently more freedom in topic choice. Closer analysis, however, reveals that this is in fact not the case; while learners certainly have more freedom to self-select or remain silent, contributions are made in response to the task. All interactions here orient to the task and there is, in fact, little freedom for learners to select topics and manage the interaction themselves.

Extract 6.5

1	L1:	was shy so didn't have a (1))=
2	L:	so it's good news (**laughter**)
3	LL:	/bad news/ ok / no no that's good news/ . . .
4	L2:	bad news . . .

5	L:	no that's bad news=
6	L3:	=ah good good news (2)
7	L1:	no no that's wrong you have to do bad news . . .
8	L2:	yes it's a bad news because [you]
9	L:	[no but that's] good news=
10	T:	=that's good news G N good news . . .
11	L2:	ok so this one? **(laughter)**
12	LL:	/oh/ yes that's correct /yeah/ . . .
13	L1:	so=
14	LL:	/((3))/ he's sick/ he's/show me this one/=
15	L1:	=no! it's my card excuse me
16	T:	so what's up you have to say the bad news=
17	L2:	=bad news because you can't ski=

In materials mode, then, patterns of interaction evolve from the material that largely determines who may speak, when and what they may say; the interaction may or may not be managed exclusively by the teacher. Though learners have varying degrees of interactional space, depending on the nature of the activity, their contributions are still bounded by the constraints imposed by the task in hand.

Skills and systems mode

In skills and systems mode, pedagogic goals are closely related to providing language practice in relation to a particular language system (phonology, grammar, vocabulary, discourse) or language skill (reading, listening, writing, speaking). Teaching objectives may also relate to the development of specific learner strategies. Typically, the interaction in this mode follows a lockstep organisation and the IRF sequence frequently occurs. Turn-taking and topic selection are determined by the target language and responsibility for managing the turn-taking usually lies with the teacher. Pedagogic goals are oriented towards accuracy rather than fluency and the teacher's concern is to get learners to produce strings of accurate linguistic forms and manipulate the target language. Direct repair and scaffolding have an important role to play, as illustrated in the next extract.

In extract 6.6 a group of intermediate level students is practising simple past forms. The teacher's pedagogic goal, as evidenced in the interaction, is to get the learners to produce patterns involving the use of irregular simple past forms *went* and *broke*. The slight pause in (218), (indicated [. . .]), provides the teacher with an opportunity to scaffold the learner's contribution in (219). Scaffolding involves the 'feeding in' of essential language as it is needed and plays an important part in assisting learners to express themselves and acquire new language. It is followed in (225) and (227) by direct repair, which is also used in (233) and (235). Direct repair, involving a short, quick correction, is a useful interactional strategy since it has minimal impact on the exchange structure. Patterns of interaction are only slightly disturbed and the 'flow' is maintained.

This combination of scaffolding and direct repair is found extensively in skills and systems mode, enabling learners to attend to specific features of their interlanguage while keeping the interaction 'on track', in line with the teacher's pedagogic goals, the agenda of the moment. Getting learners to 'notice' patterns (Schmidt 1990) and identify relationships is a central goal in skills and systems mode. Little attention is given to meaning, to communicative function; the prime objective is to enable learners to understand and produce target forms. It is widely acknowledged that form-focused instruction plays a significant part in the SLA process (c.f. Doughty and Williams 1998; Ellis 2001); clearly, the teacher's handling of learner contributions through scaffolded instruction and repair are central to that process.

Extract 6.6

218	L5:	=the good news is he went to the went to [. . .]
219	T:	he went to what do we call these things the shoes with wheels=
220	L2:	=ah skates=
221	L6:	=roller skates=
222	T:	=ROLLer skates roller skates so [he went
223	L5:	[he went to=
224	L:	=roller SKATing=
225	T:	=SKATing=
226	L5:	=he went to=
227	T:	=not to just he went [roller skating he went roller skating
228	L5:	[roller skating he went roller skating=
229	T:	=lets hear it he went the good news [is
230	L5:	[the good news is he went skating . . .
231	T:	good he went roller skating=
232	L5:	=the bad news is he . . .was broken his leg=
233	T:	=he? (2)
234	L5:	he he has . . .
235	T:	simple past . . .
236	L:	he broke=
237	L5:	=he broke he broke his leg=

In the next extract, 6.7, the teacher of an advanced group of learners is trying to elicit the phrase *military force*. Of note here is the use of display questions to guide learners to identify the missing word in (187, 189, 191, 195, 197, 199) and the very closely connected turn-taking structure, evidenced by frequent overlaps ([ ) and latched turns (=). The teacher's intention is to elicit the target vocabulary *military force*, which he eventually does (in 198). Asking display questions to guide learners to the correct answer, or at least the one that the teacher is looking for, is a notoriously complex skill, requiring deft management of learner contributions to bring them closer to the answer being sought (Johnson 1992). Frequently, 'good answers' are rejected simply because they do not conform to the one the teacher is looking for, forcing students to do the impossible and guess what's inside the teacher's head (see also Lin 2000). In extract 6.7, learners are actively involved in constructing meaning through the interaction, as opposed to being passive recipients. This 'dialogue' is, arguably, more likely to result in learning, since learners are engaged and having to think more carefully.

Extract 6.7

187	T:	=what do we call I'm going to try and get the class to tell you what this
188		word is that you're looking for . . . er we talk about military (**claps hands**) . . .
189		military what?
190	L:	((1))=
191	T:	=like fight=
192	L:	=kill=
193	T:	=no not [kill
194	L:	[action action=
195	T:	=no ((2)) military?=
196	LL:	=power=
197	T:	=power think of another word military?
198	LL:	((3))force=
199	T:	=so she believes in a FORCE for?
200	L:	that guide our lives=
201	T:	=that guides our lives

To summarise, in skills and systems mode, the focus is a specific language system or sub-skill. Learning outcomes are typically achieved through tightly controlled turn-taking and topic selection, determined by the teacher. Learners respond to teacher prompts in an endeavour to produce linguistically accurate strings of utterances. The interaction is typically (though not exclusively) form-focused, characterised by extended teacher turns, display questions and direct repair.

Classroom context mode

In classroom context mode, the management of turns and topics is determined by the local context, 'the communication potential of the L2 classroom itself' (van Lier 1988: 30). Opportunities for genuine communication are frequent and the teacher plays a less prominent role, taking more of a 'back seat' and allowing learners all the interactional space they need. The principal role of the teacher is to listen and support the interaction, which frequently takes on the appearance of a naturally occurring conversation.

In extract 6.8 with a group of advanced learners, the teacher's stated aim is 'to generate discussion prior to a cloze exercise on poltergeists' and learners have been invited to share their experiences. The turn-taking is almost entirely managed by the learners, with evidence of competition for the floor and turn gaining, holding and passing, which are typical features of natural conversation. Turns are also significantly longer, contain more overlaps and latches and pausing is more pronounced. In (261) for example, the two-second pause at the end of learner 3's turn is perceived by other learners as an invitation to take up the discussion and two learners take a turn in (262) and (263), before the original speaker (L3) regains the floor in (264). Topic shifts are also managed by the learners (in 264, 269, 281), with the teacher responding more as an equal participant, allowing the discourse to develop within the topic frames selected by the learners. Note how (in 280) the sub-topic of 'neuroses' is not developed and the original speaker retakes the floor in (281), shifting to a new topic. The only questions asked by the teacher are referential (in 276, 285, 287) and extended learner turns dominate the sequence. Errors go unrepaired, there are no evaluative comments and the only feedback given is content-based, normally in the shape of a personal reaction.

Extract 6.8

256	L3:	=ahh nah the one thing that happens when a person dies ((2)) my mother
257		used to work with old people and when they died . . . the last thing that went
258		out was the hearing ((4)) about this person=
259	T:	=aha (2)
260	L3:	so I mean even if you are unconscious or on drugs or something I mean
261		it's probably still perhaps can hear what's happened (2)
262	L2:	but it gets ((2))=
263	LL:	/but it gets/there are ((2))/=
264	L3:	=I mean you have seen so many operation ((3)) and so you can imagine

265		and when you are hearing the sounds of what happens I think you can get a
266		pretty clear picture of what's really going on there=
267	L:	=yeah=
268	L:	=and and . . .
269	L1:	but eh and eh I don't know about other people but eh ((6)) I always have
270		feeling somebody watching watch watches me=
271	T:	=yes=
272	L4:	=YEAH=
273	L1:	=somebody just follow me either a man or a woman I don't know if it's a
274		man I feel really exciting if it's a woman ((4)) I don't know why like I'm trying to
275		do things better like I'm eh . . . look like this . . . you FEEL it . . . I don't know=
276	T:	=you think it's a kind of spirit=
277	L1:	=I think it's just yeah somebody who lives inside us and ((3)) . . . visible area . . .
278	L4:	I would say it's just neurotic problems (**laughter**)
279	L1:	what what . . .
280	L4:	nothing nothing nothing . . .
281	L1:	but have you seen city of angels=
282	L4:	=no I haven't=
283	L1:	=with eh Meg Ryan and eh Nicholas Cage it's a wonderful story and I think
284		it's true actually=
285	T:	=and does this bother you=
286	L1:	=what?=
287	T:	=this feeling that you get does it bother you?=
288	L1:	=it's eh you know when I am alone I'm ok but if I feel that somebody is
289		near I would be nervous=
290	T:	=I would be very nervous . . .

The predominant interactional feature of extract 6.8 is the local management of the speech exchange system; learners have considerable freedom as to what to say and when. This process of 'topicalisation' (Slimani 1989), where learners select and develop a topic, is significant in maximising learning potential since 'whatever is topicalised by the learners rather than the teacher has a better chance of being claimed to have been learnt' (Ellis 1998: 159). In this extract, the academic task structure and social participation structure (Johnson 1995) are clearly more relaxed and opportunities for learning are increased. In many classroom contexts, it is, however, not uncommon for teachers to retain control of the interaction, interrupting students and taking control of the topic. While this may be inevitable, there are times, as in classroom context mode, when relinquishing control of turn-taking and topic choice are fundamental interactional strategies. This is, arguably, a skill that more teachers need to develop if more even, equal participation structures are to be achieved.

The defining characteristic of classroom context mode, then, is interactional space: extended learner turns predominate as participants co-construct the discourse. Teacher feedback shifts from form- to content-focused and error correction is minimal. In short, the orientation is towards maintaining genuine communication rather than displaying linguistic knowledge.

Task 6.2

Using the following extract:

1 Identify examples of each of the following modes (use Table 6.1 on page 113 to help you):

  • Skills and systems

  • Classroom context

  • Materials

2 What difficulties did you encounter?

3 How might you use this type of analysis in your own teaching?

(In the extract, a group of intermediate level adult learners are preparing to read a text called *Pot Luck Suppers*. Leslie is a character in the coursebook and Yvette, Georgia and Haldoun are all students in the class.)

29	T:	=yes olive oil yes yes must be a good quality=
30	L:	=and the other olive oil vegetable and made from maize from corn=
31	T:	=yes corn oil and yeah there's many different types of oil olive oil is the best and . . .
32		essential to Spanish omelette tortilla erm right so if you were invited to one of Leslie's
33		pot-luck suppers (**referring to the book**) erm right what would you bring . . . along . . .
34		with you?
35	L:	American or ((1))?

36	T:	yes this is this Leslie the American woman imagine she [invited you to a pot-luck
37		supper
38	L:	[a bottle of wine
39	T:	a bottle of wine yes
40	L:	a dish [of food
41	T:	[what else? a dish of food yes what=
42	L:	=dessert
43	T:	yes possibly a dessert=
44	L:	=or a starter
45	T:	or a starter . . . yes so how would you know what to bring?
46	LL:	((2)) the organiser give you a list ((1))
47	T:	that's right yes so it's it's quite well-organised you can (laughs) imagine writing a list
48		oh yes I'll ask Yvette she can bring a starter . . . oh Georgia a nice salad Italians are
49		very good with salads and then maybe a main course er Haldoun and perhaps er the
50		Japanse can do some more some more main courses so it would be very er very
51		well-organised=
52	L:	=usually((2)) like sometimes there are like 3 main courses ((2)) like graduation in
53		sometimes we have parties and we have like er roast chicken and another people
54		bring ((3)) for the main courses and we don't have nothing for nothing for dessert and
55		nothing for the starter [(laughs)]
56	T:	[(laughs)] oh dear well Georgia perhaps when you go back to Italy perhaps you can
57		organise one of these typical pot-luck suppers and organise it well so you'll have
58		plenty of desserts and plenty of starters (laughs) but er do you think it's a good idea?
59	L:	sometimes, yeah
60	L:	it's nice because you don't know what you're going to eat=
61	T:	=it's a surprise yes, yeah as long as you like everything . . . I mean some people don't
62		like certain things what adjective do we use for people who don't like that and hate
63		that and a lot of food they won't eat . . . we call it people are very . . . FUSsy fussy with

64		their food (**writes on board**) right so fussy that's don't like vegetables, never eat er
65		pasta (**laughs**)=
66	L1:	=excuse me how to say if er you ((2)) for example if you try some burger on corner
67		. . . on the the street and then you feel not very well
68	T:	er . . . I'm not quite sure what you mean Yvette if you?
69	L1:	you can buy for example ((2)) just on the street
70	T:	you mean street sellers . . . people selling food on the street yes

The SETT framework: interactures

As we have seen, the SETT framework uses four modes, each with distinctive pedagogic goals and different interactional features. In this section, the various interactional features are presented and discussed. You may find that some of these are known to you, while others may be quite new.

Task 6.3

The SETT framework is made up of the fourteen interactional features (*interactures*) below. In the table below, match the features with the descriptions given. Two have been completed for you. Compare with the original grid (see Appendix A).

Scaffolding	*Direct repair*	*Referential questions*
Content feedback	*Seeking clarification*	*Display questions*
Extended wait-time	Teacher echo	Extended teacher turn
Confirmation checks	*Teacher interruptions*	*Turn completion*
Extended learner turn	*Form-focused feedback*	

Feature of teacher talk	*Description*
A.	1. Reformulation (rephrasing a learner's contribution).
	2. Extension (extending a learner's contribution).
	3. Modelling (correcting a learner's contribution).

Feature of teacher talk	Description
B.	Correcting an error quickly and directly.
C. Content feedback	Giving feedback to the message rather than the words used.
D.	Allowing sufficient time (several seconds) for students to respond or formulate a response.
E. Referential questions	Genuine questions to which the teacher does not know the answer.
F.	1. Teacher asks a student to clarify something the student has said. 2. Student asks teacher to clarify something the teacher has said.
G.	Making sure that teacher has correctly understood learner's contribution.
H.	Learner turn of more than one sentence.
I.	1. Teacher repeats a previous utterance. 2. Teacher repeats a learner's contribution.
J.	Interrupting a learner's contribution.
K.	Teacher turn of more than one sentence.
L.	Completing a learner's contribution for the learner.
M.	Asking questions to which teacher knows the answer.
N.	Giving feedback on the words used, not the message.

The interactures used in the SETT framework can be found in varying degrees in any classroom. Some are more common than others and occur with greater regularity throughout the discourse; display questions, for example, are more widespread than referential, or genuine, questions. Using a SETT analysis allows teachers to gain a rapid profile of the kinds of features to be found in their classes and assess their appropriacy. From Table 6.1, we can identify which features, which *interactures*, belong to which mode. Content feedback, for example, is more likely to be found in classroom context mode, whereas skills and systems mode is more likely to contain examples of direct repair, which, in turn, will be less visible in classroom context mode. An interacture, then, can be defined as a particular interactional feature that 'belongs to' or is typical of a mode: display questions are interactures of materials mode, extended teacher turns of managerial mode, for example. An interacture can be regarded as being more or less appropriate, or *mode convergent*, at a given moment in a lesson according to a teacher's desired learning outcomes.

By making short recordings of your teaching and by listening to these recordings, it is possible to increase your awareness of (a) which modes are being used, and (b) which interactures appear in each mode. This combined analysis, first focusing on modes, then on interactures, will give you a detailed profile of the interactions taking place in your classes and permit you to make adjustments. For example, you may find that in classroom context mode you only ask display questions, thereby restricting the kinds of response open to learners. Or you may notice that you constantly interrupt when eliciting. These are all important features of your teaching that can be changed in order to improve learning and learning potential for your students.

Task 6.4

Using the extract below and the SETT grid, identify as many examples of *interactures* as you can. Use the coding from Task 6.3: A, B, C, etc. Were there any features that you did not find? What difficulties did you experience?

129	L5:	=I believe in trying new things and ((1)) ideas=
130	T:	=er (1) you believe in being POSitive you mean?=
131	L5:	=pardon?=
132	T:	=do you believe in always being positive is that what you mean?=
133	L5:	=no . . . I believe to (3) to have a lot of achievement
134	T:	(1) do you believe in what do you mean you you should always take opportunities is
135		that what you mean no?=
136	L5:	=no I want my life to be very (1)
137	T:	happy?=
138	L5:	=yeah and also I I do many things (1) many different experiences=
139	T:	=why don't you say you just believe in experiencing as many different things as you
140		want=
141	L5:	=oh yeah=
142	T:	=thats what I think you should say=

As I said at the beginning of this chapter, SETT has been used in a range of contexts with different teachers, some experienced, some less so. What follows is a brief account of teachers' self-evaluations where they comment on the interactures identified in their own classes and evaluate their relative merits. In the extracts that follow, there is clear evidence that interactures are interpreted by teachers as being more 'relevant', 'appropriate' or 'necessary' according to mode.

An examination of extract 6.9, for example, reveals that some interactures (content feedback) are more or less 'relevant' according to the mode 'mainly skills and systems'; in skills and systems mode, feedback typically is form- rather than content-focused. Her comments add weight to the argument that certain interactures are more appropriate in some contexts than others, that teacher talk has to reflect the focus of the lesson, that mode convergence is necessary if learning opportunities are to be maximised.

Extract 6.9

(**Reading**) 'content feedback' there was nothing because it wasn't relevant it wasn't that type of lesson part of the lesson.

(Teacher 3)

Similarly, teacher 4 in extract 6.10 indicates that certain interactures are more or less 'necessary' or 'appropriate' according to mode. While it is certainly NOT the suggestion here that teachers should be trained to ONLY use certain interactures in a certain mode, there is nonetheless a *perception* that there are different degrees of appropriacy depending on the mode in operation. In extract 6.9, for example, it is the teacher's belief that content feedback 'belongs' in a different mode, not skills and systems.

Extract 6.10

I didn't do any completing of turns, form-focused feedback didn't fit in really and there was no direct repair really because I suppose it was fluency rather than accuracy and didn't given anybody any extended wait time because I didn't think it was necessary but I would have done it if they had needed it.

(Teacher 4)

Judgments concerning the relevance or appropriacy of a particular interacture are made retrospectively in the light of desired teaching/learning outcomes or in reaction to learner needs. It is not the suggestion that such decisions are taken consciously 'in the heat' of a teaching moment, merely that they can be usefully studied as part of the reflective process of SETT. We will return to this in Chapter 7.

In extract 6.10, teacher 4 is in classroom context mode, clearly aiming to elicit longer turns from the learners and give them more interactional space – 'it was fluency rather than accuracy'. Again, there is a suggestion in his comments that certain interactures 'fit in' to certain modes more than others and that teacher talk has to be adjusted not only in line with desired learning outcomes, but also in response to learner 'needs'. In the data collected so far, it is evident that teachers vary in their abilities to fine tune their language to promote learning and make 'good interactive decisions' (Ellis 1998). Developing the kind of understanding evidenced in the comments presented here concerning the relationship between interactures and modes is perhaps one of the ways in which second language teachers' interactional choices can be improved.

Using SETT

Thus far, the impression given is that L2 classroom interaction can be classified very neatly into a finite number of modes, each with its own particular set of pedagogic and interactional features. While there are certainly examples of clearly delineated modes in the data, there are also many instances where identifying modes is more problematic and where features cannot be clearly shown. The framework, as already stated, is intended to be **representative** rather than comprehensive. The four modes depicted are quite clearly delineated by pedagogic goals and interactional features; while there are some similarities, there are also differences that make description possible. Yet the modes do not claim to account for all features of classroom discourse, nor are they sufficiently comprehensive to specify each and every pedagogic goal. The first difficulty, then, is that the framework is incapable of describing all aspects of classroom interaction. For example, interactions that are not teacher-fronted, where learners work independently of the teacher, are not described. Rather, the framework is concerned to establish an understanding of the relationship between interaction and learning; specifically, the interface between teaching objectives and teacher talk. In essence, as a tool for teacher education, the framework has to enable teachers to describe interaction relatively easily and unambiguously. Yet tensions are inevitable. The discussion now considers some of the difficulties that arise when using SETT. Because classrooms are busy places and because the interactions that take place are rapid, fast-changing and operating on many layers, description is complex. The following features of the discourse are now discussed using SETT:

(a) Mode switching: movements from one mode to another.

(b) Mode side sequences: brief shifts from main to secondary mode and back.

(c) Mode divergence: where interactional features and pedagogic goals do not coincide.

Mode switching

The overriding problem is one of demarcation; modes can be difficult to distinguish and there are times when several modes seem to occur simultaneously. The 'neat and tidy' examples presented in the earlier part of this chapter do occur, but more often than not modes occur in combination with other modes, rather than in isolation. Interactional decisions are taken in the 'here and now' of a lesson, the moment by moment sequence of planning and action, influenced by many factors, including time constraints, teacher and learner agendas, the inter-dependence of turns, unexpected occurrences. Lessons rarely progress from A to Z; like conversations, deviations, topic-shifts, back-channelling, repetitions, false-starts, overlaps all occur very regularly, making description difficult to achieve. Add to this the fact that any transcript is a reduced and idealised version of 'what really happened' and some measure of the problem can be gained.

Movements between modes, henceforth *mode-switching,* are very common in the data and may be brought about either by teacher or learner contributions, though teachers usually have prime respons-ibility. The result is the same: the interaction becomes multi-layered and more difficult to interpret and describe. In theory, any participant in the discourse can say anything at any time and the ensuing interaction takes sudden twists and turns in direction, which make analysis difficult. In practice, this rarely occurs owing to the fact that classroom interaction is goal-oriented. Understanding is gained by considering the interrelatedness of the turn-taking, the fact that turns do not occur in isolation, and by identifying pedagogic goals.

Previously, in Task 6.2, you analysed the following extract, 6.11. Here the same extract is used to consider how movements between modes – mode switching – are achieved. As we have already seen, we can identify three modes here: materials mode; classroom context mode; skills and systems mode. Mode switches are instigated by the teacher on two occasions: in line 45, from materials to classroom context, and in 47, from classroom context to skills and systems. These changes in pedagogic focus are signalled in the language of the participants.

The extract begins in classroom context mode (lines 29–32) with some open class discussion of types of oil used in cooking. The switch to materials mode occurs in line 33, marked with the discourse marker *right* and reference to the book. Lines 32 to 42 are all materials mode, and the traditional IRF routine ensues; learners respond to the material and have their answers confirmed in the teacher's echoes in lines 39, 41, 43, 45. Turn-taking is tightly managed in relation to the material, little interactional space is afforded and the role of the learners is to display knowledge and understanding, which is evaluated by the teacher. The second mode switch occurs in line 47, marked by laughter, which, here, functions as a change of state token, allowing the discourse to change focus, introduce a new topic and a new mode. At line 47, the interaction moves from materials to classroom context mode, and is marked by the mention of learners' names. This 'switch' opens the door for a personal contribution from a learner in line 52, who raises the sub-topic of graduation dinners. Note here how the personalisation of the discourse allows this learner to make an extended contribution about her personal experiences.

The interaction is brought back to the main topic, 'pot-luck suppers' by the teacher's question in line 58, preceded by the discourse marker *but*. This transition takes the discourse back to materials mode in lines 58–62, when there is a very abrupt and unmarked switch to skills and systems ('what adjective do we use for people who don't like that and hate that and a lot of food they won't eat. . . we call it people are very . . . FUSsy'). This switch again invites a learner response in line 66, which, as a vocabulary-related question, is consistent with skills and systems mode. There is a request for clarification from the teacher in line 68, followed by a self-initiated self-repair in line 69 and a confirmation check in line 70.

It is important to note here that these switches occurred very rapidly and over a short space of time. In order to 'find their way' in the discourse, learners have to be alert to these extremely rapid switches and learn to 'read the signals' so that interaction is maintained (see Breen 1998); there are many instances in the data where such rapid and often unmarked mode-switching does result in communication breakdown that may or may not be repaired.

Extract 6.11

29	T:	=yes olive oil yes yes must be a good quality=
30	L:	=and the other olive oil vegetable and made from maize from corn=
31	T:	=yes corn oil and yeah there's many different types of oil olive oil is the best and . . .
32		essential to Spanish omelette tortilla erm right so if you were invited to one of Leslie's
33		pot-luck suppers (**referring to the book**) erm right what would you bring . . . along . . .
34		with you?
35	L:	American or ((1))?
36	T:	yes this is this Leslie the American woman imagine she [invited you to a pot-luck
37		supper
38	L:	[a bottle of wine
39	T:	a bottle of wine yes

40	L:	a dish [of food
41	T:	[what else? a dish of food yes what=
42	L:	=dessert
43	T:	yes possibly a dessert=
44	L:	=or a starter
45	T:	or a starter . . . yes so how would you know what to bring?
46	LL:	((2)) the organiser give you a list ((1))
47	T:	that's right yes so it's it's quite well-organised you can **(laughs)** imagine writing a list
48		oh yes I'll ask Yvette she can bring a starter . . . oh Georgia a nice salad Italians are
49		very good with salads and then maybe a main course er Haldoun and perhaps er the
50		Japanse can do some more some more main courses so it would be very er very
51		well-organised=
52	L:	=usually((2)) like sometimes there are like 3 main courses ((2)) like graduation in
53		sometimes we have parties and we have like er roast chicken and another people
54		bring ((3)) for the main courses and we don't have nothing for nothing for dessert and
55		nothing for the starter [(**laughs**)]
56	T:	[(**laughs**)] oh dear well Georgia perhaps when you go back to Italy perhaps you can
57		organise one of these typical pot-luck suppers and organise it well so you'll have
58		plenty of desserts and plenty of starters (**laughs**) but er do you think it's a good idea?
59	L:	sometimes, yeah
60	L:	it's nice because you don't know what you're going to eat=
61	T:	=it's a surprise yes, yeah as long as you like everything . . . I mean some people don't
62		like certain things what adjective do we use for people who don't like that and hate
63		that and a lot of food they won't eat. . . we call it people are very . . . FUSsy fussy with
64		their food (**writes on board**) right so fussy that's don't like vegetables, never eat er
65		pasta (**laughs**)=
66	L1:	=excuse me how to say if er you ((2)) for example if you try some burger on cormer
67		. . . on the the street and then you feel not very well

68	T:	er . . . I'm not quite sure what you mean Yvette if you?
69	L1:	you can buy for example ((2)) just on the street
70	T:	you mean street sellers . . . people selling food on the street yes

Mode side sequences

A second and commonly found type of mixed mode occurs when there is a brief departure from main to secondary mode and back to main mode again. For example, the pattern may be classroom–context– skills–and–systems–classroom–context, with classroom context the main mode and skills and systems the secondary mode. Sequences like this are henceforth referred to as *mode side sequences*. Side sequences are a common feature of conversation and involve two speakers jointly constructing and negotiating the dialogue, 'feeling their way forward together' (Cook 1989: 54) and managing two topics and two exchange structures. Equally, in the L2 classroom, participants progress tentatively, each pursuing a particular agenda that is typically related to that of the institution. Mode side sequences occur frequently, as exemplified the following extract.

In extract 6.12, a group of advanced learners is discussing life after death. The main mode is classroom context, with a focus on personal experiences. The mode side sequence occurs (lines 114 to 123), when the learner's turn (114) switches the mode to skills and systems. Once the vocabulary question has been cleared up, the teacher brings the discussion back to classroom context mode in (125). Note that the impetus for a mode side sequence may come from either a learner or the teacher, but that it is very often the teacher who brings the discussion 'back on track', returning to the original mode. Here, there is evidence of skills and systems mode in order to clarify a language-related matter, but the departure is relatively brief and the main mode is quickly re-established.

Extract 6.12

109	T:	[no ok alright] . . . so Jan you want to live forever?=
110	L3:	=yeah if money can afford it I will freeze body=
111	L:	=ugh . . .
112	L1:	what are you going to do? . . . frozen frozen you body?=
113	L3:	=yeah=
114	L1:	cyonics? . . .
115	T:	=yeah it's cry cry cryo[genics]
116	L1:	[cryonics] cryogenics . . . no cryonics=
117	T:	=oh is it? ok=
118	L1:	=I think so I don't know . . .

119	T:	let me check it it might be in this one . . . **(looks in dictionary)**
120	L:	((4)) . . .
121	T:	cryogenics if you don't freeze your body you freeze your head isn't that the way it is?=
122	L:	=you can choose=
123	T:	=oh really?=
124	L3:	=it's eh a ((2)) . . .
125	T:	I see so if you don't believe in religion=
126	L:	=yeah=

In brief, then, we can say that mode side sequences occur when there is a momentary shift from one (main) mode to another (secondary) mode in response to a change in pedagogic goals. A number of such mode side sequences have been identified, each following a similar pattern:

- classroom–context–skills–and–systems–classroom–context

- materials–skills–and–systems–materials

- materials–classroom–context–materials

- managerial–skills–and–systems–managerial

Both teacher and learners initiate mode side sequences, but the responsibility for returning to the main mode lies with the teacher. The extent to which the teacher is able to 'keep on track' and ensure that learners do not become 'lost' is closely related to teachers' ability to move from one mode to another, adjusting language to the unfolding text of the lesson. A mode side sequence is symbolised by an immediate and obvious change in the talk-in-interaction, with different inter-actional features and a different speech exchange system.

Task 6.5

Make a fifteen-minute recording of one of your classes, or, alternatively, watch a video-clip of someone else teaching. Analyse the discourse using SETT and identify which modes are used and why and which interactures can be identified. Finally, in the light of what you now know, how effective was the teaching in terms of its potential for promoting learning?

In this section, the framework for describing L2 classroom inter-actional processes was presented and exemplified using extracts from the data. The notions of *mode switching* and *mode side sequences* were introduced, as were *mode convergent* and *mode divergent* teacher talk.

Summary

The descriptive framework presented in this chapter is designed to enable teachers to access the interactional organisation of their classes. The framework is intended as a means to an end rather than the end itself, concerned to facilitate understanding, not code every interaction. Consequently, it is representative, not comprehensive. Given the uniqueness of the L2 classroom and the fact that every interaction is locally produced, it is neither practicable nor realistic to propose that an all-encompassing view of context can be derived, or that an instrument is available that can accurately provide an emic perspective of each interaction.

The framework relates pedagogic purpose to language use, enabling teachers to identify 'recurrent segmental patterns or structures' (Drew 1994: 142) that can contribute to an understanding of what constitutes appropriate teacher talk in a particular mode. This dynamic perspective is intended to avoid the need for bland descriptive systems that adopt an invariant view of L2 classroom interaction. By getting teachers to relate their use of language to pedagogic goals and by examining interactional features in each of the four modes, it is anticipated that a greater depth of understanding can be gained in a relatively short space of time.

In the data, four modes were identified and described according to their pedagogic goals and interactional features. Managerial mode, where the goal is the organisation of learning, features a single extended teacher turn (usually an instruction or explanation) and an absence of learner involvement. In materials mode, learning outcomes are derived from materials-focused language practice: typically, the IRF sequence dominates, making extensive use of display questions, form-focused feedback and repair. Skills and systems mode typically follows a similar interactional organisation to materials mode. However, turn-taking and topic management may be less tightly controlled, and pedagogic goals are not derived from materials, but from teacher and learner agendas. In classroom context mode, on the other hand, learners are allowed considerable interactional space; the focus is on oral fluency, on the message rather than the forms used to convey it. Each mode has its own characteristic fingerprint (Heritage and Greatbatch 1991), specific interactional features that are related to teaching objectives. While the characteristics identified in each mode have a certain uniformity, there is also some degree of heterogeneity

(Seedhouse 1996) determined by the precise nature of the local context and including factors such as the level of the students and the methodology being used.

Modes are not static and invariant, but dynamic and changing. There are movements from one mode to another, *mode switching,* and between main and secondary modes (*mode side sequences*). Although learners may initiate a switch, the responsibility for returning to the main mode typically lies with the teacher. Switches from one mode to another are marked by *transition* or *boundary* markers (*right, now, ok,* etc.) with a corresponding adjustment in intonation and sentence stress. A mode may last for one whole lesson or for much shorter periods, with more frequent changes.

A teacher's use of language may be *mode convergent,* where pedagogic goals and language use are congruent, facilitating learning opportunities, or *mode divergent,* where inconsistencies in pedagogic goals and interactional features hinder opportunities for learning. Occurrences of mode convergent or mode divergent verbal behaviour may be purely 'accidental' in that teachers do not consciously plan to coincide language use and teaching aims (however, see Chapter 7), or more deliberate.

7 Classroom discourse as reflective practice

Introduction

The aim of this chapter is to introduce readers to the idea that reflective practice can be enhanced by making classroom discourse the main focus of the reflection. We have already seen that interaction underpins everything that takes place in a classroom. Here, I argue that there is a compelling need to put classroom discourse at the centre of reflective practice by advocating a more structured approach to the process of reflection on practice. Why do I say this? The first, and perhaps most important reason, is that the notion of reflective practice had become a little tired and even dated. Without doubt, and as we shall see below, the case for reflective practice is very strong; few would argue that if we are to improve as teachers, we need to reflect on and change our practices on a regular, ongoing basis. Practitioners and researchers alike have been saying this for many years now. And yet, I argue, reflective practice is only taking place in a limited way and with minimal impact (see below). Perhaps reflective practice needs a makeover: using classroom discourse as the focus might just be one way of doing this.

Second, and as we shall see below, few teachers are actually *taught* how to 'do' reflective practice. Most teachers have experienced being told to reflect on their practice, both on pre-and in-service teacher education programmes. But very few, I suggest, are given the tools and skills needed to do just that and to make reflection a part of a teacher's professional life.

Third, I am going to argue that in order to reflect on practice we need to know exactly 'what is happening' when we are teaching. The best way to understand teaching is to collect data and the best kind of data is based on classroom interaction. By identifying a problem, collecting data and then beginning the process of reflection and change, I am very confident that reflective practice will not only occur on a much larger scale, it will also have a greater impact on performance.

In the first part of the chapter, I present a critique of the notion of teacher as reflective practitioner, while the second part deals with a classroom discourse oriented approach to reflective practice.

The teacher as reflective practitioner

The notion of reflective practice for teachers has been with us for almost thirty years. First proposed by Schön (1983, 1996) as a means of continuous professional development for educators and other professionals, reflective practice is now regarded as a fundamental principle of teacher education and teacher development. Essentially, reflective practice entails thinking about a particular aspect of one's teaching and trying to change or improve it. The broadly-defined process involves cycles of thoughtfully considering the effectiveness of practice, taking steps to improve practice, and assessing the effectiveness of those efforts, often in conjunction with other professionals with complementary experience (Ferraro 2000). Hatton and Smith (1995) described reflection as 'a deliberate thinking about action with a view to its improvement (34). It should be noted, however, that, according to Sparks-Langer (1992), there does not appear to be a single definition of reflective practice (henceforth, RP) in the literature, a point that we'll return to below.

Zeichner and Liston (1996) presented five features that they consider to be key in reflective teachers. Reflective teachers are those who:

1 examine, frame and attempt to solve the dilemmas of classroom practice;

2 are aware of and question the assumptions and values they bring to teaching;

3 are attentive to the institutional and cultural contexts in which they teach;

4 take part in curriculum development and school change efforts;

5 take responsibility for their own professional development.

The case for RP among a variety of practitioners has been advocated for some time since Schön (see, for example, Eraut 1995; Edge 2001). Many years ago, Dewey (1933) suggested that learning to teach must include opportunities for new teachers to develop the capacity for reflective action. More recently, in teacher education, it has been acclaimed as a goal in many programmes (Hatton and Smith 1995).

Personal reflection

What does the term 'reflective practice' mean to you? Can you think of any occasions where you have used reflective practice in your own teaching or as a learner? What aspects of your teaching would you like to reflect on and how might you do this?

Furthermore, Bartlett (1990) suggested that initial teacher training involves more than skills and competencies, and that teachers need to be equipped with the tools that will enable them to analyse their own classroom practices and make adjustments to the teaching and learning environment.

There is, then, plenty of evidence for the need for RP: it is, essentially, seen as a 'good thing' and something that any structured programme of professional practice should include. In initial teacher education programmes, trainee teachers are told at a very early stage that they must 'reflect on their practice'; indeed, many written and practical assignments include the ability to reflect critically on practice as one of the main assessment criteria. What is less clear is the precise meaning of RP and, more importantly, *how* to do it. Teacher educators, I suggest, are quite content to tell their trainee teachers to reflect on practice; few teach them how to do it. And yet what is needed is for teachers in training to be taught *how* to reflect so that reflection plus action becomes an integral element of their professional practice. The only way that teachers can develop the skills needed to constantly improve and refine their teaching is for them to become researchers of their own practice. This is something that must be taught.

In the words of Russell (2005: 200), 'The absence of any clear agreement about what reflective practice is and how we recognise it helps us to understand why it is not clear how to teach it.' While acknowledging that this is the current state of affairs, he then went on to say that it 'can and should be taught – explicitly, directly, thoughtfully and patiently (204). Other writers have suggested how RP might be taught. Alger (2006), for example, suggested that reflection could be fostered through activities such as action research, case studies, microteaching and reflective writing assignments, while Park (2003) has identified reflective journals as potentially valuable tools for developing reflective practitioners. He claimed that the

Task 7.1

What aspects of classroom practice can we reflect on? Think of three examples relating to teachers and three for learners. It's probably best to write each example as a question as I have done below. Then decide HOW you would reflect and improve your practice in response to each question.

Teachers	Learners
How can I improve the questions I ask?	How can I involve my students more in my classes?

journaling process did a number of things including stimulating critical thinking, allowing teacher educators some insights into the minds of the candidates, and helping the candidates to understand better the process of learning.

Under the notion of second language teacher *education*, as distinct from second language teacher *training* (Richards and Nunan 1990; Wallace 1991), the focus of attention is on the need to enable teachers to develop themselves. There is clearly more to teacher preparation than skills training; teachers need to be equipped with the tools that will enable them to find out about their own classrooms and make adjustments (Bartlett 1990). In short, teachers must learn to change their role from teacher to teacher-researcher, a logical extension of what Wallace (1991: 8) terms 'the applied science model' of teacher education (c.f. Schön 1983). This model of teacher education involves a process of *reflection in action* whereby teachers and teachers in training are involved in critical thought, questioning and re-appraising their actions in the second language classroom. More recently, there has been a call for the concept of *reflection in action* to be re-interpreted as 'reflection after action' (Eraut 1995), since teachers cannot reflect as they teach; instead, a cycle of action–reflection–further action is preferred, with a slight distancing between each of the stages.

Under reflective practice, in addition to reflecting on present classroom procedures, teachers adopt a retrospective stance and reflect on past actions in an endeavour to increase their understanding of the teaching/learning process (Wallace 1998). Competencies are acquired through and by the participants who have an active role in their own development, which in turn is based on two types of knowledge: *received knowledge*, 'the intellectual content of the profession' (Wallace 1991: 14), including the specific knowledge (linguistic and pedagogic) that language teachers need in order to perform their role; and *experiential knowledge*, based on the experience gained in the classroom and reflection on that experience. To use Wallace's terms, experiential knowledge is based on knowledge-in-action plus reflection on that knowledge. Mann makes a similar distinction (2001: 58):

> Received knowledge is the stuff of dictionaries and is more verifiable. Experiential knowledge is not a matter of fact, but a complex mix of feeling, thought and individual perspective.

Clearly, both types of knowledge are important, but it is the second that is of most concern here since it rests on the assumption that teachers can and should reflect on their practices and learn from them. Central to the notion of experiential knowledge is collaborative discussion, where thoughts and ideas about classroom practice are articulated (Taylor 1985). To use Taylor's term, articulation involves the 'shaping' of ideas, the reformulation of concepts in a progression towards enhanced understanding. Reflection on practice does not occur in isolation, but in discussion with another practitioner, a form of cooperative development, involving a 'Speaker' and an 'Understander', who enhances professional understanding through dialogue (c.f. Edge 1992).

Perhaps one of the best ways to promote reflective practice is for teachers to engage in a process of action research. Action research rests on the premise that teachers can and should investigate their own classrooms (Cohen *et al*. 2007: 226). The starting point is the identification of a problem; the process continues with data collection, data analysis and finally outcomes are suggested. According to Carr and Kemmis (1983: 220–221), action research can be defined as:

> a form of self-reflective inquiry undertaken by participants in social situations in order to improve the rationality and justice of their own practices, their understanding of these practices, and the situations in which the practices are carried out.

Action research involves identifying a specific classroom problem and considering ways of solving the problem. The process of problem posing is actually as important as problem solving and the process is normally a collaborative one, involving discussion and dialogue with a colleague or 'critical friend'.

Cohen *et al*. (2007) identify eight stages in the process:

1 Identify the problem.

2 Develop a draft proposal.

3 Review what has already been written on the issue.

4 Restate the problem or formulate a hypothesis.

5 Select research procedures.

6 Choose evaluation procedures.

7 Collect data, analyse the data and provide feedback.

8 Interpret the data and make inferences.

The value and relevance of action research are self-evident: helping teachers to focus on problems in their own classrooms and to identify solutions is desirable from the position of both professional development and learning. Perhaps the most important aspect of the action research process is that it is data-led. Improvement in teaching performance comes about through the collection and analysis of a small amount of data. Here, 'data' are things like: recordings of a teaching session; a set of test results; a completed observation schedule; minute papers[1] and so on. In short, collecting data means collecting evidence that will help a teacher address a particular problem or issue. As Johnson points out, this process of collecting and analysing data is central to the professionalisation of teaching (1995: 29): 'The more research-driven knowledge teachers have, the better their teaching performances will be.'

Under this view, 'research-driven knowledge' is data-driven and, more importantly, based on data derived from a teacher's own classroom. According to Nunan (1989: 3), there are a number of reasons why teachers might be interested in researching their own classrooms:

- teachers have to justify educational innovations;

- teachers are constantly involved in intellectual and social change;

- becoming a teacher–researcher is a logical stage in the process of professional self-development.

To this list is added another reason, that of *ownership*. I'd like to suggest that ownership of the data is the single, most important factor contributing to enhanced understanding and professional development. Ownership of the data is, arguably, far more likely to result in a change in teaching behaviour since one of the stages in getting teachers to modify their teaching behaviour is for them to *experience* the change (Thornbury 1996), a point echoed by Harmer (1999: 5), 'It's no good talking about or imposing change [. . .], you have to let the changes experience what you are talking about first.' Because teacher-researchers are both the producers and consumers of their research (Kumaravadivelu 1999), since they own the data and are responsible for effecting changes to classroom practices, the process is more private and, arguably, less intimidating. The concern is to enhance understanding of local context rather than generalise to a broader one. Teachers engaged in action research are concerned to enhance their understandings of the local context: a specific class, teacher or group of students. As we have already seen, the process entails data collection, analysis, reflection and discussion. Enhancing understandings of a specific problem in a particular context rests on the following three assumptions that will be dealt with in turn in the remainder of this section:

- the research takes place in the classroom;

- teacher-researchers reflect and act on what they observe;

- understanding emerges through dialogue.

Task 7.2

Consider each of the following scenarios. For each situation, say why this might be a problem, then suggest what kind of data you would collect to help you make improvements to your practice:

- Students refuse to speak English when working independently.

- Your instructions never seem to 'work' and are always mis-understood.

- Your teaching is dominated by question–answer routines.

- Your students constantly do badly in the end of unit tests you set them.

Assumption 1: the research takes place in the classroom

The kind of research we are describing here is small-scale, localised, context-specific and private. This type of research contrasts starkly to the kind that dominates second language teaching. According to Nunan, much of the research that goes on in second language teaching is deemed irrelevant, resulting in a 'wedge between researcher and practitioner' (1996: 42). One of the reasons is that teachers' voices are often unheard, replaced by the researcher's perspective; another is that much research is still conducted under experimental conditions in class-rooms created for research purposes (ibid.). This startling revelation suggests an urgent need for research that is located in 'ordinary' classrooms, conducted by teachers for their own ends; understanding and professional development can only be enhanced when the process of inquiry is carried out *in situ*, in the teacher's natural environment. This was termed 'ecological research' by van Lier, drawing comparisons with any natural environment in which the slightest change in one sub-system will impact other systems (2000: 11):

> Ecological research pays a great deal of attention to the smallest detail of the interaction, since within these details maybe contained the seeds of learning. The reflective teacher can learn to 'read' the environment to notice such details.

The main attraction of this view of reflection in action is that teachers work very closely with the data they collect in their own context, their own 'environment', to use van Lier's term. The understandings gained from working with the detail of the data belong to teachers. Public ownership does not come into question, neither does generalisability; research is a process of inquiry, conducted by the teacher for the teacher. The main advantage is that there is a unification of theory and practice since the smallest details can be studied, changes implemented and then evaluated (van Lier 2000). The main reason for the potential for such microscopic analysis is the fact that the research is located in a context that is both clearly defined and familiar to the teacher-researcher.

Assumption 2: teacher-researchers reflect and act on what they observe

The second assumption is very much in tune with the broad philosophy of reflective practice: reflection results in a change in practice, based on evidence in the form of data. Ideally, any change in practice should benefit students. As mentioned previously, the first step in the process is to identify a problem: the very act of 'posing problems' and coming to understand them is, in itself, developmental. Problems may or may not be solved; the real value lies in discussing options and considering possibilities. Reflection and action result in a kind of 'emergent understanding', an ongoing process of enhanced awareness.

For most second language teachers, this view of class-based research might appear somewhat daunting – teachers are not automatically equipped with classroom observation skills and may know even less about how to process and analyse data. Not only are L2 teachers normally too busy to take on additional duties such as data collection and analysis, few have actually been trained in class-based research techniques. The other issue is that many of the research methods currently available have been designed for and by researchers, not by teachers. There is a real paucity of research tools that can be used as part of a reflective practice cycle and that do not require enormous amounts of time and energy to master. My aim in the next section is to demonstrate how classroom interaction data can be collected and analysed quickly and easily and have an immediate impact on understandings and teaching performance.

Assumption 3: understanding emerges through dialogue

Action research has always been regarded as a collaborative process involving dialogue (Kemmis and McTaggart 1992; Winter 1996; Zuber-Skerritt 1996). Dialogue is a crucial part of the reflection–action–further–action cycle, since it allows for clarification, questioning and ultimately enhanced understanding. Conversation is the means by which new ideas are expressed, doubts aired and concerns raised

(Wells 1999). It is through talk that we gain fuller understandings; I can think of many occasions when a discussion with friends or colleagues has helped me understand a new concept or a new idea more fully. I am sure that readers will agree that a conversation is often the best means of accessing new ideas and gaining closer understandings of complex processes such as teaching.

From a theoretical perspective, socio-cultural views of learning are very helpful here (see also Chapter 3). The main 'message' of this view of learning is that all human development is underpinned by language, often talk. Quite simply, if we wish to develop or improve in any aspect of our lives, one of the first steps is to talk about it. New ideas and new knowledge are 'appropriated'; in other words, we gain ownership of them. This process occurs through talk. Often, through a dialogue with, possibly, a more experienced professional, we are 'scaffolded' or assisted in making sense and acquiring deeper insights of complex phenomena. Consider this extract of interview data in which the researcher (R) is talking to a teacher (T) about her use of teacher 'echo':

Extract 7.1

T: I was struck by how much echoing I did before and sometimes there was a justification for it . . . but a LOT of the time . . . it was just echo for the sake of echo so I was fairly consciously trying NOT to echo this time.

R: And what effect did that (**reduced echo**) have on the interaction patterns or the involvement of learners in the class, did it have any effect that you noticed?

T: I think that it made them more confident perhaps in giving me words because it was only going to come back to them if the pronunciation WASn't right rather than just getting ((1)) straight back to them. When you're eliciting vocabulary if they're coming out with the vocabulary and it's adequate and it's clear, there's no need for you to echo it back to the other students . . . you're wasting a lot of time by echoing stuff back.

(Teacher 1, interview 1)

Here we see very clearly the value of dialogue in promoting closer understandings. The teacher is reflecting on her use of 'echo', the repetition of student contributions – a common feature of classroom discourse. Her realisation that echo can become a kind of habit ('echo for echo's sake') is probed by the researcher who asks about the effect of echo on learner involvement. The teacher's response is quite revealing: she says that reduced echo makes learners more confident and that a lot of echo is unnecessary. Arguably, this realisation may not have occurred without an opportunity to discuss echo and reflect on its effects. The researcher's question allows her to think about her language use and give reasons, possibly for the first time. It is this kind of 'light bulb moment' that professional dialogue can create. Through talk, new realisations and greater insights come about and get their first airing. Dialogue can establish 'proximal processes', or contexts that create opportunities for learning potential, which, according to Bronfenbrenner and Ceci (1994: 578), 'offer development growth in terms of:

- differentiated perception and response;
- directing and controlling one's own behaviour;
- coping successfully under stress;
- acquiring knowledge and skill;
- modifying and constructing one's own physical, social and symbolic environment.'

Again, using a socio-cultural construct, teachers are 'scaffolded' through their 'Zones of Proximal Development' (ZPD) to a higher plane of understanding through the dialogues they have with other professionals (van Lier 1996). Under this perspective, reflection and action alone are insufficient means of allowing professional development – scaffolded dialogues, where issues are clarified and new levels of understanding attained, are central to reflective practice.

Task 7.3

Think of a time in your professional life when a conversation with a friend or colleague helped you to understand something better. What was the effect of the dialogue on your professional practice and what changes did you make to your teaching, if any?

Developing reflective practices through SETT

In the last chapter, I presented the SETT framework, designed to enable teachers to evaluate and analyse their interactions with students as a means of improving classroom practice. The final task, Task 6.4, of Chapter 6 invited you to make a short recording of your teaching and analyse that recording using SETT.

In this section, I consider how the SETT framework might be used as a tool to promote and foster reflective practice. The data used in this section are taken from interviews with teachers who have used the framework to evaluate and improve their teaching. To summarise the previous section in this chapter, the central argument here is that if teachers are to become effective reflective practitioners, three conditions are necessary:

1 Teachers need a *tool*, such as the SETT framework, to help focus attention and direct reflections to specific features of their teaching.

2 Teachers need an appropriate *metalanguage* with which to discuss their reflections. An appropriate terminology that is understood by all parties is central to this.

3 There needs to be *dialogue*. Teachers engaged in reflective practices should have an opportunity to discuss their reflections with a colleague or other professional in order to make sense of their self-observations.

The SETT framework (see Appendix A) was designed to help teachers gain closer understandings of the complex relationship between language, interaction and learning. It can be seen as a tool that promotes and guides reflection and that, when accompanied by dialogue, will result in changes in classroom practice that will, ultimately, benefit learners. Similar frameworks have been advocated by other researchers with an overall goal of making classrooms more dialogic and more engaging for learners (see, for example, Mortimer and Scott (2003) and Alexander (2008)). The SETT framework is intended to be used by teachers evaluating their own language use: it therefore offers an emic, insider perspective designed to facilitate reflection and action.

In the original study (2006), users of SETT made short (fifteen-minute), 'snapshot' recordings of parts of their classes and analysed these recordings using the framework. This entailed listening to the tape twice: once to identify the four modes (see Table 6.1, Chapter 6), then a second time to identify and make a note of specific interactures such as teacher echo, direct repair, scaffolding, etc. This process was repeated over a period of time in order to allow emergent under-standings of classroom interaction to develop. From this dual analysis (modes plus interactures), it is then possible to produce a kind of profile of one's teaching, taken from a purely interactional perspective. This allows teachers to answer questions like these:

• Which modes seem to occur most frequently in my classes?

• How mode convergent (see Chapter 6) is my teaching?

• Are some interactional features (display questions, for example) more common than others?

• How much interactional space do I give to my learners?

- Are there any particular features of the interaction in my classes that I need to change or improve?

And so on. . .

Over time, and with repeated used, teachers gain in their classroom interactional competence (see Chapter 8) and become much better at promoting more dialogic, engaged interaction in which learners really play a role. By completing the SETT reflective practice cycle in Figure 7.1 on p. 149 and by engaging in a structured process of focused reflection, action and further reflection, I suggest that improvements to practice will occur naturally and relatively easily. Teachers become genuine researchers of their own practice: collecting and analysing data, reflecting and modifying teaching behaviour, discussing this process with a colleague, collecting more data, and so on. The SETT reflective practice cycle is summarised below; in the remainder of this section, I present and analyse interview data from step 5 of the cycle as a means of demonstrating this process in action. Pseudonyms have been used throughout to protect the identities of the participating teachers.

In the first example, extract 7.2 below, the focus of the discussion is 'wait time', one of the interactional features that the teacher, Nick, had chosen to discuss. For Nick, there is a growing realisation of the value of wait-time in whole class open discussion (*I just gave them whatever time they needed*). He comments on what actually happens following a teacher prompt (*they're processing the question [. . .] and they HAVE to literally look into their own minds and do they have an experience which relates to the question*) and makes the interesting observation that for some students, this takes more time and they need to be given that time (*the wait-time is ALways more extensive for them*).

It is apparent from Nick's comments that this is the first time he has been in a position to actually think about wait time as an important phenomenon and one that teachers need to incorporate into their teaching. Arguably, using the SETT procedure allowed him to analyse this aspect of his teaching in far greater detail and make changes by increasing wait-time where necessary. A simple change in practice maybe, but it is one that is likely to have a huge impact on the kind of interaction that occurs and a change that is likely to open up space for learning. Note too in extract 7.2 how the interviewer (I) plays an important role in guiding the discussion and in helping Nick to clarify his own thinking around a particular issue.

Extract 7.2

T: I just found it was very enjoyable and the feedback, like extended wait-time. Lots of GAPS here where you think there's nobody replying and then they suddenly come in

I: Was that conscious or was that just something . . .?

T: No I deliberately because I know that the far-easterne
    problems speaking and therefore I gave them I just gav
    whatever time they needed you know. In some cases t
    processing the question and they're processing the inform
    and they HAVE to literally look into their own minds and do
    have an experience that relates to the question. And this is
    case I think particularly with Roy with Yung rather and Jang
    who are Korean I think the wait-time is ALways more extensive
    for them.

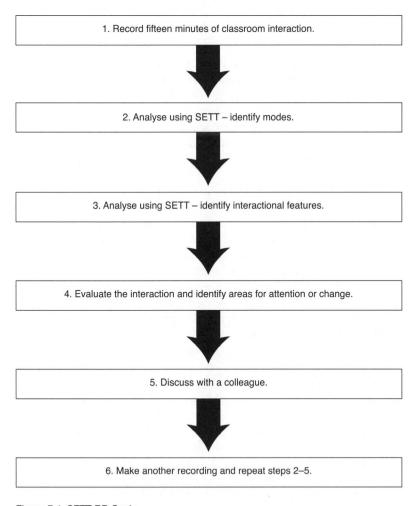

Figure 7.1 SETT RP Cycle

In extract 7.3, we can see how the same teacher actually incorporates extended wait time into his teaching. Here, we see Nick trying to elicit a particular piece of vocabulary (*shopping centre*). Note the three-second pauses between questions. This use of extended wait time and the accompanying strategy of using a different question each time leads to an extended learner turn in 3. Again, arguably, it is this use of extended wait time that results in a longer response than the one that might be expected by the teacher. The learner not only provides the piece of vocabulary, she also comments on why people go to shopping centres (*it's very convenient*). The point I am making here is that Nick is able not only to articulate and discuss a particular aspect of his teaching (the use of extended wait time), he is able also to demonstrate this practice while teaching.

Extract 7.3

1	T:	what are the things that we have today with shopping? what do we have today? (3)
2		what do we call these places today? (3) what's the word we're talking about? (3)
3	L:	shopping centres because you just go the shopping centre you can buy everything its
4		very convenient

Under a *dialogic* approach to RP, a process of collaborative meaning-making occurs, as evidenced in the next extract, 7.4. Here, teacher and interviewer jointly construct understandings through their talk and in relation to a particular tool. Notice how the interactants 'feel their way' in the discourse, seeking and giving clarification and trying to apply a new metalanguage to help them advance their understandings. In line 1, for example, there is a request for clarification by this teacher, Jill, relating to teacher echo. This is answered in lines 2–5, in which the interviewer attempts to offer alternatives to echo (*requests for clarification* and *direct repair*). In lines 7–9, the interviewer clarifies the distinction between direct repair and teacher echo. He also makes the point that teacher echo can have positive consequences (*to allow the whole class to HEAR it*) or negative ones (*it can be just a habit*). Compare the role of the interviewer in lines 2–5, where there is a lot of hedging, frequent use of the modal *could*, and the use of softeners (*I would have thought*) with his role in 7–9, where he is more directive, more teacher-like we might say. In lines 7–9, there is a sense that the interviewer is actually teaching the difference between direct repair and teacher echo. This could be in response to Jill's comment (*I wasn't quite sure about that*), or it could be stemming from a perceived need to clarify the terminology.

In the second part of this extract (lines 10–21), there is a justification by Jill for her use of echo, possibly in response to the interviewer's comment *it can be just a habit*. In lines 10–12, Jill is able to rationalise her use of teacher echo (*so the rest of the class can hear*), before moving on to explain that, from her completed SETT grid, some of her contributions were examples of teacher echo, some examples of direct repair. There is evidence here that this teacher is 'sorting out' in her own mind not only the differences in meaning between the various inter-actional features, but also her reasons for using them at specific points in the lesson. The use of dialogue and the framework are central to this process: she is essentially uncovering the interactional decisions taken and describing – probably for the first time – her 'online decision-making'. We'll come back to this below. Central to the process is the potential, brought about by the presence of the interviewer, to air her ideas and clarify interactional strategies taken 'in the heat of the moment', while teaching. Note the assurance given by the interviewer in lines 16–19, a kind of affirmation that Jill's use of language and online decision-making were appropriate for that stage in the lesson.

Extract 7.4

1	T:	Yes yes, repeating what the students say. Is that teacher echo?
2	I:	It's teacher echo but it could also be a kind of clarification in a way or you could
3		actually even interpret it as direct repair, couldn't you because if they say 'busy'
4		(**mispronounced**) or something instead of 'busy' and you just say 'busy' that's more
5		direct repair I would have thought than echo.
6	T:	Yes I wasn't quite sure about that.
7	I:	If what you're doing is correcting their pronunciation, then that's direct repair, if what
8		you're doing is just regurgitating what they've said that's echo and again echo can be
9		to allow the whole class to HEAR it or it can be just a habit.
10	T:	Yep. I mean I do actually with this class I do use quite a lot of teacher echo simply
11		because they do tend to speak very quietly and mumble sometimes and it IS really so
12		the rest of the class can hear. This was pronunciation so 'busy' (**referring to SETT**
13		**grid**) so that should have gone up to direct repair, however, THESE were teacher

14		echoes 'noisy expensive interesting' because the pronunciation was ok, but then I
15		repeated them for the reasons I mentioned they were mumbled.
16	I:	And I think everyone needs to HEAR a contribution. I think that's a GOOD use of
17		teacher echo and I think the sort of that we all probably have the slightly negative one
18		is when somebody says something and you just repeat it for no apparent reason.
19		I think that's the one to be more aware of.
20	T:	So again perhaps in the upper level classes when the pronunciation is good and
21		clear, then it's not necessary to repeat.

In the SETT RP data, many of the comments made by teachers were about justifying their 'online decision-making'. By 'online', I mean the decisions that teachers make while teaching; a decision to cut an activity short, or allow more time, or to get students to finish some writing at home. Essentially, good teaching is about making the right decision at a particular moment – I would go further and argue that good decisions are often related to the ways in which interaction is managed at a particular point in time. In extract 7.5 below, for example, the teacher (Barbie) is talking about scaffolding, perhaps for the first time. Her comments indicate that she is trying to both understand for herself and explain to the interviewer how scaffolding occurs in practice (*I'm going to re-formulate it [. . .] I'm going to give them a lot of examples so that's all scaffolding isn't it?*). Barbie goes further and explains that scaffolding occurs more in skills and systems mode because this is the mode where the main focus is the language itself (*it's so focused on language*). What is actually happening in these, and other, extracts then is that teachers are reflecting *through* the dialogues they have with the interviewer, based on an earlier analysis of their own interactions with students. I would suggest that this is a far more effective means of promoting RP than simply asking people to reflect on their practice. Not only are teachers able to discuss particular aspects of their teaching, they are also able to give reasons for a particular strategy and make observations about its appropriacy at a given moment.

Extract 7.5

I: Is scaffolding something you think you do more of in that type of mode for example you're in a skills and systems mode here. Do you think it's something that happens more in some modes than others or is it maybe too difficult to say at this stage?

T: *My first feeling would be yes because it's so focused on language that anything they give me that might not be correct and not clear then I'm going to re-formulate it or anything they don't understand I'm going to give them a lot of examples so that's all scaffolding isn't it?*

(Teacher 3, interview 2)

As an alternative to simply talking about classroom interaction in a semi-structured interview, it is also possible to get teachers to make a video-recording of their teaching and discuss the recording. This procedure, known as *stimulated recall*, has the immediate advantage of allowing both interviewer and teacher to watch something together and comment on it together. It is a very powerful research tool and an excellent means of raising awareness about specific features of the interaction. Stimulated recall was used in the SETT RP cycle as an alternative to simply discussing a teacher's performance. Teachers were asked to make a video recording of part of a lesson, complete the SETT framework and then discuss the playback with a colleague or critical friend. The extracts that follow are taken from the stimulated recall interviews. The classroom interaction is presented on the left side of each extract; the teacher's commentary on the right side.

In extract 7.6, the teacher, Joe, is commenting on an early part of a lesson in which he is setting up a task. We can see from the interaction that this is clearly managerial mode and the teacher's goal is to locate the activity in time and space (*we're going to be reading; last Christmas we did a quiz*). He is providing a context for the activity and helping learners to understand what comes next, an instruction and organisation of the groups. Joe comments on the mode (managerial) and interactional feature (extended teacher turn). He then offers an evaluation of the final part of the extract, the question, which, in Joe's own terms was rather 'vague' and 'problematic'. Although we do not know exactly what happened next, there is a suggestion by Joe that the wording of his question created problems later on because it was too vague. His comments highlight a problem that we are all only too aware

Task 7.4

How might you use this approach (stimulated recall) to collect data on your own teaching? What aspects of your classroom language might you focus on using this approach and what problems do you foresee in using it?

of: the need for clarity when setting up tasks and giving instructions. Joe's reflections and self-evaluation, by pointing at specific features of the interaction, enable a much finer grained analysis, both for us, as outsiders, and for Joe commenting on his own teaching.

Extract 7.6

T: this morning we're going to be reading about and talking about er music and pop stars and famous people. Last Christmas we did a quiz do you remember and it was a picture quiz and some of the pictures were people from your countries. Erm let me see could you work with Ben and could you three guys work together (**T organises groups**). If you recognise any of those people who they are and what you know about them and then what kind of lifestyle do you think these people have?

So here I'm setting up the activity so this is managerial and an extended teacher turn. So this is me setting up the activity, more managerial.

It's a very sort of vague question which is problematic later on but I thought this was . . . I want them to speak to each other but it was kind of problematic, maybe it was too vague . . .

In the second stimulated recall extract, 7.7, we see a continuation of Joe's lesson in which he elicits information about the various pop-stars. As Joe's own comments reflect, he is asking genuine or referential questions here in which there is a real exchange of information. As we can see from the interaction, in many respects the extract resembles casual conversation. Turn-taking is rapid (indicated by latching =) and there are requests for clarification (e.g. from?) and acknowledgement tokens (uh uh). It is not immediately evident who the teacher is: this could be two friends chatting and roles are pretty symmetrical. Perhaps one of the things Joe could have mentioned in his commentary is the fact that there are opportunities here for extending learner contributions and for eliciting further information. We might even argue that learning opportunities, in the form of speaking practice, have been missed in this short extract. Nonetheless, what this and other extracts show quite clearly is the relationship between classroom interaction and teachers' comments on it; this kind of data is both highly revealing and highly suited to the promotion of reflective practice.

Extract 7.7

(Teacher stops the activity)

T: so you can help me because I don't know some of these people er who's that who's that person in picture A?

L: Mei Chung

T: Mei Chung. What does she do?

L: she's a pop singer=

T: =she's a a pop singer . . . from?

L: from Taiwan=

T: =Taiwan is she famous in lots of countries?

L: I think Taiwan and Hong Kong=

T: =uh uh and in Malaysia too?

L: yes

I'm asking referential questions here because I didn't really know the answer to some of these. They just told me. These are genuine questions.

In the final stimulated recall extract 7.8, we see another teacher, Mary, clarifying a piece of vocabulary, 'discographics'. Our analysis of the interaction reveals a number of interesting features:

- In 1, L1 comes up with an 'invented' piece of vocabulary, 'discographics', which is immediately met by surprise by Mary in 2.

- L1 tries to explain (in 3) and encounters some perturbation, indicated by self-initiated self-repair and a four-second pause, which Mary ignores, preferring to let L1 struggle a little longer.

- In 4, Mary interrupts L1 (indicated =) and seeks clarification, offering an acknowledgement of L1's previous contribution ('like you said'). Mary also scaffolds a more 'precise' term, offering 'the music business' as a more appropriate phrase for 'discographics'.

- In 5, it is apparent that L1 is not satisfied with this attempted clarification, as indicated by her two questions, both suggesting some doubt and confusion.

- Mary again interrupts (in 6), possibly preventing a fuller explanation from L1 and possibly causing further confusion.

Mary's own self-reflections on her data are equally interesting. Her insights offer a detailed analysis of a repair strategy that may have backfired and caused more confusion. She is able to rationalise the whole process and take stock of the different courses of action taken, and alternatives rejected (*I was going to say it's a false friend but I decided not to because I thought that might confuse her*). Mary is also able to accept that she may have understood L1's explanation and that she possibly could have allowed more time, further evidence of the interruption mentioned above. By her own admission, and as evidenced in 5 (see above), there was some uncertainty about the outcome of this repair being successfully achieved. There is doubt both in Mary's comments (*there was still a doubt in my mind. . . .*), and in the questions asked by L1 (the music business? what is the name of industry?).

Extract 7.8

(The teacher is eliciting vocab items and collecting them on the board. Learner 1 is trying to explain a word)

1	L1:	discographics=	*I was going to say it's a false friend*
2	T:	=ooh what do you mean?	*but I decided not to because I thought that might confuse her . . .*
3	L1:	the people who not the people the (4) the business about music record series and=	*maybe I misunderstood her now when I look back at it . . . I understood at the time that she meant that this was a particular industry but maybe she meant a business . . . but*
4	T:	=is this a word you're thinking of in Basque or Spanish in English I don't know this word 'discographics' what I would say is er **(writes on board)** like you said 'the music business'=	*I wasn't prepared to spend a long time on that because it didn't seem important even though there was still a doubt in my mind . . .*
5	L1:	=the music business? what is the name of of er industry?=	
6	T:	=the music industry as well it's actually better	

It is clear, I believe, from these extracts, that stimulated recall is a potentially very powerful approach that has much to offer reflective practice, especially when the focus of the reflection is classroom interaction. Even without the transcripts, much can be learned by participants and it is a methodology that brings together very nicely the various elements that I have argued are necessary for reflective practice to work effectively, namely, a tool, some data and dialogue. Stimulated recall is relatively easy to organise, is inexpensive and unobtrusive; yet its potential for influencing professional development is enormous.

Summary

In this chapter I have considered how reflective practice (RP) might be realigned and improved if the focus of the reflection is classroom interaction. By analysing extracts of classroom discourse and using them for reflection, I have argued that teachers will learn how to reflect on their practice in a structured and systematic way. Moreover, a classroom discourse focused approach to RP allows the key elements of the process to be addressed: first, a problem is identified; then data are collected (here, in the form of classroom recordings); data are then analysed using an appropriate tool and there is some reflection; finally, new understandings and changes to practice emerge through dialogue and discussion. The entire cycle is then repeated.

Using interview data, we have seen how emergent understandings are collaboratively achieved; teacher and interviewer co-construct meanings and uncover the detail of interactions in a bid to improve practice. Taking this a little further, we have seen how stimulated recall has much to offer RP in terms of its potential for providing a fine-grained analysis of classroom discourse. The main point of this chapter has been to demonstrate how teachers can become effective researchers of their own practice and acquire some of the skills and tools that they will be able to use in their professional lives. A classroom discourse oriented approach to RP, I suggest, is more likely to result in sustainable professional development and enable teachers to really gain close understandings of the contexts in which they work.

Note

1   Minute papers are short, written evaluations by students on a teacher's teaching. They are quick to complete (hence 'minute paper') and give useful feedback on specific teaching sessions.

8 Classroom interactional competence

Introduction

In this chapter, I present and develop the notion of classroom interactional competence and consider how it can be characterised in different contexts. Classroom Interactional Competence (CIC) is defined as, 'Teachers' and learners' ability to use interaction as a tool for mediating and assisting learning' (Walsh 2006: 132). It puts interaction firmly at the centre of teaching and learning and argues that by improving their CIC, both teachers and learners will immediately improve learning and opportunities for learning. Building on many of the ideas put forward in this book and elsewhere, I aim to show how a better understanding of classroom discourse will have a positive impact on learning, especially where learning is regarded as a social activity that is strongly influenced by involvement, engagement and participation; where learning is regarded as *doing* rather than *having* (c.f. Sfard 1998).

The chapter falls into three sections. In the first, we look at the work that has been completed on Interactional Competence, a construct that has existed for more than twenty years and yet which continues to attract a great deal of attention. In the second section, I characterise classroom interactional competence (CIC), using data extracts to examine the strategies open to both teachers and learners to enhance interaction and improve opportunities for learning. In the final section, we consider how teachers and learners might, in a very practical sense, develop their own classroom interactional competence.

Personal reflection

What do you understand by the term 'interactional competence'? What is the difference between, for example, interactional competence, communicative competence and spoken fluency?

Interactional competence

It is apparent when studying spoken interaction that different speakers have different levels of competence and varying abilities to express their ideas and achieve understanding. This is true both in and outside classrooms, of native and non-native speakers, regardless of their language proficiency. Put simply, some people seem to be better able to communicate than others, while some people seem to have difficulty in conveying the most simple meanings. If we put this in the context of the second language classroom, the situation becomes both more complex and less understood. We'll return to this in the next section.

Much of what happens in language classrooms, I suggest, is concerned with individual performance rather than collective competence. In other words, we, as teachers are constantly evaluating and assessing our learners' ability to produce accurate, fluent and appropriate linguistic forms. Think about your own teaching and/or learning context. Your focus of attention will almost certainly be on the ways in which learners produce correct forms, articulate a particular point of view, etc. Think too about the ways in which we test spoken language. Again, the emphasis is on an individual's ability to produce correct utterances, rather than to negotiate meanings or clarify a point of view or idea. Speaking tests focus heavily on accuracy, fluency, grammatical structures, range of vocabulary and so on. They rarely consider how effectively a candidate interacts or how well a candidate co-constructs meanings with another interlocutor. In short, the focus of attention is on individual performance rather than joint competence.

There may be many reasons for this position, not least of which is the fact that a solo performance is easier to teach and easier to test than a joint, collective one. To produce materials and devise tasks that focus on interaction is far more difficult than to devise materials and activities that train individual performance. Although contemporary materials claim to adopt a task-based approach to teaching and learning, they do not, I suggest, train learners to become better interactants. All attention is directed towards the individual's ability to produce accurate, appropriate and fluent utterances.

In the 'real world', of course, effective communication rests on an ability to interact with others and to collectively reach understandings. Interactional competence, then, is what is needed in order to 'survive' most communicative encounters. Being accurate or fluent, in themselves, are, I suggest, insufficient. Speakers of an L2 must be able to do far more than produce correct strings of utterances. They need to be able to pay attention to the local context, to listen and show that they have understood, to clarify meanings, to repair breakdowns and so on. All of this requires extreme mental and interactional ability, the kind of ability that will not, arguably, be trained by taking part in pair-work tasks or group discussions.

The notion of interactional competence was first coined by Kramsch (1986: 370):

I propose (. . .) a push for interactional competence to give our students a truly emancipating, rather than compensating foreign language education.

What Kramsch seems to be saying here is that much foreign language teaching adopts what Cook (2001) terms a 'deficit' model, where second language speakers are perceived as being in some way inferior to first language speakers, and where the performance of second language speakers is somehow measured against that of first language speakers. Indeed, in language testing contexts, many of you will have come across descriptors or assessment criteria that use a wording like 'shows native-like fluency of the language' in speaking tests and so on. Kramsch, by contrast, argues that a focus on interactional competence allows us to concentrate more on the ability of learners to *communicate* intended meaning and to establish joint understandings. Essentially, interactional competence is concerned with what goes on *between* interactants and how that communication is managed. Rather than fluency, we are concerned with what McCarthy (2005) terms *confluence*: the act of making spoken language fluent together with another speaker. Spoken confluence is highly relevant to the present discussion since it highlights the ways in which speakers attend to each other's contributions and focus on collective meaning-making. It is also a concept that lies at the heart of most classroom communication, where interactants are engaged in a constant process of trying to make sense of each other, negotiate meanings, assist and query, support, clarify and so on. We might say that, both inside and outside the classroom, being confluent is more fundamental to effective communication than being fluent.

Since Kramsch's 1986 paper, many researchers have struggled with the notion of interactional competence without really coming to a convincing and workable definition. More recent references emphasise the fact that interactional competence is context-specific and concerned with the ways in which interactants construct meanings *together*, as opposed to looking at features of *individual* performance that lie at the heart of communicative competence. For example, consider the differences between the interactional resources needed in a context where the emphasis is on a transaction, such as ordering a coffee, to the interactional resources needed to take part in a conversation. Clearly, in the first context, a basic knowledge of English will allow you to order a coffee with minimal interactional competence. In the second, however, and in most classroom contexts, much more sophisticated interactional resources will be required if you are to successfully compete for the floor, gain and pass turns, attend to what the speaker has said, interrupt, clarify and so on. We can see, from these two examples, that interactional competence is highly context specific and related very closely to speaker intent and to audience.

In an attempt to identify specific features of interactional competence, Young (2003) points to a number of 'interactional resources' including specific interactional strategies, such as turn-taking, topic management, signalling boundaries and so on. Markee (2008) proposes three components, each with its own set of features:

- language as a formal system (including grammar, vocabulary, pronunciation);

- semiotic systems, including turn-taking, repair, sequence organisation;

- gaze and paralinguistic features.

As Markee (2008: 3) says, developing interactional competence in a second language involves learners 'co-construct[ing] with their interlocutors locally enacted, progressively more accurate, fluent, and complex interactional repertoires in the L2'. While I agree with the first part of this definition and acknowledge, indeed emphasise, that interactional competence is a joint enterprise, I have some issues with Markee's focus on accuracy, fluency and complexity as indicators of interactional competence. I would go further and suggest that a person who has a high level of interactional competence is not necessarily an accurate speaker. As I hope to show in the next section, there are alternative ways of characterising interactional competence.

Young (2008: 100) offers this definition of interactional competence:

Interactional competence is a relationship between participants' employment of linguistic and interactional resources and the contexts in which they are employed . . .

Here then, Young focuses on the relationship between 'the linguistic and interactional resources' used by interactants in specific contexts. At this stage, it might be helpful to look at some data in order to clarify some of the ideas we have discussed so far on interactional competence.

In extract 8.1 below, students are working independently of the teacher in what might be termed an oral fluency practice activity. They roll a dice and discuss a topic corresponding to the number shown on the dice. If they have already discussed that topic, they simply select another one. What is immediately obvious from the extract is the amount of interactional work that students engage in to keep the discussion moving and on track. Students have been asked to talk about pictures of people that they are close to and in line 1 the topic is launched with a question by L1 and an extended response plus justification by L3 in lines 2–3. L2 shows empathy towards L3, making the point that L3 is very busy and has little time to 'play' (sic) with her boyfriend, a point taken up by L1, who says that they can at least live together as a means of improving their relationship. Note how the word search in line 6 is dealt with very quickly by L4 in line 7, allowing the discussion to continue and avoiding a potential breakdown. L4 extends her contribution with an interruption (*and know each other*). The four-second pause in line 9 indicates an opportunity for a change of speaker or change of topic and this is proposed by L3. However, the change of topic does not occur immediately as L2 interrupts in line 10 with an anecdotal story about registration and the fact that the students doing the registration are able to know who is single.

L2's interruption prompts L3 to conclude her discussion about her boyfriend in lines 14–19 (*he's not very handsome, he's clever and serious about his work*). L1's overlaps are in support of what L3 is saying and offer some kind of affirmation or approval of the comments made by L3. Note too how laughter is used as a way of offering approval and affirmation throughout this extract. Finally, in line 20, L1 brings the discussion back to the original topic switch proposed by L3 in line 9, where there was no switch. Note the extended ten-second pause at the end of the extract, suggesting that the students are considering another topic and that there is now going to be a switch.

Task 8.1

Before you read any further, look at extract 8.1 and comment on these students' ability to manage and direct the interaction, unaided and with no teacher involvement. How would you evaluate this in terms of the students' oral fluency? Are there any examples of what you might call interactional competence?

Extract 8.1

1	L1:	do you bring his photo with you
2	L3:	eh . . . yeah but we have only a few photos because we get together (.)only one year or
3		so=
4	L2:	=and your work was very busy so you have no time to play with him [<LO3> Yeah]

5	L1:	but I suppose that you must (.)leave some enough money to(.)live with your boyfriend
6		and in this way you can (.)improve the (.)eh (3 sec unintelligible) how do you say=
7	L4:	=relationship=
8	L1:	=relationship yes [<L04> and know each other]=
9	L3:	=yeah I think I now him very well now (laughs) (4) well lets talk another topic=
10	L2:	=I remember one thing when they choose register in Coleraine and they organiser
11		know you [reg . . . register . . . register]
12	L:	∟ are single girl and they don't know you have a boyfriend
13	LL:	((laugh))
14	L3:	I think eh that is is humerous ok he is not very handsome and not very but I think he
15		is very clever ehm and he [<L01> a lot like you] no (laughs) I think he is clever than
16		me and (laughs) (3) he do everything very . . . [seriously
17	L1:	[seriously
18	L3:	yeah (3 sec unintelligible) eh and eh in some eh . . . in some degree . . . eh I . . . admire
19		him (laughs)=
20	L1:	=thats a good thing [<L> Yeah] lets change another topic (10)

In terms of the interactional competence demonstrated in this extract, we can make a number of observations about the interactional resources employed and their impact on the overall flow and coherence of the discussion:

- Turn-taking. It is apparent that all four students manage the turn-taking very well and are able to interrupt, hold and pass turns. Interruptions occur, but naturally and in a supportive way. There are no major breakdowns and the discussion flows well.

- Repair. It is interesting to note that even though errors do occur, they are largely ignored. (c.f. lines 1, 2, 4 etc., all containing errors). This is what Firth (1996) refers to as the 'let it pass' principle; in many business contexts where English is used as a lingua franca, interactants largely ignore errors unless an error causes a problem for understanding. In extract 8.1, the main repair comes in lines 6–8, where the word 'relationship' is needed in order to clarify meaning.

- Overlaps and interruptions. Note how overlaps and interruptions occur frequently (for example, in lines 4, 8, 12, 16, 20), but they are supportive and designed to ensure that the interaction flows smoothly. These overlaps and interruptions are examples of what McCarthy (2003) refers to as good 'listenership': they signal to a speaker that she has been understood, that the channels are open and that the communication is working well. Essentially, they 'oil the wheels' of the interaction and help to prevent trouble and breakdowns from occurring. As a deliberate strategy, overlaps give vital clues to speakers that they are being understood and that something is being communicated.

- Topic management. One of the key indicators of the coherence of a piece of spoken interaction is topic management and development. In extract 8.1, we can see how the main topic of 'relationships' is introduced, developed and discussed at length despite one attempt to switch topic in line 9 – which is ignored until much later in line 20. Interactants are genuinely engaged with the topic and succeed in maintaining it for some time and from a range of perspectives. In short, we can say that this is a good example of coherent discourse in which all participants are concerned to engage with and develop a topic to the full.

To summarise this section, I present, in a table, the main features of interactional competence and compare them with some of the ideas proposed under what is referred to as communicative competence (c.f. Hymes 1972; Canale and Swain 1980):

As a final word and pointing towards the future, it is important to recognise the important work that is underway at the time of writing. Research projects such as *English Profile,* led by Cambridge University Press, working with a number of partner institutions (www.englishprofile.org), now acknowledge that there is much work to be done in terms of characterising interactional competence as the 'fifth skill' (in addition to speaking, listening, reading and writing). It is almost certain that the results of this and related research projects will have enormous implications for language teaching, language testing and materials design. In the next section, we therefore consider how interactional competence might manifest itself in the classroom.

Task 8.2

Based on the discussion so far and what you may have read, how would you define interactional competence as it relates to your own teaching and learning context? What are the specific features of interactional competence that you would like your learners (or yourself) to acquire?

Table 8.1 interactional competence versus communicative competence

Interactional competence	Communicative competence
Emphasises the ways in which interactants co-construct meanings and jointly establish understanding.	The focus is on individual differences in competence and the fact that one of the aims of learning a language is to move to the next level of competence.
Includes both interactional and linguistic resources, but places more emphasis on the way the interaction is guided and managed through turns-at-talk, overlaps, acknowledgement tokens, pauses, repair and so on.	Emphasises the knowledge and skills needed to use language in specific contexts as opposed to knowledge of language as an idealised system.
Is highly context specific: the interactional competence required in one context will not always transfer to another. Different interactional resources will be needed in different contexts	Context is everything: what we say is dependent on who we are talking to, where we are, why we are talking, what we have to say and when this takes place (c.f. Hymes, 1972).
Largely rejects individual performance in favour of collaborative enterprise.	Emphasises individual performance and recognises that this can and will change.
Less concerned with accuracy and fluency and more concerned with communication; this means that speakers must pay close attention to each others' contributions and help and support where necessary.	Accuracy, fluency and appropriacy lie at the heart of communicative competence and are also the measures used to evaluate it.
Places equal emphasis on attending to the speaker as producing one's own contribution; listening plays as much a part in interactional competence as speaking.	Focuses more on individual speech production than on the listener and acknowledgement of what has been said.

Classroom interactional competence

Turning now to a conceptualisation of classroom interactional competence (CIC), defined here as 'teachers' and learners' ability to use interaction as a tool for mediating and assisting learning' (Walsh 2006: 132), the starting point is to acknowledge the centrality of interaction to teaching and learning. In the same way that we have seen that interactants display and orient to learning through interactions that are co-constructed, they also demonstrate differing abilities to jointly create discourse that is conducive to learning. CIC focuses on the ways in which teachers' and learners' interactional decisions and subsequent actions enhance learning and learning opportunity. From the extracts of data below, we will consider how teachers and learners display CIC and discuss the implications of this for gaining closer understandings of the relationship between L2 learning and interaction. The assumption is that by first understanding and then extending CIC, there will be greater opportunities for learning: enhanced CIC results in more learning-oriented interactions.

Given the context dependency of interactional competence, we are attempting here to identify some of the features of *classroom* interactional competence (CIC). How are meanings co-constructed in the unfolding interaction? What do participants do to ensure that understandings are reached? How do they deal with repair and breakdown? More importantly, how does CIC influence learning? In what ways are interactants able to create, maintain and sustain 'space for learning'? Space for learning refers to the extent to which teachers and learners provide interactional space that is appropriate for the specific pedagogical goal of the moment. It does not simply mean 'handing over' to learners to maximise opportunities for interaction. Rather, creating space for learning acknowledges the need to adjust linguistic and interactional patterns to the particular goal of the moment. Again, the emphasis is on promoting interactions that are both appropriate to a particular micro-context and to specific pedagogic goals.

In language assessment circles, I have already mentioned that it is now widely predicted that interactional competence will become the 'fifth skill' (see previous section). Given that interlocutors display varying degrees of competence in their joint construction of meanings, I am suggesting here that teachers and learners also need to acquire a fine-grained understanding of what constitutes classroom interactional competence and how it might be achieved. Not only will such an understanding result in more engaged and dynamic interactions in classrooms, it will also enhance learning.

In the data, there are a number of ways in which CIC manifests itself. First, and from a teacher's perspective, a teacher who demonstrates CIC uses language that is both convergent to the pedagogic goal of the moment and that is appropriate to the learners. Essentially, this entails an understanding of the interactional strategies that are appropriate to teaching goals and that are adjusted in relation to the co-construction of meaning and the unfolding agenda of a lesson. This position assumes that pedagogic goals and the language used to achieve them are inextricably intertwined and constantly being re-adjusted (Walsh 2003; Seedhouse 2004). Any evidence of CIC must therefore demonstrate that interlocutors are using discourse that is both appropriate to specific pedagogic goals and to the agenda of the moment.

In extract 8.2 below, a stimulated recall methodology has been used (see Chapter 7). On the left side is the actual classroom interaction and on the right the teacher's commentary on it. I have selected this extract because I believe it shows very clearly that this teacher's pedagogic goals and the interaction used to achieve them are at one, they are working together – we can say they are 'mode convergent' (see Chapter 6). Essentially, his comments on the right indicate quite clearly why certain interactional decisions were taken. For example, in the interaction, we see evidence of the teacher constantly seeking clarification, affirming and re-affirming and helping the learner to articulate a full response (in 5, 7 and 9). Each of these responses is designed, according to the teacher to 'get it flowing' and 'to reinterpret for the benefit of the class'. Not only is he helping the learner to articulate his ideas more clearly, he is helping the rest of the class to understand what is being said. From his comments and the evidence provided in this extract, we can say quite clearly that pedagogic goals and the language used to achieve them are at one and that this teacher knows why he has made certain interactive decisions. We might say that he is demonstrating a level of interactional awareness here: his actions and his comments both highlight this.

Extract 8.2

1	T:	what was the funniest thing that happened to you at school (1) Tang?	*Basically he's explaining that on a picnic there wasn't this gap that there is in a classroom – psychological gap – that's what I'm drawing out of him. There's a lot of scaffolding*
2	S1:	funniest thing?	*being done by me in this monitoring,*
3	T:	the funniest	*besides it being managerial, there's*
4	S1:	the funniest thing I think out of school was go to picnic	*a lot of scaffolding because I want to get it flowing, I want to encourage them, keep it moving as it were.*
5	T:	go on a picnic? So what happened what made it funny?	*I'm clarifying to the class what he's saying because I know in an extended turn – a broken turn – and it's not exactly fluent and it's not articu-*
6	S1:	go to picnic we made playing or talking with the teacher more closely because in the school we have a line you know he the	*late – I try to re-interpret for the benefit of the class so that they're all coming with me at the same time and they all understand the point being made by him*

| | | teacher and me
the student= |
7	T:	=so you say there was a gap or a wall between the teacher and the students so when you=
8	S1:	if you go out of the school you went together with more (**gestures 'closer' with hands**)=
9	T:	=so you had a closer relationship [outside the school]
10	L1:	[yeah yeah]

A second feature of CIC is that it facilitates interactional space: learners need space for learning to participate in the discourse, to contribute to class conversations and to receive feedback on their contributions. Interactional space is maximised through increased wait-time, by resisting the temptation to 'fill silence' (by reducing teacher echo), by promoting extended learner turns and by allowing planning time. By affording learners space, they are better able to contribute to the process of co-constructing meanings – something that lies at the very heart of learning through interaction. Note that this does not necessarily mean simply 'handing over' to learners and getting them to complete pair and group work tasks. While this may facilitate practice opportunities and give learners a chance to work independently, it will not, in itself, necessarily result in enhanced learning. The same point has been made by others (c.f. Rampton 1999).

What is needed, I would suggest, is a re-think of the role of the teacher so that interaction is more carefully understood, and so that the teacher plays a more central role in *shaping* learner contributions. Shaping involves taking a learner response and doing something with it rather than simply accepting it. For example, a response may be paraphrased, using slightly different vocabulary or grammatical structures; it may be summarised or extended in some way; a response may require scaffolding so that learners are assisted in saying what they really mean; it may be recast (c.f. Lyster 1998): 'handed back' to the learner but with some small changes included. By shaping learner contributions and by helping learners to really articulate what they mean, teachers are performing a more central role in the interaction, while, at the same time, maintaining a student-centred, decentralised approach to teaching.

Extract 8.3 is taken from a secondary class in China, where students are talking about visits to museums. This teacher successfully creates space for learning by using a number of key interactional strategies:

1 Extensive use of pausing throughout, some of these pauses are quite extensive (c.f. lines 1, 3, 6 and 17, for example). Remember that typically teachers wait for less than one second after asking a question or eliciting a response. Pausing serves a range of functions:

  • It creates 'space' in the interaction to allow learners to take a turn-at-talk.

  • It allows thinking or rehearsal time (c.f. Schmidt 1993) enabling learners to formulate a response (see lines 44 and 46 where a teacher pause is followed by a learner pause).

  • It enables turn-taking to be slowed down, helping to make learners feel more comfortable and less stressed.

  • Increased wait time often results in fuller, more elaborated responses, as in lines 40ff and 46ff.

2 A lack of repair. Students make some mistakes in this extract (line 34, word order; line 46, verb form 'wasting of time'). These are ignored since they do not impede communication and do not fulfil the teacher's pedagogic goal here: elicitation and sharing of personal experiences. In this type of micro-context, error correction is not seen as being necessary and the teacher disregards errors since they are not of central concern.

3 Signposting in instructions. This teacher twice calls for a choral response (in lines 23 and 28). She marks her instruction and signposts that she wants the whole class to respond ('together'). This is a useful strategy in a multi-party conversation like a classroom where calling out and 'ragged' choral repetitions are very common.

4 Extended learner turns (in lines 46–47, for example). The teacher allows learners to complete a turn and make a full and elaborated response. Often teachers interrupt and close down space when learners are attempting to articulate something quite complicated. Here, she does the opposite and allows the student space in the interaction to make a full and useful contribution.

5 Seeking clarification (lines 34–37). The teacher is not entirely satisfied with the first response and insists on the insertion of 'often'

to make sure that this contribution is as accurate as possible. This is a good example of a recast (see above).

In addition to creating space, in the same extract we can see how space can be 'closed down'. One of the main causes of this is where teachers make excessive use of echo, repeating their own or students' contributions, sometimes with no apparent reason or need. Note that there are two types of echo:

- Teacher–learner echo: where a teacher repeats a learner's utterance for the benefit of the class (lines 8, 11, 20 and 22 for example). This is helpful and ensures that a class progresses together and that everyone is 'in the loop'. It is an inclusive strategy, which ensures that the whole class comes along together and that there is commonality of understanding (see extract 8.2 where the teacher comments on the need to ensure that the whole class is 'coming with me at the same time').

- Teacher–teacher echo: where a teacher simply repeats her own utterance almost like a kind of habit (lines 4–5, 14–15, 32–33, 44). This serves no real function, arguably, and may impede opportunities for learning since the teacher is taking up learners' space in the dialogue. It may be used as a kind of defence mechanism since silence can be quite threatening.

Extract 8.3

1	T:	class begins (3) good afternoon everyone
2	SS:	good afternoon teacher
3	T:	sit down please (3) so our topic today is museums(.)
4		talking about museums (.) have you ever <u>been</u> to museums
5		(1)? Have you ever been to museums (2)? Yes of course.
6		And what ↑<u>kind</u> of museums have you been to (4) NAME?
7	S:	(unclear)
8	T:	The national museum ↑yes thank you very much and how
9		about you NAME?
10	S:	(unclear)
11	T:	History museum (.) thank you very much (.) so as you
12		mentioned just <u>now</u> (1) you have been to ((**puts powerpoint**
13		**slides of museums up**))many kinds of museums (.) but (.)do

14		you still remember ↑when did you <u>go</u> to those museums for
15		the <u>last</u> time (2)? When did you go there for the <u>last</u>
16		time? For example when did you go to the national museum
17		(.) the last time (4)? ((**gets microphone from another**
18		**student**)). Thank you
19	S:	er maybe several month ago
20	T:	several month ago thank you ok how about you?
21	S:	I think several years ago
22	T:	several <u>years</u> ago. Ok ((laughs)). Thank you very much (3)
23		ok actually can you tell me together do you often go to
24		museums?
25	Ss:	no
26	T:	No so what you said is <u>just</u> the same as what I <u>read</u> in
27		the newspaper the other day(.) would you please read the
28		title of this piece of news together ((**points to**
29		**powerpoint slide**))
30	Ss:	((**reading aloud**)) why are young people absent from
31		museums?
32	T:	thank you (.) what does it <u>mean</u>? (.) NAME what does the
33		title <u>mean</u>?
34	S:	(.) why young people don't go to museums
35	T:	they don't go to museums very?
36	S:	often
37	T:	very often thank you very much (.) and (.)so actually
38		you are young people ↑<u>why</u> don't you go to museums very
39		often(3)? NAME
40	S:	(2) er because erm there's nothing in the museums that
41		er attracts us and er even the mus- things in museums are
42		usually very (.) old
43	T:	old thank you very much ok so nothing can att<u>ract</u> you
44		((**writes on board**)) (3) what else? What else?
45		<u>why</u> don't you go to museums very often? NAME
46	S:	(3)I think going to museums is a wasting of time because
47		because I'm not interested in those old-fashioned things
48	T:	ok thank you very much so you're not in↑terested in it
49		it's not interesting right? ((**writes on board**)) not
50		interesting (5) ok.

So far, we have seen that two important features of CIC are the convergence of language use and pedagogic goals, and the need for interactional space. A third feature or strategy entails teachers being able to *shape* learner contributions by scaffolding, paraphrasing, reiterating and so on, a point that has already been mentioned. Essentially, through shaping the discourse, a teacher is helping learners to say what they mean by using the most appropriate language to do so. The process of 'shaping' contributions occurs by seeking clarification, scaffolding, modelling, or repairing learner input. In a decentralised classroom in which learner-centredness is a priority, these interactional strategies may be the only opportunities for teaching and occur frequently during the feedback move (c.f. Cullen 1998). Elsewhere (see, for example, Jarvis and Robinson 1997), the process of taking a learner's contribution and shaping it into something more meaningful has been termed *appropriation;* a kind of paraphrasing that serves the dual function of checking meaning and moving the discourse forward.

We turn now to a further consideration of how these features of CIC manifest themselves in classroom data. The extract below is taken from an adult EFL class where the teacher is working with an upper-intermediate group of learners who are preparing to do a listening comprehension about places of interest. There are a number of features in the extract that show evidence of CIC:

Extract 8.4

```
1    T:    okay, have you have you ever visited any places
           ↑outside London?=
2    L1:   =me I stay in (.) Portsmouth and er:: in Bournemouth
3    T:    [where've you been?
4    L1:   [in the south
5    T:    [down (.) here? (pointing to map)
6    L1:   yeah yeah
7    T:    ↑why?
8    L1:   er my girlfriend live here and (.) I like this student
9          place and all the people's young and a lot (.) er go out
10         in the (.) evening its very [good
11   T:    [right
12   T:    anybody else? (4) Have you been anywhere Tury?
13   L2:   Yes I have been in er (.) Edinbourg ((mispronounced)),
14         (())=
15   T:    =so here here ((pointing to map))=
16   L2:   =yes er Oxford (.) Brighton (.) many places (())=
17   T:    =and which was your favourite?=
```

18	L2:	=my favourite is London
19	T:	(.) ↑why?
20	L2:	because it's a big city you can find what what you [want
21	T:	[mmhh
22	L2:	and do you can go to the theatres (1) it's a very (.)
23		cosmopolitan [city
24	L:	[yes
25	L2:	I like it very much=
26	T:	=do you all (.) agree=
27	LL:	=yes (laughter)
28	T:	((3)) laughter)
29	T:	has anybody else been to another place outside London?
30	L:	no not outside inside
31	T:	(.)mm? Martin? Anywhere?
32	L3:	=no nowhere=
33	T:	=would you like to go (.) [anywhere?
34	L3:	[yes yes
35	T:	[where?
36	L3:	(well) Portsmouth I think it's very (.) great=
37	T:	=((laughter)) cos of the students [yes (.) yes
38	LL:	[yes yes
39	L3:	and there are sea too
40	T:	Pedro?
41	L4:	it's a (.) young (.) place
42	T:	mm anywhere else? (3) no well I'm going to talk to
43		you and give you some recommendations about where you
44		can go in (.) England (.) yeah

(Carr 2006)

We can ascertain from this context (and from the lesson plan accompanying these published materials) that the teacher's main concern is to elicit ideas and personal experiences from the learners. The corresponding talk confirms this in a number of ways. First, there is no repair, despite the large number of errors throughout the extract (see, for example, lines 2, 8, 13, 36, 39), the teacher chooses to ignore them because error correction is not conducive to allowing learners to have space to express themselves. Second, the questions she asks are often followed with expansions such as 'why'? (see for example, 7, 19), which result in correspondingly longer turns by learners (in 8, and 20). Again, we would claim that both the teacher's questioning strategy and the longer learner turns are evidence of CIC since they facilitate opportunities for both engaged interaction and learning opportunity. Third, we note that there are several attempts to 'open the space' and allow for wider participation of other learners. This occurs, for example, in 12 (*anybody else* plus a four-second pause), in 26 (*do you all agree?*), in 42 (*anywhere else* plus a three-second pause). On each of these occasions, the teacher is attempting to include other students in the interaction in a bid to elicit additional contributions. Again, her use of language and pedagogic goals are convergent, ensuring that learning opportunities are maximised.

Other features that show evidence of CIC include:

- the use of extended wait time, pauses of several seconds (in 12 and 42) that allow learners time to think, formulate and give a response. Typically, teachers wait less than one second after asking a question (see, for example, Budd Rowe 1986), leaving learners insufficient time to respond.

- the use of requests for clarification (in 3, 5, 15) that serve to ensure that understandings have been reached. Not only do such requests give important feedback to the students, they allow the teacher to ensure that the other students are included by clarifying for the whole class.

- Minimal response tokens that tell the other speaker that under-standings have been reached without interrupting the 'flow' of the interaction (see, for example, 11 (*right*), 21 (*mmhh*). Again, the use of such feedback is further evidence of convergence of pedagogic goals and language use.

- Evidence of content feedback by the teacher who responds to the message and not the linguistic forms used to articulate a particular message. In extract 3 above, for example, the teacher responds in an almost conversational way to almost all of the learners' turns. She offers no evaluation or repair of learner contributions, as would be the 'norm' in many classroom contexts. Instead, she assumes an almost symmetrical role in the discourse, evidenced by the rapid pace of the interaction (note the overlapping speech in 3–5, 33–35, and latched turns in 14–18 and 25–27).

In the same extract, there are a number of features of CIC that we can highlight from a learner's perspective. First, there is recognition on the part of L1 that the appropriate reaction to a question is a response, the second part of that adjacency pair, as evidenced in lines 2, 4, 6, 8. Not only does L1 answer the questions posed by the teacher, he is able to recognise the precise type and amount of response needed, ensuring that his contributions are both relevant and timely. He is also sufficiently competent to appreciate that a question like 'why' in line 7 almost always requires an extended response, which he provides in 8.

His CIC is sufficiently advanced to appreciate that the teacher's focus here is on eliciting personal experiences – while his responses are adequate and appropriate, they are certainly not accurate; yet this is of little or no concern given the pedagogic focus of the moment. This learner has correctly interpreted the teacher's question as a request for further information where accuracy is less important than the provision of that information.

L1 also displays CIC in terms of his ability to manage turns, hold the floor and hand over his turn at a particular point in the interaction. He responds quickly to the teacher's opening question, as indicated by the latched turn in 2 and turn continuation in 4, indicated by the overlapping speech. As well as being able to take as turn and hold the floor, this learner (L1) also recognises key signals that mark a transition relevance place – the teacher's 'right' and accompanying overlap in lines 9 and 10 signal to this learner that it is time to relinquish his turn at talk and hand over to another learner. While it is the teacher who 'orchestrates the interaction' (Breen 1998), nonetheless, L1 has to be able to take cues, observe key signals and manage his own turn-taking in line with what is required by the teacher. He must also recognise that his own contributions are largely determined by the teacher's and by the specific pedagogic goals of the moment.

Task 8.3

Read the extract below, which is again taken from a senior high school class in China where the topic for discussion is visiting a museum. Based on what you now know about CIC, make a list of the features of interactional competence in this extract for (a) the teacher and (b) the learners.

Extract 8.5

1	T:	ok now <let's start>(.) er today our topic is museum (1)
2		are you going to a museum in the coming summer holiday?
3		NAME are you (4)
4	S:	no I don't
5	T:	why?
6	S:	because a museum is very boring if I have some spare
7		times er I would like to choose do something interesting
8	T:	mmh so it's boring to you right?
9	S:	er yes

10	T:	ok (2) erm how about NAME [how about you are you going
11	S:	[me either me neither because I
12		think it's boring too
13	T:	why?
14	S:	and er at first I don't have the spare time and if I have
15		I will do something er in my hobbies
16	T:	mmhh so you are not interested?
17	S:	yes
18	T:	thank you (2) well how would you (.) complete this
19		sentence((**writing on board**)) museum is a place where (.)
20		visitors can(.)how would you complete this sentence erm
21		say NAME
22	S:	look around [look around
23	T:	[look around °thank you° (.) look around how
24		about you NAME?
25	S:	a museum is a place er where visitors can have fun
26	T:	[have fun
27	S:	[have fun
28	T:	have fun by? by
29	S:	have fun by getting knowledge (3) by getting new
30		((mispronounced))knowledge
31	T:	getting no knowledge (.)
32	S:	(1) new new knowledge so- so- sorry
33	T:	new kn- knowledge ok don't be nervous (.) well yeah well
34		you (.) learn some new knowledge in the museum mainly
35		by (.) looking or (.) listening or (.) reading (5) who's
36		got the microphone? NAME (.)
37	S:	(3) I think it's by reading something
38	T:	mm by reading some material ↑or how about photos?
39	S:	er yeah read some photos and maybe some films
40	T:	mmhh some films thank you or you look at some photos
41		right? Thank you (.) well it's very clear that museums
42		are not so attractive to ↑you is that true (1) mmhh?

In this section, we have seen how CIC is portrayed in a number of contexts. By 'context', I mean the physical, geographical and temporal setting of the interaction in addition to the specific micro-context, or mode, of the moment. As we have seen (both here and in Chapter 6), the interactional and linguistic resources used by both teachers and learners will vary considerably according to specific teaching and learning goals at a particular point in time. One aspect of CIC is the extent to which teachers match their use of language to their intended goals. The point we are making here is that CIC is one aspect of learning in formal contexts: teachers and learners, by making appropriate interactional choices through their online decision-making, both facilitate the co-construction of meaning and display to each other their understandings. CIC manifests itself through the ways in which interactants create space for learning, make appropriate responses 'in the moment', seek and offer clarification, demonstrate understandings, afford opportunities for participation, negotiate meanings, and so on. These interactional strategies help to maintain the flow of the discourse and are central to effective classroom communication. They offer a different but complementary view of learning through interaction to that provided by a conversational analytic perspective that focuses mainly on turn design, sequential organisation and repair.

In the next section, we consider how CIC can be developed in both teachers and learners by looking at some practical applications of the construct.

Developing CIC in teachers and learners

Elsewhere in this book (see, for example, Chapter 7), I have commented on the need for appropriate tools, reflection and dialogue in order to help teachers become more aware of the interactions taking place in their local context. I have also made the point that in order to enhance learning, we need to begin by gaining a closer understanding of context and that one of the best ways of doing that is to gain a fuller understanding of interaction; specifically, the relationship between interaction and learning.

Personal reflection

How would you like to develop CIC in the context in which you teach? What particular skills would you like to acquire or improve so that interaction is enhanced? What might you do to help learners improve *their* CIC?

Task 8.4

In the following extract, identify any evidence of CIC from (a) the interaction (on the left), (b) the teacher's own commentary on the interaction (on the right). Based on your analysis, how might you change your own classroom practice?

Extract 8.6

Students are preparing to do a board game and clarifying vocabulary (fifteen minutes)

L: what does it mean singe, singed my eyebrows?

T: singed, singed (**writes on board**) (4) to singe means really to burn but it always has the sort of the meaning to burn something with hair=

L: =some people you know too close to the fire so it singed your eyebrows burns your eyebrows

T: yeah, yeah

L: (12) bump into cupboard door is it like hit?

T: yeah it's like knock into

L: (20) fractured means like twist

T: no fractured [means broken]

L: [broken] (12)

What I liked about this is that they were all asking questions. So for me, that would point up the use of providing a structured type of activity; although there's a lot management time setting it up, because they know they've got that time, they'll play a far more active role in it. So again, shutting up and letting them get on with it.

My aim in this section is to offer some specific strategies, activities, tasks etc. designed to help both teachers and learners enhance their CIC. Many of the suggestions that follow will entail you making recordings or using transcripts and recordings of your, or a colleague's, classes, or, alternatively using published materials. You may want to re-read Chapter 3 that deals with recording and transcribing classroom data.

Task 8.5

One of the ways in which teachers can improve their CIC is to develop a metalanguage for talking about interaction in their teaching. The following extract is taken from an interview with a teacher who has just analysed a recording of a class. Comment on her use of metalanguage: how well is it used and how does it help her to explain and understand her own practice?

There were quite a lot of display questions which I think is appropriate for low level classes, pre-intermediate, you tend to use a lot of display questions so I had plenty of examples of those like 'How do you spell exciting?' and then later I was asking questions based on the text 'Does she like Rome?' of course were questions I knew the answers to 'What's the adjective for the noun pollution?' There would be more referential questions if it was more a discussion with a higher level group so that's one thing that came out. I used referential 'polluted'? 'Is your city in China polluted?' to Lee which enabled them to use a bit more free sort of speech. But these were very limited the referential questions to extend or reinforce the vocabulary.

Task 8.6

Make a 15–20 minute recording of part of a lesson. This can be a class that you either teach or observe. If this is too difficult to organise, watch a video of someone teaching . Focus on the teacher's use of language and identify examples of the following interactional features (taken from SETT). How would you rate your CIC? Are their any changes you would like to make to your practice based on this analysis?

FEATURE	DESCRIPTION
A. Scaffolding	• Reformulation (rephrasing a learner's contribution) • Extension (extending a learner's contribution) • Modelling (providing an example for learner(s))
B. Direct repair	Correcting an error quickly and directly.
C. Content feedback	Giving feedback to the message rather than the words used.
D. Extended wait-time	Allowing sufficient time (several seconds) for students to respond or formulate a response.
E. Referential questions	Genuine questions to which the teacher does not know the answer.
F. Seeking clarification	1 Teacher asks a student to clarify something the student has said. 2 Student asks teacher to clarify something the teacher has said.

FEATURE	DESCRIPTION
G. Extended learner turn	Learner turn of more than one utterance.
H. Teacher echo	1 Teacher repeats teacher's previous utterance. 2 Teacher repeats a learner's contribution.
I. Teacher interruptions	Interrupting a learner' contribution.
J. Extended teacher turn	Teacher turn of more than one utterance.
K. Turn completion	Completing a learner's contribution for the learner.
L. Display questions	Asking questions to which teacher knows the answer.
M. Form-focused feedback	Giving feedback on the words used, not the message.
N. Confirmation checks	Confirming understanding of a student's or teacher's contribution.

Task 8.7

Make a recording of one of your classes or use a recording of a class (published or personal). Based on what you now know about CIC, evaluate the recording in terms of:

- the teacher's use of ability to create 'space' for learning;

- evidence of learner engagement and involvement;

- specific strategies used by teacher or learners to promote understanding and establish shared meanings.

Summary

In this chapter, I have presented and characterised the construct classroom interactional competence. Placing interaction at the centre of learning, I have argued that in order to enhance learning and learning opportunity, teachers should begin by developing their own interactional competence. While I suggest that classroom interactional competence is highly context specific (both in the general social/ geographic sense and in the more specific sense of 'context of the moment'), there are certain features of CIC that can be encouraged and promoted in any setting. By adopting specific interactional strategies, CIC can be greatly enhanced. These strategies include the need for teachers to create space for learning, the importance of jointly created understandings, the value of shaping learner contributions, the need to engage and involve learners in dialogue, and so on.

Clearly, it is important for teachers to decide for themselves how to improve their CIC. What I have attempted to do in this chapter is to offer some thoughts on the various elements that make up CIC and suggested how teachers might enhance their own understandings. Like all professional development, there is no one 'right way' to improve. However, understanding a specific context and developing skills appropriate to that context are central to any endeavour towards becoming a better teacher. Developing an understanding of classroom interaction and improving the way that interaction is managed are, I suggest, central to improving your teaching.

9 Conclusions

In this, the final chapter of the book, I try to bring together some of the main themes that have been presented and discussed, and point to future directions for the study of classroom discourse. For ease and economy, the chapter is divided into two sections:

• Classroom discourse: looking back.

• Classroom discourse: future directions

Classroom discourse: looking back

At the beginning of this book, I gave a number of reasons for studying classroom discourse. After more than fifty years of research, it would be fair to say that the reasons for studying interaction in second language classrooms have not changed very much; what has changed, is our approach and how we use the information we obtain. The principal reason for studying classroom discourse is that it lies at the heart of everything that takes place in classrooms; to restate van Lier, it is 'the most important thing on the curriculum' (1996: 5). Understanding interaction helps us to understand teaching and learning and improve the ways we, as teachers, go about our professional lives. Like any human enterprise, we need to understand classrooms if we are to improve them; analysing interactions is one of the most useful ways of gaining insights into what goes on there.

Of course, one of the prime motives for looking at interaction so closely is that it should help us to further our understanding of learning. Views on this differ. For example, in 1994, Rod Ellis claimed that L2 classroom interaction studies 'have contributed little to our understanding of how interaction affects acquisition' (1994: 239). In contrast, in 1998, Michael Breen made the following, opposing statement:

> Social relationships in the classroom orchestrate what is made available for learning, how learning is done and what we achieve.

These relationships and the purposeful social action of teaching and learning are directly realised through the discourse in which we participate during lessons. [...] Furthermore, because the data made available to learners in a classroom are a collective product with which teachers and learners must interact actively as both creators and interpreters, because what learners actually learn from the classroom is socially rather than individually constructed, any explanation of how language is learned must locate the process *within* the discourse of language lessons.

(1998: 119)

Space does not permit a full examination of these polarised perspectives, but suffice it to say, at least for the time being, that one reason for such differing points of view is that in order to understand the role of interaction in learning, we need to understand what we mean by *learning*. Our view of learning is conditioned very much by our own experiences as learners, teachers and researchers. If we adopt, for example, a largely cognitive view of learning, we may not see why interaction is important at all (c.f. Ellis above). If, on the other hand, we adopt a more social view of learning, where learning is seen as being directly related to participation and involvement (c.f. Sfard 1998), then, clearly an understanding of interaction is both relevant and important. (For a fuller discussion on this debate, see Seedhouse *et al.* 2010). The position adopted here and throughout this book is that learning is very much a social process; learners learn best, I would suggest, when they are actively engaged in some kind of task, activity or discussion. This position coincides very closely with the one advocated under socio-cultural theories of learning and the work of scholars such as Vygotsky and Lantolf.

In the context of understanding learning, much of the research on classroom discourse has focused on describing the features that can be found in classroom interaction. In the early chapters of this book, we looked at the ways in which teachers modify their speech, ask questions, correct errors and maintain overall control of the interaction. A huge body of research now exists on repair (see, for example, Seedhouse 2004) and questioning (see, for example, Walsh 2006), perhaps the most commonly found features of classroom discourse in any classroom, anywhere in the world. Similarly, stemming from the work of Sinclair and Coulthard (1975), it would be fair to say that in most classrooms the IRF/E exchange structure still prevails; teachers typically ask questions, learners respond and have their responses evaluated. This is how much classroom discourse is structured and this is how interaction typically advances in any educational setting.

The 'discovery' of the IRF exchange structure by Sinclair and Coulthard has been fundamental in fostering our understanding of the very fabric of classroom discourse. For example, we know that one reason for the prevalence of IRF is that all classroom interaction is goal-oriented and that the main responsibility for setting goals lies with the teacher. By understanding the interconnectedness between pedagogic goals and the language used to achieve them, much has been done to unveil how learning takes place and how language, interaction and learning are inextricably entwined (c.f. Seedhouse 2004). Put simply, by developing understandings of interaction, we are advancing our understandings of learning.

While IRF is the dominant type of discourse structure to be found in classrooms, I am not suggesting that it is something we should be advocating or encouraging; indeed, quite the reverse. By appreciating that it does exist, we as teachers are in a position to ensure that we do not fall into the trap of promoting a rather mechanical, rigid kind of interaction in which there is little scope for creativity and spontaneity. In earlier chapters, we have seen how it is quite feasible to promote a different type of discourse in which learners play a fuller role and in which there is far more evidence of engagement and dialogue (c.f. Alexander 2008).

More recent studies of classroom discourse have adopted a variable approach, in which the relationship between language and pedagogic goals has been studied more closely. These studies provide us with an alternative approach to describing classroom according to specific micro-contexts or modes (see, for example, Seedhouse 2004; Walsh 2006). Rather than assuming that classroom discourse is all of a oneness, a variable approach makes the important point that language use and interaction vary according to a teacher's agenda and what is happening at a particular moment in a classroom. By understanding how pedagogic goals and language use are interconnected, we obtain a different perspective on classroom discourse, and one which is more closely aligned to the decisions made by teachers and learners. Perhaps most importantly, this perspective allows us to consider how the discourse is advanced *jointly*; both teachers and learners play important roles in collectively co-constructing meanings through their interactions. An understanding of the give and take that occurs in the interaction is fundamental to understanding learning (c.f. Pekarek Doehler 2010).

Having made some mention of the *what* and *why* of classroom discourse, I now turn to a consideration of the *how*. The early chapters of this book and, indeed much of the research that has been conducted to date, focused on the features and structure of classroom discourse (the what) and offered reasons for studying it (the why). The ways in which teachers and researchers have gained access to the complexities of classroom interaction have changed over the past forty years or so. Chapter 4 offered an overview of the main approaches to the study of classroom discourse, reviewing the work that has been conducted from interaction analysis, discourse analysis and conversation analysis perspectives. Each approach has its own merits and shortcomings and should be adapted to local contexts. For example, it would be unrealistic, in most situations, for teachers to provide detailed transcripts of their classes using conversation analysis; equally, for most classroom research, interaction analysis does not provide the kind of detail needed to gain a close understanding of the interaction. One of the central arguments of this book has been that teachers' professional development should be data led; if teachers are to improve their practice, I suggest, they need to make recordings of their classes. Clearly, however, it would be unrealistic to expect teachers to spend hours transcribing and analysing their data. By using an appropriate tool, such as the SETT framework, I have tried to offer alternative approaches to collecting and analysing data, though it is also apparent that there is still much to be done in helping teachers access usable data (see below).

SETT, by aligning language use and pedagogic goals in a limited number of modes, permits closer scrutiny of the discourse, identifying interactional features that *construct* or *obstruct* opportunities for learning (Walsh 2002, see also Nystrand 1997; Lin 2000; Nassaji and Wells 2000). The relationship between learning and interaction is understood from the teacher's perspective in the light of intended learning outcomes. Using SETT, the socially constructed discourse of the language classroom can be scrutinised in teaching and learning 'moments'; instances in the discourse where a particular interactional decision appears to either facilitate or hinder learning opportunity. The use, for example, of a display question in classroom context mode might be examined; or the deliberate and careful use of verbal scaffolds to facilitate understanding might result in enhanced understanding on the part of the teacher. It is the framework that allows interactive decisions to be related and compared to both teaching objectives and learning opportunities. Essentially, the SETT framework is intended to enable teachers to gain close, detailed understandings of their local context. While it may need to be adapted to that context, it permits a dynamic analysis of L2 classroom discourse by paying close attention to intentions and events.

To summarise this section, I make the following observations on the current position of classroom discourse research before turning to a consideration of what the future holds:

1 Despite developments in teaching materials, understandings of SLA, approaches to teaching and changes in teacher education pro-grammes, the basic structure of classroom discourse has changed very little; most classrooms are still dominated by IRF routines.

2 That said, when teaching goals and the language used to achieve them are considered together, a different perspective emerges, enabling more detailed, microscopic analysis of micro-contexts.

3 Different theories of learning impact greatly on our understanding and perceptions of classroom interaction: the greater the emphasis on learning as a social process, the greater the importance attached to interaction.

4 In recent years, there has been greater emphasis on using our knowledge about classroom discourse to train teachers and to advance their professional self-development; however, this is only happening on a relatively small scale.

5 Technological advances coupled with alternative approaches to studying classroom discourse have resulted in the emergence of different perspectives on the nature of classroom discourse and the relationship between interactional and linguistic features.

Classroom discourse: future directions

So what does the future hold? At the beginning of this book, I posited a number of challenges for teachers and learners in relation to understanding classroom discourse. One of these was to make an observation that very little time is actually spent making language teachers aware of the importance of classroom discourse. Although most second language teacher education programmes offer some kind of subject-based preparation and training in classroom methodology, there is very little emphasis on promoting an understanding of classroom interaction. As I have tried to demonstrate in this book, an understanding of interaction is crucial to effective teaching for a variety of reasons:

- Interaction is at the heart of learning.

- Understanding interaction is the first step to improving awareness of context.

- Reflective practice is more effective when the focus is classroom interaction.

- Learners are more engaged and more involved in classes where teachers understand how to make effective use of interaction.

- Teachers can research their own practices by focusing on interaction.

As mentioned in Chapter 1, it would not require too much imagination to introduce a 'third strand' on initial teacher education programmes to supplement the two currently in use: language awareness and teaching methodology. The third strand would be called something like 'interactional competence' and would focus exclusively on ways of helping teachers to understand classroom interaction as a means of improving their own practice. Not only will this result in more engaged, dialogic teaching, arguably it will make the whole process of teaching and learning more enjoyable for all concerned.

A second, and related, direction for the future is the need to further our understandings of interactional competence and classroom interactional competence (see Chapter 8). As we have already seen, interactional competence, the 'fifth skill', is set to become one of the major influences on language teaching, testing and materials design. I suggest that both interactional competence and CIC are highly context specific and that teachers have a responsibility to gain understandings of what they mean in their own context. It would be unrealistic to adopt a 'one size fits all' approach to this. Instead, there is a need to characterise interactional competence for both teachers and learners in a range of contexts. This will entail collecting and analysing classroom data and using appropriate tools to analyse the data. Such an opportunity provides an opening for teachers to become researchers of their own practice and to enhance understandings of their own professional practice. In short, it presents teachers with an occasion to engage in research that will ultimately benefit themselves and their learners, as opposed to 'having research done to them' by outside researchers.

A third challenge for the future is that we will need to develop new understandings of classroom discourse as our understanding of what we mean by 'classroom' changes. When we consider that many of us now work in contexts in which technology plays a considerable role, the traditional physical boundaries of the classroom no longer apply. Instead, we find ourselves teaching and supporting learning by means of virtual learning environments (VLEs), computer mediated communication (CMC), through the use of email, blogs, podcasts and so on. Clearly, the impact of technology in the last twenty years has been huge and is set to grow even further. These developments have to be incorporated into our understandings of interaction and of the ways in which interaction impacts on teaching and learning.

In the same way, we can see that our understanding of spoken discourse in classrooms is also in a constant state of flux. This can be explained in part by developments in technology that have enabled us to capture and describe more effectively spoken interactions in classroom settings. But this is only part of the story. Thanks to the endeavours of researchers and practitioners and their efforts to approach old problems in new ways by, for example, combining different research methodologies, asking different questions, introducing new theoretical perspectives, we are now better able to explain and uncover the complexities of multi-party spoken interaction. Research methods focusing on the micro-analysis of spoken classroom interaction, such as conversation analysis, have played a huge role in promoting understandings. Similarly, researchers looking at multimodality and the interplay of the various features of any spoken interaction – the words used, intonation and speech quality, gaze, gestures, embodied actions, etc. – have contributed enormously to this process.

If one of the prime motives for studying classroom interaction is to advance our knowledge about learning, we should recognise that views and attitudes towards learning are also changing. For a significant number of researchers following what has come to be known as a 'CA-for-SLA' agenda, learning can be studied 'in the moment' by looking at participation, interaction, orientations and so on. Current views of learning emphasising its social dimension lead me to believe that a fourth future direction for classroom discourse research is to advance understandings of learning as doing, participating, engaging, etc. Learning is about far more than 'having', and while we cannot ignore the cognitive dimensions of learning, these are much more difficult to access. If we want to look for evidence of learning, we should begin by focusing on the words and interactions of learners. It is here that we will gain the most useful insights and be in a position to influence the process of learning. This view of learning also resonates with the kinds of skills that employers are looking for in their employees: an ability to communicate effectively, to work as part of a team, to demonstrate interpersonal and problem-solving skills, and so on. Classroom discourse research that focuses on learning as participation has much to offer not only in terms of education and second language learning, but also in terms of informing workplace practice and enhancing professional development.

On a more practical level, what does the future hold for classroom practice? How might future classroom discourse research directions inform teaching methodologies and help learners? If task-based learning is as widespread as is claimed (see, for example, Ellis 2003), what is the relationship between task-type and interaction and vice versa? How might more effective management of classroom interaction result in a more engaged, more dialogic type of learning? And what do we know of the importance of interaction during feedback following a task? This, according to many researchers (c.f. Willis 1996) is the most important part of the task-based cycle and the one most likely to lead to learning. There is much work to do in this area.

In many parts of the world, classrooms are still dominated by the IRF routine, with teachers doing 90 per cent of the talking and learners playing a minimal role in the interaction. A future research direction in contexts such as this is for teachers and researchers to consider how the IRF cycle might be broken, allowing for more engaged, dialogic teaching and encouraging learners to play a more central role in the interaction. While there are clearly cultural sensitivities around such a proposal, I would suggest that changes might begin by looking more closely at the interactions that take place and not by importing expensive, Western teaching methodologies into contexts where they are clearly not appropriate. Learning and learning opportunity can be enhanced in any context in the world, but the starting point must be to develop an understanding of that context. This can be best achieved, I suggest, by encouraging practitioners to study classroom interaction.

From a learner's perspective, a number of challenges lie ahead. In earlier sections of the book, I talked about the importance of creating 'space for learning'. I argued that the mains responsibility for doing this lies with the teacher and that learners need to play a more equal role in the discourse. When we consider the ways in which learners are socialised into certain types of classroom behaviour, this is a huge challenge. In most content-based subjects, learners answer questions, respond to cues, follow the teacher's initiative, avoid interrupting and so on. And yet, in a language classroom, a very different set of interactional traits is needed if learners are to play a more equal part in the discourse. In language classrooms, we need learners to both ask and answer questions, to interrupt where appropriate, to take the initiative, seize the floor, hold a turn and so on.

By following learnt behaviours, which are the product of many years of being socialised into classroom rituals and practices, we may be facilitating the kind of 'smooth' discourse profile, which prevails at the moment. But are we helping to create interactions that result in learning? I suggest that we need to encourage interactions that have a more 'jagged' profile in which learners play a more central role in co-constructing meanings and in ensuring that there are opportunities for negotiation, clarification and the like. A jagged classroom inter-action profile has more of the features that would be found in naturally occurring interactions such as everyday conversation, business encounters and the like. While not denying that the language classroom is a social context in its own right, many of its features are determined by the fact that control of the communication lies with the teacher. In other contexts, roles are much more equal, resulting in different interactional features. Turns are longer, for example, and there are more frequent topic changes. Overlaps and interruptions are more common, as are pauses. I am suggesting that it is in this kind of inter-action that learners have the opportunity to acquire the kinds of linguistic and interactional resources that will help them develop as learners. Teachers, while still playing a more central role, would need a far more sophisticated understanding of classroom discourse in order to be able to manage the interaction, create learning opportunities and shape learner contributions.

Finally, in terms of possible future directions in the methods used for studying classroom discourse, we need to be clear about who the user is. In particular, there is a need to make a distinction between research tools for teachers and research tools for researchers. Up until recently, I suggest, the same set of tools has been used by both teachers and researchers, not always to good effect. As mentioned earlier in this chapter, it is unrealistic to expect teachers to devote hours of their time to recording, transcribing and analysing classroom data. What they need is a tool that offers a 'snapshot' of their classes and that allows them to develop understandings and acquire interactional competence. For most teachers, their main concern is to grow in professional expertise and make sure that learners have a rewarding and enjoyable experience. Short recordings, analysed using some kind of tool or framework, preferably developed by teachers for their own use, is a much more realistic goal than wholesale transcription of a full lesson. The aim should be to collect small amounts of data from a sample of lessons and build up a profile of a teacher's classroom interactional competence. From this, changes to practice can be made and evaluated over time.

For researchers, future challenges will be concerned with collecting data that offers greater insights into what really happens in classrooms. Advances in technology are sure to play a part in this – for example, we have already seen in Chapter 7 how corpus linguistics might be combined with other methods to further understandings. Multiple method research is likely to play an important part in helping researchers uncover what is going on in language classrooms. In addition to using technology, another aspect of this is to involve participants more in the analysis. So many corpus-based studies do not interview participants – this is surely essential if we are to maximise our understanding of classroom interaction. We need to talk to teachers and learners and get their perspective.

There are sure to be many other future directions that classroom discourse research might take. What is clear is that there has to be a continuation of the current trend of involving practitioners and ensuring that they both benefit from new advances in knowledge and play a key role in producing that new knowledge.

Task commentaries

Chapter 1

Task 1.1

This is an interesting piece of classroom discourse in many respects. The most striking feature is the predominance of long teacher turns and short learner contributions. In terms of speech modification, we can observe that this teacher uses quite a complex range of vocabulary for this level, pre-intermediate. It is unlikely that they would be able to understand many of the words used here: *steroids, contaminated, as a matter of course, scandal,* etc. A second observation is the way in which this teacher moves from one topic to another: opening with intensive farming, moving on to antibiotics, steroids, street vendors in a very short period of time. Again, learners may find rapid topic changes like this very difficult to follow unless they are marked in some way. Note too that learners interrupt the teacher in lines 74 and 83 to ask language-related questions. In each case, there is some confusion on the part of the teacher (in lines 75 and 84), followed by a further clarification by the learner (in lines 76 and 85). Perhaps the most interesting feature of this teacher's classroom idiolect (her individual way of talking in a classroom) is the fact that there is almost no signposting for learners. Note how little use is made of discourse markers like *ok, right, so* to mark the beginning and ends of transitions. Note too how little evidence there is here of pausing, normally a particular feature of modified speech and one that is essential for learners trying to follow the discourse. This is especially important in the final teacher turn, especially in lines 92–93 where the focus of the discourse is language and the word *hygienic*. This change in focus is not marked in any clear way, it is somehow embedded in the discussion on street vendors and likely to cause great confusion for learners. In response to the task questions, there is minimal guiding here by the teacher. Learners are likely to feel lost and excluded owing to the high level of vocabulary used, the lack of pausing, the absence of discourse markers, the rapid topic changes, their perceived need to interrupt to seek clarification.

Task 1.2

Other reasons for asking questions include:

- to get a piece of information from a student (a genuine question);
- to check concepts;
- to engage learners;
- to elicit full responses;
- to motivate learners.

While there are plenty of reasons for asking questions and this is by far the most frequently used strategy by teachers for eliciting a learner response, there are other strategies available, which might be equally effective. These include the use of pictures as prompts for a response, getting learners to ask questions across the class, using single word cues, getting students to ask questions as well as answer them, and so on. The point is that, although the teacher's aim is to elicit a response, it is not always necessary to ask questions to do so.

Task 1.3

The first thing to note is the two-second pause at the beginning of the learner's response, possibly indicating that this learner is not sure how to reply. Silence usually indicates some kind of interactional 'trouble' – here some doubt as to how to respond to the teacher's question. The latched turn in 12/13 (marked =) suggests that the teacher has interrupted in order to correct the error * I am agree. This is followed in 13–14 with an explanation by the teacher and an acknowledgement (in 15) by the student. We are not sure what happens next (marked ((3)), three seconds of confusion), so it is difficult to evaluate the extended explanation in lines 17–20. However, what we can say is that this explanation is quite disruptive to the flow of the open type of interaction, which is in evidence here. In other words, the teacher, through her choice of repair strategy, has actually disturbed the interaction and minimised learner involvement. A short, direct repair might have been the answer here so as to avoid disruption and ensure that learners' involvement was maximised. Given that the teacher's aim is to elicit feelings, her choice of error correction strategy is at cross-purposes with her pedagogic goal. A very quick correction and return to the main focus of the lesson would have been more appropriate.

Chapter 2

Task 2.1

The main difference between these two tasks is that A is much more open and discursive than B, which has a more definitive end-point. Essentially, the focus of A is the topic, whereas B is more closely oriented to the task and to task achievement. To complete Task A, students will need to know how to make suggestions, agree/disagree, evaluate each others' ideas and so on, whereas task B could actually be achieved with very little language (student A: 'parachute'; student B: 'ok', etc.). Tasks that are more topic-oriented such as Task A, normally require more preparation if they are to produce longer, fuller student contributions. Depending on the level of the learners, teachers may offer some structure to the task to ensure that it is achieved. Here for example, students could be asked to individually list their own arguments, compare in pairs, then fours, before coming up with one common list and providing reasons for their choices to the class as a whole. In terms of enjoyment, this will vary hugely from learner to learner. In many ways, Task B is easier because it has a clear structure and a definite end-point; learners know when they have finished the task. On the other hand, Task A might appeal to an international group of students because it allows a genuine exchange of opinions – students always like to hear about their classmates!

In terms of interaction, Task A may have more breakdowns, more long pauses, more errors and so on, while B may be complete with only a cursory use of language. A will require more effective topic and turn management, while B will pose a challenge in terms of the group coming to some kind of agreement. To summarise, we can distinguish between topics and tasks in the following way:

Topics

- good topics are ones which learners can identify with; depends on their world knowledge;

- topics normally should be controversial (c.f. *converging* and *diverging* topics);

- can be done as a formal debate;

- allow preparation time: *language, task.*

Tasks

- tasks are goal-oriented;

- tasks have a definite **end-point** (5 differences, 3 minutes to complete, 4 reasons);

- objectives should be non-linguistic;
- objectives should require interaction;
- visual stimulus may be helpful.

Task 2.2

Extract 1
This is clearly pre-task and set up. The teacher is locating learning in time and place ('this morning, last Christmas', etc.) before organising the groups and setting the task. While it seems quite clear, the instruction is very short and is not checked in any way.

Extract 2
This is clearly the 'task' phase and learners are working quite independently of the teacher in a free-flowing discussion. The teacher takes a 'back seat' and acts more like a member of the group, simply showing understanding (256 and 260) and letting learners get on with the task. Learners, for their part, manage all the turn-taking and topic management on their own and for all intents and purposes, the discussion resembles everyday conversation. This teacher succeeds very well in using language that is highly appropriate to the stage of the TBLT process and gives learners the space they need to complete the task.

Extract 3
This is the language focus or post-task phase of the cycle, where teachers typically get feedback following a task and offer their own input. There are some problems in this extract: a misunderstanding in 74–76, a breakdown and repair in 82–84. Note too the excessively long turn of the teacher and the fact that the topic seems to 'meander' somewhat. While the teacher seems concerned to engage learners in a discussion, the students want to check their answers and learn new vocabulary. There seems to be a mis-match between what the teacher's pedagogic goals are and what the learners perceive.

Task 2.3

This is a very good example of what is often referred to as 'guiding questions'. The teacher, by skilfully asking follow-on questions, succeeds in helping learners to the answer she is looking for, which eventually happens in line 34. This strategy requires great mental agility on the part of the teacher who must listen carefully to what students say. Note how it pays off in the extended learner turn in line 34. Her first question is very open and is met with an inappropriate response, in terms of what she is looking for. Rather than reject the response 'scary' in 29, she seeks clarification (in 30) before bringing the discourse back on track with her question in 33. This teacher is very effective in her questioning strategy and is 'rewarded' with a comprehensive response in 34.

Chapter 3

Task 3.1

In extract 3.1, the teacher is trying to elicit *military force*. He uses a number of devices to guide learners towards a correct response and to 'shape' their contributions:

- In 188, he alerts the learners to the phrase he is looking for by first clapping his hands and then saying *military what?*
- In 190, he provides the synonym *fight* as means of guiding learners towards the correct response.
- In 192 and 194, he uses direct repair as a means of minimising interruptions to the flow of the interaction and leaving the floor open to learners.
- In 194 and 196, he uses a rising intonation to guide learners towards the phrase *military force*.
- In 198, he emphasises the word *force* to show that this is the correct response.

We can make the assumptions above (a) by analysing the interaction carefully and paying close attention to the specific features of the discourse and (b) by using our experience of classrooms and what typically occurs when teachers elicit vocabulary. There is too the methodological argument that encouraging learners to use intelligent guessing is a useful strategy for helping them to both deal with unknown lexical items and guess what might be the most appropriate word – as in this case.

Task 3.2

In this extract, the teacher's stated aim is 'to promote oral fluency and discussion'. While her choice of questions seems to suggest that this is indeed her aim (*what about in Spain if you park your car illegally?*), she manages the interaction in such a way that learners are unable to fully articulate a response. Throughout this extract, the teacher interrupts and corrects errors (in 275, 277, 279, 281, 283, 285), resulting in minimal responses from learners. We can say that this teacher, by her use of language and interactional strategies is actually obstructing learning and learning opportunity. Her pedagogic goal (oral fluency) and the language used to achieve that goal are actually in opposition. Learners, in this micro-context, need interactional space and an opportunity to express themselves; both are constantly denied here.

In terms of interaction and learning, the position adopted here is that the relationship is a very strong one, especially when learning is seen as participation. If learners are unable to participate, it is, arguably, unlikely that learning can take place.

Chapter 4

Task 4.1

Choosing a transcription system is very much dependent on how much detail you need to show in the data. If you are following a strict CA approach, then every detail is important. If, on the other hand, you are following a DA approach, you may find that less detail is needed. The one below is appropriate in that it does show pauses (though not in any great detail), overlapping speech and latched turns. It also includes some prosodic features of spoken language such as rising and falling intonation and emphatic speech. On the other hand, it does not include details such as voice quality (such as 'smiley voice'), nor does it show in detail pauses of less than one second.

The guideline, then, has to be 'fitness for purpose'. The transcription system must show enough detail to be workable and to enable interpretation of the data. On the other hand, if it has too much detailed information it may be unusable by readers or other analysts; it may also make the task of transcription so onerous that it becomes self-defeating.

Task 4.2

The main difficulty associated with using FIAC is that we are trying to apply language functions to classroom discourse as outsiders, without really being sure what is happening at a particular point in time. For example, using FIAC in this extract, line 11 may function as (4) *teacher asks a question* or (6) *teacher gives direction*. Do we classify line 13 as (6) *gives direction* or (7) *criticises or uses authority*? We face similar difficulties when looking at student talk. While line 12 is clearly (8) *pupil response*, how do we classify the remaining learner utterances? Is line 15 a response or is it an initiation?

The point is that all utterances can perform more than one function and it is almost impossible to say, with conviction, what a particular utterance is 'doing' at any given moment in classroom interaction. For this reason, using FIAC is fraught with difficulty.

11	T:	ok does anyone agree with his statement?
12	L:	(2) erm I am agree with=
13	T:	=agree be careful with the verb to agree there you as well Ensa that it's we! agree it's not to
14		be agree it's to agree! Ok=
15	L:	[oh I agree]
15	L:	((3))
16	T:	I agree with you but not I AM agree with you the verb is to agree ok so ((3)) to agree with
17		**(writing on board)** is the preposition that follows it I so it's I agree with you I disagree with
18		you . . . ok em Silvie can you em what were you going to say?
19	L2:	I agree with you because em when when we talk about something em for example you
20		saw a ((2)) on TV=

Task 4.3

Extract 4.6 (see below) has been included in order to illustrate some of the limitations of a DA approach. The first obvious feature is that the discourse is almost entirely managed by the students, with only one teacher turn (in 10). The absence of IRF patterns of discourse is also noticeable, as is the way in which turns are self-selected, passed, seized or held. There are overlapping turns, where several students speak at once (indicated by / /, or [ ]), and evidence of meanings being negotiated by students independently of the teacher, as in 4–5, 6–7. Interactional space is maximised, and there is a sense that the floor has been 'handed over' to the learners, with the teacher taking a 'back seat'. In many respects, this piece of discourse can be likened to casual conversation: turn-taking is rapid, roles are symmetrical and participants have complete freedom as to when they speak and when they remain silent. Such instances are not uncommon in the contemporary L2 classroom, stemming perhaps from learner-centredness and communicatively-oriented teaching methodologies. Were a strictly DA approach adopted, it is highly unlikely that the unfolding discourse could be adequately captured, resulting in idealisation of the data or misrepresentation of 'what actually happened'.

Extract 4.6

1	L:	no that's bad news=
2	L:	=so it's good news (**laughter**)
3	LL:	/bad news/ ok / no no that's good news/. . .
4	L2:	bad news . . .
5	L:	no that's bad news=
6	L3:	=ah good good news (2)
7	L1:	no no that's wrong you have to do bad news . . .
8	L2:	yes it's a bad news because [you]
9	L:	[no but that's] good news=
10	T:	=that's good news G N good news . . .

Chapter 5

Task 5.1

Go to the Collins Bank of English website at www.collins.co.uk/
Corpus/CorpusSearch.aspx. Use this free software to perform the
following operations for *not really*.

1 Under the corpus concordance sampler, type in not+really in the
'type in your query' box. Now tick the 'British transcribed speech'
box.

2 Click 'show concs' (concordances). You'll get a list of concordance
lines for *not really*.

3 Read through the concordance lines. What observations about
not really can you make? How might you use this with a group
of learners?

4 Consider how this approach could be used with a corpus of
classroom discourse. What might it reveal?

Task 5.2

I have marked in possible options here, there may be others. In the
opening lines, the teacher locates the class temporally (*today, last
class/last week*). This is important so that learners have a point of
reference and can relate today's session to a previous one. The teacher
then goes on to remind learners what happened in the last class (*we
did a quiz ok/right/yes*). Not only does this serve to remind learners
what happened last time, it also creates 'shared space', a sense that
we're all in this together and we can now move forward with the work
we did last time. Shared space is crucial if learning is to take place

and most teachers work very hard to create such an environment (see the discussion on shared space in Chapter 5).

The final two discourse markers (*right/ok/now*) mark the discourse and function almost like punctuation in a written text. Their purpose is to get learners' attention and to draw attention to the instruction that follows.

> T: <u>Today</u> we're going to be reading about and talking about er music and pop stars and famous people Last <u>class/week</u> we did a quiz <u>right/ok/yes</u> and it was a picture quiz and some of the pictures were people from your countries. <u>Right/ok/now</u> let me see could you work with Ben and could you three guys work together (**T organises groups**). If you recognise any of those people who they are and what you know about them and then what kind of lifestyle do you think these people have. <u>OK/now/right</u> you can begin when you're ready.

Task 5.3

I have given a suggested answer to the task below. Note that decisions concerning 'real' or 'artificial' may be based on how real or authentic an activity is in class. For example, discussing homework is a very 'real' activity in class, as is planning a composition. Both activities require language to be used for genuine communication. Other activities, however, such as doing a role play, or answering comprehension questions are artificial in the sense that they are designed to promote language practice, but not to encourage genuine communication. Clearly, most classes will include a combination of both 'real' and 'artificial' activities.

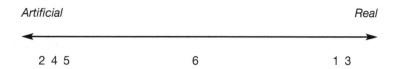

Artificial   *Real*

2 4 5   6   1 3

7 Planning a composition with a group of students

8 Doing a role play

9 Discussing homework with students

10 Modelling new language

11 Watching a video and answering comprehension questions

12 Taking part in a class debate

Chapter 6

Task 6.1

While there are no 'right' answers to this question, it is very likely that managerial mode will be present in your teaching:

- when setting up a new activity;
- when concluding a task;
- when giving an instruction;
- when organising learners into pairs or groups;
- when monitoring a task, giving advice, etc.;
- when giving feedback after a task.

There may be other occasions. Essentially, the management of learning occupies a great deal of time and it is something that most of us, as teachers, are concerned to improve. Note too that, in many contexts, the management of *learners* takes up a lot of class time. While managerial mode does not specifically include things such as dealing with difficult students, discipline and so on, these are clearly important features of classroom life and cannot be ignored.

Some of the difficulties associated with managing learning include:

- giving clear instructions;
- setting and adhering to time limits;
- using signpost words appropriately;
- making a distinction between an 'instructional voice' and a 'teaching voice' so that learners are able to understand instructions more easily;
- moving learners in and out of group-work and plenary (open class) activities.

There may be others specific to your own context. One of the best ways of improving class management is to make short recordings of stages in a lesson that involve close class management and analysing them (see Chapter 6).

Task 6.2

This extract opens in skills and systems mode (lines 29–33). The teacher is dealing with a language question concerning the difference between olive oil and sunflower oil so this is skills and systems mode. The slight hesitation and reference to the coursebook (*erm* in 33) signals a transition to materials mode (lines 33–46). Note how the turn-taking is tightly controlled, there are a lot of IRF sequences and all the interaction evolves around the materials being used. There is little scope for students' personal opinions and the teacher's role is to get students to display their understanding.

In line 47, we see a transition to classroom context, signalled by laughter and the reference to students' names (Yvette, Georgia and Haldoun). This has a striking effect on the interaction that ensues; note the long learner turn (53–56) and the more personalised responses. Students here have been given the floor and are free to comment on their past experiences of pot luck suppers. Classroom context mode continues until line 61 when the teacher switches modes, rather suddenly, by asking a language focused question (fussy). Lines 61–70 are skills and systems mode and the focus is on language, with learners seeking clarification and asking questions. There is some confusion here (in 68), possibly caused by the rather rapid mode switch in 61.

The main difficulty with this kind of analysis is that we are outsiders trying to work out what has happened in a particular context. This problem does not arise when you use SETT to evaluate your own teaching since you are more aware of the decisions taken and the local context.

29	T:	=yes olive oil yes yes must be a good quality=
30	L:	=and the other olive oil vegetable and made from maize from corn=
31	T:	=yes corn oil and yeah there's many different types of oil olive oil is the best and . . .
32		essential to Spanish omelette tortilla erm right so if you were invited to one of Leslie's
33		pot-luck suppers (**referring to the book**) erm right what would you bring . . . along . . .
34		with you?
35	L:	American or ((1))?
36	T:	yes this is this Leslie the American woman imagine she [invited you to a pot-luck
37		supper
38	L:	[a bottle of wine
39	T:	a bottle of wine yes
40	L:	a dish [of food
41	T:	[what else? a dish of food yes what=
42	L:	=dessert
43	T:	yes possibly a dessert=
44	L:	=or a starter

45	T:	or a starter ... yes so how would you know what to bring?
46	LL:	((2)) the organiser give you a list ((1))
47	T:	that's right yes so it's it's quite well-organised you can **(laughs)** imagine writing a list
48		oh yes I'll ask Yvette she can bring a starter ... oh Georgia a nice salad Italians are
49		very good with salads and then maybe a main course er Haldoun and perhaps er the
50		Japanse can do some more some more main courses so it would be very er very
51		well-organised=
52	L:	=usually((2)) like sometimes there are like 3 main courses ((2)) like graduation in
53		sometimes we have parties and we have like er roast chicken and another people
54		bring ((3)) for the main courses and we don't have nothing for nothing for dessert and
55		nothing for the starter [(**laughs**)]
56	T:	[(**laughs**)] oh dear well Georgia perhaps when you go back to Italy perhaps you can
57		organise one of these typical pot-luck suppers and organise it well so you'll have
58		plenty of desserts and plenty of starters **(laughs)** but er do you think it's a good idea?
59	L:	sometimes, yeah
60	L:	it's nice because you don't know what you're going to eat=
61	T:	=it's a surprise yes, yeah as long as you like everything ... I mean some people don't
62		like certain things what adjective do we use for people who don't like that and hate
63		that and a lot of food they won't eat... we call it people are very ... FUSsy fussy with
64		their food (**writes on board**) right so fussy that's don't like vegetables, never eat er
65		pasta (**laughs**)=
66	L1:	=excuse me how to say if er you ((2)) for example if you try some burger on cormer
67		... on the the street and then you feel not very well
68	T:	er ... I'm not quite sure what you mean Yvette if you?
69	L1:	you can buy for example ((2)) just on the street
70	T:	you mean street sellers ... people selling food on the street yes

Task 6.3

You should have the following if you have completed the grid correctly:

Feature of teacher talk	Description
A. Scaffolding	1. Reformulation (rephrasing a learner's contribution) 2. Extension (extending a learner's contribution) 3. Modelling (providing an example for learner(s)
B. Direct repair	Correcting an error quickly and directly.
C. Content feedback	Giving feedback to the message rather than the words used.
D. Extended wait-time	Allowing sufficient time (several seconds) for students to respond or formulate a response.
E. Referential questions	Genuine questions to which the teacher does not know the answer.
F. Seeking clarification	1. Teacher asks a student to clarify something the student has said. 2. Student asks teacher to clarify something the teacher has said.
G. Extended learner turn	Learner turn of more than one utterance.
H. Teacher echo	1. Teacher repeats teacher's previous utterance. 2. Teacher repeats a learner's contribution.
I. Teacher interruptions	Interrupting a learner' contribution.
J. Extended teacher turn	Teacher turn of more than one utterance.
K. Turn completion	Completing a learner's contribution for the learner.
L. Display questions	Asking questions to which teacher knows the answer.
M. Form-focused feedback	Giving feedback on the words used, not the message.
N. Confirmation checks	Confirming understanding of a student's or teacher's contribution.

Task 6.4

129	L5:	=I believe in trying new things and ((1)) ideas=
130	T:	=er (1) you believe in being POSitive you mean?= **(F)**
131	L5:	=pardon?=
132	T:	=do you believe in always being positive is that what you mean?= **(F)**
133	L5:	=no . . . I believe to (3) to have a lot of achievement
134	T:	(1) do you believe in what do you mean you you should always take opportunities is
135		that what you mean no?= **(N)**
136	L5:	=no I want my life to be very (1)
137	T:	happy?= **(A)**
138	L5:	=yeah and also I I do many things (1) many different experiences=
139	T:	=why don't you say you just believe in experiencing as many different things as you

```
140           want= (A)
141   L5:     =oh yeah=
142   T:      =thats what I think you should say=
```

I have marked the most obvious features by using letters: each letter is taken from the SETT grid in the previous task. So, in lines 130 and 132, the teacher is seeking clarification, and in line 134, this becomes a confirmation check. I am interpreting 137 and 139 as examples of scaffolding; the teacher is trying to help L5 articulate a response more clearly by 'feeding in' the language required. Note that as we have seen, 'labelling' utterances in classroom discourse in this way is notoriously difficult and there may be other possible answers here. I have used my knowledge of the context and of the data to present the most plausible answers.

Task 6.5

This task has no commentary. The main rationale is to give you an opportunity to try out the SETT framework for yourself and evaluate its usefulness. It might be worth comparing your evaluation with that of a colleague if this is possible.

Chapter 7

Task 7.1

There are literally hundreds of ways of completing this table. I have offered just a few questions here. When devising reflective practice questions, the main consideration should be their 'answerability'. While it may be possible to come up with lots of areas of focus, it is important to recognise that only some questions can be answered, while others may lie outside your control. Choose questions that give a clear focus, which can be answered and which you have the capacity to control.

Teachers	Learners
How can I improve the questions I ask?	How can I involve my students more in my classes?
What alternative ways of giving feedback can I try?	How can I encourage students to ask questions?
How can I improve my instructions?	What is the effect on interaction of allowing 'rehearsal time'?
I ask too many display questions; what can I do about this?	How can I get students to use English more actively in class?
What can I do to improve the ways in which I elicit from my students?	What techniques can I use to get students to scaffold each other?
How can I reduce my teacher echo?	

Task 7.2

Each of the following situations may cause problems, at least some of the time. Obviously, my suggested solutions may have to be adapted to your own context.

- Students refuse to speak English when working independently. This is a 'problem' that teachers often comment on – 'how can I get them to speak English all the time?' The solution might be simply: don't even try! It is probably more realistic to get students to use English for short 'bursts' of activity and then allow them to use L1 again. Set time limits and challenge students to use English for five, ten minutes or longer or just for the completion of a single task. Get them to reflect on the problems they experienced; record them during a task and let the class comment. And don't forget, there is nothing wrong with using L1 in class – it can be very useful indeed.

- Your instructions never seem to 'work' and are always misunderstood. This is something we all experience. Instructions are just difficult to give and to be understood. Try the following:

  - Break all instructions down. It should be possible to organise all activities using 1, 2, 3.

  - Check instructions by getting one student to summarise.

  - Give part of an instruction and have students complete that before moving on to the next part: instruction-action-instruction-action, etc.

  - Record your instructions and analyse them – where is it going wrong and how might you improve?

- Your teaching is dominated by question–answer routines. This needs a recording to be made or the help of an observer or 'critical friend'. You need to identify moments in your teaching when it would be possible to elicit without asking a question. Use cues, prompts, silence, pictures, etc. But most important, you need to be more conscious about the use of questions and look at their purpose in relation to what you want to achieve at a particular point in time. Plan whole sections of a lesson where you ask no questions and do encourage students to ask more questions so that you spend more time answering their questions and less time asking your own.

- Your students constantly do badly in the end of unit tests you set them. You need to analyse the tests and look at the teaching you have done: are the tests fair? Do they include the content of what you have been teaching and do they test in the *way* that you have taught? For example there's no point getting students to read long texts if you want to test their grammar – choose an alternative.

Task 7.3

I believe that talking to colleagues is one of the most effective means of improving your professional practice. Try it if you haven't already done so. Better still, get them to come and watch you teach having first discussed a problem or issue and tried to implement a change. The combination of observation plus dialogue is incredibly beneficial and, in my experience, always gets results.

Task 7.4

Following on from the commentary on the previous task, the idea here is to get you to appreciate the value of professional dialogue. Stimulated recall is an excellent way of recording yourself teaching and then discussing with a colleague. It works like this: make a recording of one of your lessons (10–15 minutes is plenty, audio or video). Find some time to watch or listen to the recording first on your own and then with your colleague. Focus on one aspect of the recording and discuss this, recording the conversation you have with your colleague. Finally, use both recordings (of your teaching and the discussion with a colleague) to try to reflect on, understand and make some changes to your professional practice. The whole process is designed to give you greater insights into your teaching and to allow you to share problems and possible solutions with another professional. It should take place in a friendly, supportive environment and trust and mutual respect must be upheld at all times.

Chapter 8

Task 8.1

See the commentary in Chapter 8, pages 162–3.

Task 8.2

Like all of the tasks so far, the answer to this one will be very context-specific and dependent on local conditions. If, for example, you work mainly with adult learners who are highly motivated, your conception of interactional competence will be very different to that of someone working in a state school with very young learners. The following list is neither exhaustive nor applicable to every context; it is merely indicative of some of the things you may want to include in your definition of IC in your context. Note that the features I have listed below are different to those often used to characterise oral fluency; here, we are interested in what goes on between speakers, not in solo performance (see Chapter 8 for a fuller discussion on this).

Interactional competence: teachers	Interactional competence: learners
Uses language appropriate to the goal of the moment.	Recognises the kind of response required: short or full response.
Listens and responds carefully to learners.	Is able and prepared to talk about personal experiences.
Avoids interrupting all the time.	Helps other learners by scaffolding,
Allows learners to have 'interactional space'.	suggesting, prompting, ignoring errors where appropriate.
Takes care to support learners by scaffolding where necessary.	Is prepared to ask and answer questions.
Allows learners to 'struggle' some of the time; avoids giving the answer.	Seeks opportunities to use English both with teachers and classmates.
Tries to help learners by 'shaping' responses and not always accepting the first answer.	Is not afraid of making mistakes and will take risks in open class discussions.
	Respects the views of others and is prepared to be open-minded.
Avoids asking display questions all the time.	Manages turn-taking well and is able to 'bring in' other students in pair and group-work tasks.
Is not afraid of silence and is prepared to use it to allow learners more 'space'.	Is able to open and develop a range of topics.
Uses error correction that is appropriate to the moment.	Makes use of both linguistic and interactional resources to communicate effectively.
Creates a friendly, supportive learning environment.	Uses acknowledgement tokens (or backchannels) – words like *uh uh,*
Avoids persistent use of IRF and is aware of its consequence on interaction.	*mmm, ok, right, yeah,* etc. – to signal understanding to a speaker.

Task 8.3

The following features of CIC can be identified in extract 8.5:

1 An absence of repair. Repair is again either totally lacking (examples) or it is done in a very constructive way. For example, the other-initiated, other-repair in line 31 'feels' more like a request for clarification than a direct error correction. This serves the purpose of making students feel at ease and willing to take risks. Again, in this micro-context where the prime focus is elicitation and the sharing of personal experiences, repair has to be handled in a sensitive way in order to maximise space for learners and for learning. Note too the subtle error correction in line 40 ('look at some photos'). This is simply fed into the dialogue, a strategy that serves to minimise interruption and maximise the 'flow' of the discourse.

2 Seeking extensions. This teacher does not always accept the first response she gets and tries to 'push' learners to say more (for example, in lines 5 and 13 where she asks learners to justify their

response: 'why'?). On both occasions she succeeds in getting an extended response from learners who give reasons for a previous contribution. (Note that the strategy of constantly asking 'why' might have the opposite effect and cause learners not to offer an elaborated response. It should, therefore, be used sparingly).

3 Increased wait time – note the pausing:

- Line 4 (four seconds). This pause allows the student to formulate a response and then go on to justify it.

- Lines 10 and 18 (both two seconds). Here the pause is used to signpost the end of a particular stage in the lesson and mark a transition to a new focus. This allows students to effectively 'navigate the discourse' (Breen 1998) and move on to a new stage in the lesson. Pausing, then, has many different functions, in the same way it has several functions in everyday conversation.

- Line 35 (five seconds). While this may not be deliberate, she is looking for the microphone, this extended pause allows the student to formulate a response. . .

4 Using 'interactional pointers'. To help learners follow the discourse and take part, this teacher uses specific spoken strategies that help learners know what is expected of them and what their role is at a specific point in time. These include: nominating a student (3, 10, 21, 24, 36); signpost words to mark transitions or a change in focus (*well* (18, 41); locating learning in time and space (1). These 'navigational aids' help learners stay together and prevent them from becoming lost in the discourse (c.f. Breen 1998).

5 Use of acknowledgement tokens (8, 16, 38, 40) is very important in keeping channels open and 'oiling the wheels of the interaction' (McCarthy 2003). Arguably, listeners – here the teacher – play a key and fundamental role in helping speakers to hold the floor and stay focused.

Extract 8.5

1	T:	ok now <let's start>(.) er today our topic is museum (1)
2		are you going to a museum in the coming summer holiday?
3		NAME are you (4)
4	S:	no I don't
5	T:	why?
6	S:	because a museum is very boring if I have some spare
7		times er I would like to choose do something interesting
8	T:	mmh so it's boring to you right?

9	S:	er yes
10	T:	ok (2) erm how about NAME [how about you are you going
11	S:	[me either me neither because I
12		think it's boring too
13	T:	why?
14	S:	and er at first I don't have the spare time and if I have
15		I will do something er in my hobbies
16	T:	mmhh so you are not interested?
17	S:	yes
18	T:	thank you (2) well how would you (.) complete this
19		sentence((**writing on bb**)) museum is a place where (.)
20		visitors can(.)how would you complete this sentence erm
21		say NAME
22	S:	look around [look around
23	T:	[look around °thank you° (.) look around how
24		about you NAME?
25	S:	a museum is a place er where visitors can have fun
26	T:	[have fun
27	S:	[have fun
28	T:	have fun by? by
29	S:	have fun by getting knowledge (3) by getting new
30		((mispronounced))knowledge
31	T:	getting no knowledge (.)
32	S:	(1) new new knowledge so- so- sorry
33	T:	new kn- knowledge ok don't be nervous (.) well yeah well
34		you (.) learn some new knowledge in the museum mainly
35		by (.) looking or (.) listening or (.) reading (5) who's
36		got the microphone? NAME (.)
37	S:	(3) I think it's by reading something
38	T:	mm by reading some material ↑or how about photos?
39	S:	er yeah read some photos and maybe some films
40	T:	mmhh some films thank you or you look at some photos
41		right? Thank you (.) well it's very clear that museums
42		are not so attractive to ↑you is that true (1) mmhh?

Task 8.4

1 Evidence of CIC in the interaction:

- Frequent and extended pauses.

- Learners asking questions.

- Direct error correction (no fractured [means broken]).

- Extended learner turns.

- Interactional space given to learners by teacher.

2 Evidence of CIC in the teacher's own commentary on the interaction:

- Her observation that students are asking questions.

- Her observation that she needs to stay silent some of the time (*So again, shutting up and letting them get on with it*).

- Her comments on the value of spending time setting up an activity to maximise the learning potential of the task.

Extract 8.6

Students are preparing to do a board game and clarifying vocabulary (fifteen minutes)

L: what does it mean singe, singed my eyebrows?

T: singed, singed (**writes on board**) (4) to singe means really to burn but it always has the sort of the meaning to burn something with hair=

L: =some people you know too close to the fire so it singed your eyebrows burns your eyebrows

T: yeah, yeah

L: (12) bump into cupboard door is it like hit?

T: yeah it's like knock into

L: (20) fractured means like twist

T: no fractured [means broken]

L: [broken] (12)

What I liked about this is that they were all asking questions. So for me, that would point up the use of providing a structured type of activity; although there's a lot management time setting it up, because they know they've got that time, they'll play a far more active role in it. So again, shutting up and letting them get on with it.

Task 8.5

This teacher uses a number of metalinguistic expressions to analyse her own use of language. Her main focus is the questioning strategies she used and the difference between display and referential questions. What is interesting about her commentary is not so much that she knows the difference, but that she appears to be very aware of *why* she uses different types of questions. She comments on the fact that display questions are more appropriate with lower levels and for checking learning, whereas referential questions allow greater 'freedom' of expression.

Task 8.6

The main purpose of this task is to familiarise yourself with the SETT framework and to evaluate your teaching using an instrument that does not require wholesale transcription. Follow the procedure given and Appendix A and repeat this 2–3 times. Each time you should focus on one aspect of your teaching and try to make some changes. If possible, get a colleague to observe you once you have completed this procedure and identify examples of CIC in your teaching (see Task 8.7).

Appendix A

SETT: Self Evaluation of Teacher Talk

Procedure

- Make a 10-15 minute audio-recording from one of your lessons. Try and choose a part of the lesson involving both you and your learners. You don't have to start at the beginning of the lesson; choose any segment you like.

- As soon as possible after the lesson, listen to the tape. The purpose of the first listening is to analyse the extract according to classroom context or mode. As you listen the first time, decide which modes are in operation. Choose from the following:

  1 Skills and systems mode (main focus is on subject content, skills or knowledge).

  2 Managerial mode (main focus is on setting up an activity)

  3 Classroom context mode (main focus is on eliciting feelings, opinions, attitudes, etc.)

  4 Materials mode (main focus is on the use of text, tape or other materials).

- Listen to the tape a second time, using the SETT instrument. Write down examples of the features you identify.

- If you're not sure about a particular feature, use the SETT key (attached) to help you.

- Evaluate your teacher talk in the light of your overall aim and modes used. To what extent do you think that your use of language and pedagogic purpose coincided? That is, how appropriate was your use of language in this segment, bearing in mind your stated aims and the modes operating.

- The final stage is a feedback interview with another colleague or with me. Again, try to do this as soon as possible after the evaluation. Please bring both the recording and SETT instrument with you.

SETT: Self Evaluation of Teacher Talk

Lesson Cover Sheet

A. Lesson details:
Name:

Class:

Level:

Date:

Overall aim:

Age:

Materials:

B. Lesson modes identified

C. Self-evaluation of teacher talk
Evaluate your teacher talk in the light of your overall aim and modes used. To what extent do you think that your use of language and pedagogic purpose coincided? That is, how appropriate was your use of language in this segment, bearing in mind your stated aims and the modes operating. Continue on the next page if necessary.

SETT: Self Evaluation of Teacher Talk

Feature of teacher talk	Description
A. Scaffolding	1. Reformulation (rephrasing a learner's contribution) 2. Extension (extending a learner's contribution) 3. Modelling (providing an example for learner(s)
B. Direct repair	Correcting an error quickly and directly.
C. Content feedback	Giving feedback to the message rather than the words used.
D. Extended wait-time	Allowing sufficient time (several seconds) for students to respond or formulate a response.
E. Referential questions	Genuine questions to which the teacher does not know the answer.
F. Seeking clarification	1. Teacher asks a student to clarify something the student has said. 2. Student asks teacher to clarify something the teacher has said.
G. Extended learner turn	Learner turn of more than one utterance.
H. Teacher echo	1. Teacher repeats teacher's previous utterance. 2. Teacher repeats a learner's contribution.
I. Teacher interruptions	Interrupting a learner' contribution.
J. Extended teacher turn	Teacher turn of more than one utterance.
K. Turn completion	Completing a learner's contribution for the learner.
L. Display questions	Asking questions to which teacher knows the answer.
M. Form-focused feedback	Giving feedback on the words used, not the message.
N. Confirmation checks	Confirming understanding of a student's or teacher's contribution.

SETT: Self Evaluation of Teacher Talk

Feature of teacher talk	Examples from your recording
A. Scaffolding	
B. Direct repair	
C. Content feedback	
D. Extended wait-time	

E. Referential questions

F. Seeking clarification

H. Extended learner turn

I. Teacher echo

J. Teacher interruptions

K. Extended teacher turn

L. Turn completion

M. Display questions

N. Form-focused feedback

_____

Appendix B

Transcription system

The transcription system is adapted from van Lier (1988) and Johnson (1995). Language has not been corrected and standard conventions of punctuation are not used, the aim being to represent 'warts and all' the exchanges as they occurred in the classroom. Many parts of the transcripts are marked unintelligible; it should be noted that the lessons were recorded under normal classroom conditions with no specialist equipment. Consequently, background noise, simultaneous speech and other types of interference have, at times, rendered the recordings unintelligible.

T:	-	teacher
L:	-	learner (not identified)
L1, L2, etc.:	-	identified learner
LL:	-	several learners at once or the whole class
/ok/ok/ok/	-	overlapping or simultaneous utterances by more than one learner
[do you understand?]		
[I see]	-	overlap between teacher and learner
=	-	turn continues, or one turn follows another without any pause.
. . .	-	pause of one second or less marked by three periods.
(4)	-	silence; length given in seconds
?	-	rising intonation – question or other
!	-	emphatic speech: falling intonation
((4))	-	unintelligible 4 seconds a stretch of unintelligible speech with the length given in seconds
Paul, Peter, Mary	-	capitals are only used for proper nouns
T organises groups	-	editor's comments (in bold type)

Glossary

Acknowledgement token
a term used in Conversation Analysis (CA) to refer to words like *ok, right, yeah, sure, mm, uhuh*. These words are used by listeners to acknowledge speaker contributions and to help communication proceed smoothly.

Asymmetrical roles
in many professional or workplace settings, speaker roles are not equal. Consider, for example, doctor/patient or teacher/student contexts: one speaker has more knowledge and power than the other, thus affecting the way interaction progresses.

Backchannels
a term used by discourse analysts to refer to words like *ok, right, yeah, sure*. These words are essentially discourse markers that refer back to a previous contribution in spoken interaction.

Clarification request
where one speaker asks another for clarification.

Classroom idiolect
a teacher's individual way of talking in class.

Classroom interactional competence (CIC)
the ways in which teachers and learners use language to mediate learning (see Walsh, 2006).

Concept checking
teachers check key concepts, usually by asking questions, as a way of ensuring that learners have understood a particular teaching point. Example: to check the concept of past time:

> T: Mary went to London yesterday. OK? So is she still there today?

Concordancing/concordance line
a term used in corpus linguistics to describe the way in which key words are presented in context. A concordance line allows us to see how a particular word is used with other words, how words combine in context.

Confirmation check
where speakers check that they have understood a previous utterance correctly.

Content feedback
feedback (normally from a teacher) on the message, not the language used to express it.

Corpus
a corpus is a collection of texts that is stored on a computer. These texts may be spoken or written, but must be 'real' and taken from natural contexts. A corpus can be searched quickly and easily, making it very suitable for analysing language in use.

Direct repair
where errors are corrected quickly and directly, with little explanation or exemplification.

Discourse marker
words like *sure, ok, right, now, so*, which mark spoken discourse in some way. In classrooms, these words often mark the beginning and end of an activity, or enable movement from one stage of a lesson to another.

Display question
questions to which teachers already know the answer. Their function is to get learners to 'display' what they know about something.

Echo
repeating (a) what a learner has said for the benefit of other learners, (b) what a teacher has already said. Echo may help the flow of the interaction or it may 'get in the way' if used excessively.

Elicitation
getting responses from students, normally, but not exclusively, by asking questions.

Extended learner turn
a learner contribution of several utterances. Most contributions are very short, one or two words only. Extended learner turns give students greater opportunity to express themselves and say what they really want to say.

Extended teacher turn
a teacher contribution of several utterances.

Extended wait-time
the time a teacher waits after asking a question or seeking a response. Typically, this is very short, less than one second. Extended wait-time (of 2 seconds or more) allows learners more time to think and prepare their contribution.

Form-focused feedback
teacher feedback that focuses on language rather than message.

Input hypothesis
first proposed by Stephen Krashen in 1981, who argued that second language acquisition depends largely on students receiving comprehensible input.

Interaction hypothesis
first proposed by Michael Long in 1983 and based on Krashen's theory. Long proposed that learners acquire a second language when they negotiate meanings through interaction with others. This was the hypothesis on which CLT was based.

Interactional competence
see Kramsch (1986). Considers the competence speakers need to communicate effectively and emphasises what goes on *between* speakers rather than solo performance.

Interacture
(Walsh 2006). Refers to the specific interactional features of classroom discourse that may help or hinder communication. Includes things like wait time, confirmation check, display question, etc.

IRF Exchange
based on the work of Sinclair and Coulthard (1975), who noted that most classroom discourse follows a three-part structure:

Teacher	**I**nitiates:	what's the past tense of go?
Student	**R**esponds:	*went*
Teacher	**F**ollows-up/**E**valuates:	*went, excellent*

The IRF exchange is still the basic unit of all classroom interaction and can be found in almost any classroom, anywhere in the world.

Latching/latched turn
a term used in CA to describe the way in which one turn may follow another with no pausing or silence.

Micro-context
refers to the ways in which interactants create contexts through their talk. Each micro-context comprises specific pedagogic goals and the language used to achieve them.

Mode
(Walsh 2006). A mode is a particular second language classroom micro-context, which has specific and identifiable pedagogic goals and specific linguistic and interactional features.

Mode convergence
when teachers use language that is appropriate to a particular micro-context. Typically, mode convergence occurs when pedagogic goals and the language used to achieve them are working together.

Mode side sequence
a brief departure from one mode (for example, *classroom context*) to another (for example, *skills and systems*) and then back again.

Mode switching
rapid movements from one mode to another.

Modelling
teachers frequently model new language by articulating a particular word, phrase or structure with correct pronunciation, stress and intonation. This is important for learners if they are to acquire the new language.

Negotiation of meaning
(see also, interaction hypothesis). Meanings are negotiated through interaction and when speakers seek clarification or confirm intended meanings. According to Long, negotiation of meaning is central to second language acquisition (SLA).

Noticing
(c.f. Schmidt 1993). The process of making connections, links etc. between one word, phrase or structure and another. Noticing is considered by some to be a crucial element in the process of SLA.

Online decision-making
the interactive decisions made by teachers while 'online', while teaching. 'Good' interactive decisions are those which promote learning and SLA.

Output hypothesis
first proposed by Merrill Swain (1985), who maintained that, for SLA to occur, the focus of attention should be on the words used by learners, their output.

Overlaps
where one utterance occurs at the same time as another, a very common feature of all spoken interaction.

Referential question
a genuine question, one to which a teacher does not know the answer (c.f. display question).

Reflective practice
the process of reflecting on one's teaching and making changes to practice.

Reformulation
refers to ways in which one speaker (normally the teacher) takes an utterance of a learner and 'reformulates' it so that it is more accurate, more precise. (See also the work of Lyster on *recasts*.)

Repair
a form of error correction.

Scaffolding

a term first coined by Bruner (1983) to denote the ways in which verbal scaffolds are used to assist learners. In a classroom, this may entail teachers 'feeding in' specific words or structures as and when needed by learners. It has to be said that learners also scaffold each other.

SETT

(self-evaluation of teacher talk, (Walsh 2006)). A framework designed to allow teachers to gain a closer understanding of interactional processes in the classroom as a means of improving their teaching (see Appendix A).

Shaping

refers to the ways in which teachers help learners to express themselves more clearly by 'shaping' their contribution: rewording, adding additional language, modifying, etc.

Stimulated recall

a research technique that can also be adapted for professional development. It entails making a short recording of your teaching, listening or watching with a colleague, discussing together and recording that discussion as a way of improving your practice.

Teacher Talking Time (TTT)

the amount of time teachers spend talking while teaching, typically around 70–80 per cent of the total class-time.

Transition markers

typically, discourse markers such as *right, now, ok, so, well* used to mark transitions or changes from one part of a lesson to another or from one activity to another.

Turn completion

used in CA to indicate where one speaker completes another's turn.

Turn taking

all human interaction is underpinned by turn-taking. Understanding the process is the domain of CA and entails looking at the ways in which turns are held, passed, taken or given. An understanding of turns at talk offers unique insights into the ways in which people interact and convey meaning.

ZPD

Zone of Proximal Development. A term first proposed by Vygotsky (1978) to refer to the difference between learning alone or learning with a more experienced 'knower'. As Lantolf (2000: 17) puts it: '[the ZPD is] the collaborative construction of opportunities for individuals to develop their mental abilities.' Key to this is collaborative: we learn better, proponents of ZPD argue, when we are learning with someone else.

Further reading

The following is a suggested list of additional reading that you might like to consult. Some of the references below appear in the main text, others have been added. The brief comment after each reference is intended for guidance only.

Books

Alexander, R.J. (2008) *Towards Dialogic Teaching: Rethinking Classroom Talk* (4th edition), York: Dialogos.
Excellent introduction to the importance of classroom interaction and talk to learning in a variety of contexts.

Bailey, K. and Nunan, D. (eds) (1996) *Voices from the Language Classroom*, Cambridge: CUP.
This is a very useful collection of papers from a variety of ELT contexts documenting the complexities of classroom life and classroom interaction.

Burns, A. (2009) *Doing Action Research in English Language Teaching: A Guide for Practitioners*. London: Routledge.
This is a practical and comprehensive guide to conducting action research projects.

Hall, G. (2011) *Exploring ELT: Language in Action*, London: Routledge.
Looks at the relationship between practice and theory when considering some of the key issues that have emerged in English Language Teaching.

Johnson, K.E. (1995) *Understanding Communication in Second Language Classrooms*, Cambridge: Cambridge University Press.
A very thorough overview of the various elements that need to be taken into account in any study of classroom discourse.

Kramsch, C. (1993) *Culture and Context in Language Teaching*, Oxford: OUP.
An exploration of the links between cultural knowledge and second language learning.

Lantolf, J.P. and Thorne, S. (2006) *Sociocultural Theory and the Genesis of Second Language Development*, Oxford: Oxford University Press.
Looks at the relevance of socio-cultural theories of learning to second language acquisition, adopting a largely social view of learning.

Mortimer, E. and Scott, P. (2003) *Meaning Making in Secondary Science Classrooms*, Buckingham, UK: Oxford University Press.
Offers useful insights into the ways in which classroom interaction can be studied as a means of facilitating learning and making teaching more effective.

Nunan, D. (1989) *Understanding Language Classrooms*, London: Prentice Hall.
Though quite old now, this is still a very useful and thought-provoking volume that considers alternative ways of approaching the study of language classrooms.

Sargeant, P. (forthcoming) *World Englishes: Language in Action,* London: Routledge.
An overview of the spread and current role of English and Englishes in the world.

Seedhouse, P. (2004) *The Interactional Architecture of the Second Language Classroom: A Conversational Analysis Perspective,* Oxford: Blackwell.
An excellent book that promotes the use of conversation analysis in the study of classroom discourse.

ten Have, P. (2007) *Doing Conversation Analysis: A Practical Guide*, London: Sage.
One of the best introductions to conversation analysis currently available.

Walsh, S. (2006) *Investigating Classroom Discourse*, London: Routledge.
This book offers a framework for studying classroom interaction as a means of improving second language learning and teaching.

Young, R.F. (2008) *Language and Interaction: An Advanced Resource Book*, London and New York: Routledge.
An excellent resource for studying language, social interaction and human communication.

Young, R.F. (2009) *Discursive Practice in Language Learning and Teaching,* Michigan: Wiley-Blackwell.
Provides a comprehensive account of discursive practices and social context in second language acquisition.

Journal articles and chapters in books

The following is a list of some of the key papers that have been published on issues relating to classroom discourse in the last thirty years.

Allwright, R.L. (1984) 'The importance of interaction in classroom language learning'. *Applied Linguistics*, 5: 156–71.
One of the most influential papers on the relationship between classroom interaction and learning.

Breen, M.P. (1998) 'Navigating the discourse: on what is learned in the language classroom', in W.A. Renandya and G.M. Jacobs (eds), *Learners and Language Learning. Anthology Series 39*, Singapore: SEAMO Regional Language Centre.
Looks at the ways in which learners 'get lost' in classroom interaction and at the role of the teacher in preventing this from happening.

Fung, L. and Carter, R. (2007) Discourse markers and spoken English: native and learner use in pedagogic settings, *Applied Linguistics, 28*(3), 410–439.
Provides a taxonomy of the most frequently found discourse markers used in classroom settings and offers a description of their functions.

Howard, A. (2010) 'Is there such a thing as a typical language lesson?' *Classroom Discourse*, 1: 82–100.
Considers the effect of the observer on classroom discourse and tries to uncover what really happens in 'typical' language classrooms.

Larsen-Freeman, D. (2010) 'Having and doing: learning from a complexity theory perspective', in P. Seedhouse, S. Walsh, C. Jenks (eds), *Reconceptualising Learning in Applied Linguistics*, London: Palgrave Macmillan.
Provides a stimulating discussion on polarised views of learning as either 'having' or 'doing', before turning to a critique of complexity theory as a means of seeing language as a complex adaptive system.

Markee, N. (2008) 'Toward a learning behavior tracking methodology for CA-for-SLA'. *Applied Linguistics, 29*: 404–427.
Considers the role of conversation analysis in tracking learning in spoken classroom interactions.

McCarthy, M. J. and Walsh, S. (2003) 'Discourse' in D. Nunan (ed) *Practical English Language Teaching*, San Francisco: McGraw-Hill.
Offers a view of classroom interaction where teacher–learner discourse is characterised by micro-contexts or discourse modes.

Pekarek Doehler, S. (2010) 'Conceptual changes and methodological challenges: on language, learning and documenting learning in conversation analytic SLA research', in P. Seedhouse, S. Walsh, C. Jenks (eds), *Reconceptualising learning in applied linguistics*. London: Palgrave-MacMillan.
Looks at the conceptions of language and learning proposed by proponents of CA-for-SLA, whereby conversation analysis is used in the study of second language acquisition.

Richards, K. (2006) 'Being the teacher': identity and classroom conversation ... A response to Sheen and O'Neill (2005), *Applied Linguistics* 27: 135–141.
Considers the ways in which teachers' identities are co-constructed through their interactions with learners and other teachers.

Seedhouse, P. (2005) 'Conversation analysis and language learning', *Language Teaching* 38: 1–23.
A state of the art article on the role of conversation analysis in the study of second language learning.

Sfard, A. (1998) 'On two metaphors for learning and the dangers of choosing just one', *Educational Researcher*, 27: 4–13.
Proposes and evaluates two metaphors for learning: learning as *having* and learning as *doing*.

Walsh, S., O'Keefe, A. and Morton, T. (2011) 'Analyzing university spoken interaction: a corpus linguistics/conversation analysis approach', *International Journal of Corpus Linguistics* [waiting for volume number].
Offers a methodology for studying classroom interaction that combines highly qualitative conversation analysis methodologies with more quantitative methods using corpus linguistics.

References

Ädel, A. (2010) 'How to use corpus linguistics in the study of political discourse', in A. O'Keeffe and M.J. McCarthy (eds), *The Routledge Handbook of Corpus Linguistics*, London: Routledge, pp. 591–604.

Alexander, R.J. (2008) *Towards Dialogic Teaching: Rethinking Classroom Talk* (4th edition), York: Dialogos.

Alger, C. (2006) 'What went well, what didn't go so well: growth of reflection in pre service teachers', *Reflective Practice, 7* (3), 287–301.

Allen, J.P.B., Frohlich, M. and Spada, N. (1984) 'The communicative orientation of language teaching: an observation scheme', n J. Handscombe, R. Orem and B.P. Taylor (eds), *On TESOL 83: the Question of Control*, Washington D.C.: TESOL.

Allwright, R.L. (1984) 'The importance of interaction in classroom language learning', *Applied Linguistics*, 5: 156–71.

Bailey, K. and Nunan, D. (eds) (1996) *Voices from the Language Classroom*, Cambridge: CUP.

Bartlett, L. (1990) 'Teacher development through reflective teaching', in J.C. Richards and D. Nunan (eds), *Second Language Teacher Education*, Cambridge: Cambridge University Press.

Batstone, R. (1994) *Grammar*, Oxford: Oxford University Press.

Bellack, A., Kliebard, H., Hyman, R. and Smith, F. (1966) *The Language of the Classroom*, New York: Teachers College Press.

Biber, D., Conrad, S. and Reppen, R. (1998) *Corpus Linguistics: Investigating Language Structure and Use*, Cambridge: Cambridge University Press.

Breen, M.P. (1998) 'Navigating the discourse: on what is learned in the language classroom', in W.A. Renandya and G.M. Jacobs (eds), *Learners and Language Learning*, Anthology Series 39, Singapore: SEAMO Regional Language Centre.

Bronfenbrenner, U. and Ceci, S.J. (1994) 'Nature-Nurture reconceptualised in developmental perspective: a bioecological model', *Psychological Review*, 101/4: 568–586.

Brown, J.D. and Rodgers, T. (2002) *Doing Applied Linguistics Research*, Oxford: Oxford University Press.

Brown, P. and Levinson, S. (1987) *Politeness: Some Universals in Language Usage*, Cambridge: Cambridge University Press.

Brumfit, C.J. (1995) 'Teacher professionalism and research', in G. Cook and B. Seidlhofer (eds), *Principle and Practice in Applied Linguistics*, Oxford: Oxford University Press, pp. 27–42.

Bruner, J. (1983) *Child's Talk*, Oxford: Oxford University Press.

—— (1990). 'Vygotsky: A historical and conceptual perspective', in L.C. Moll (ed), *Vygotsky and Education: Instructional Implications and Applications of Sociohistorical Psychology*, Cambridge: Cambridge University Press.

Bucholtz, M. (2007) 'Variation in transcription', *Discourse Studies*, 9/6: 784–808.

Budd Rowe, M. (1986) 'Wait time: slowing down may be a way of speeding up', *Journal of Teacher Education*, 37: 43–50.

Bygate, M. (1988) *Speaking*, Oxford: Oxford University Press.

Canale, M. and Swain, M. (1980) 'Theoretical bases of communicative approaches to second language teaching and testing', *Applied Linguistics*, 1: 1–27.

Carr, D. (ed) (2006) *Teacher Training DVD Series* (set of 15 DVDs). London: International House.

Carr, W. and Kemmis, S. (1983) *Becoming Critical: Knowing through Action Research*, Victoria, Australia: Deakin University Press.

Carter, R. and McCarthy, M.J. (2006) *Cambridge Grammar of English. A Comprehensive Guide*. Cambridge: Cambridge University Press.

Cazden, C.B. (1986) 'Classroom discourse', in M.C. Wittrock (ed) *Handbook of Research on Teaching*, New York: MacMillan.

Chaudron, C. (1988) *Second Language Classrooms: Research on Teaching and Learning*, New York: Cambridge University Press.

Cohen, L., Manion, L. and Morrison, K. (2007) *Research Methods in Education*, London: Routledge-Falmer.

Cook, G. (1989) *Discourse*, Oxford: Oxford University Press.

Cook, V. (2001) *Second Language Learning and Language Teaching* (3rd edition), London: Arnold, co-published by Oxford University Press.

Cotterill, J. (2010) 'How to use corpus linguistics in forensic linguistics', in A. O'Keeffe and M.J. McCarthy (eds), *The Routledge Handbook of Corpus Linguistics*, London: Routledge, (pp. 578–590).

Cullen, R. (1998) 'Teacher talk and the classroom context', *English Language Teaching Journal*, 52: 179–187.

Dewey, J. (1933) *How we think: A restatement of the relation of reflective thinking to the educative process*, Boston: D.C. Heath and Company.

Donato, R. (1994) 'Collective scaffolding in second language learning', in J.P. Lantolf and G. Appel (eds) *Vygotskyan Approaches to Second Language Research*, Norwood, New Jersey: Ablex Publishing Corporation.

Doughty, C. and T. Pica (1986) '"Information-gap" tasks: Do they facilitate second language acquisition?' *TESOL Quarterly*, 20/2, 305–326.

Doughty and Williams (1998) *Focus on Form in Classroom Second Language Acquisition*, Cambridge: Cambridge University Press.

Drew, P. (1994). 'Conversation Analysis', in R.E. Asher (ed) *The Encyclopaedia of Language and Linguistics*, Oxford: Pergamon.

Drew, P. and Heritage, J. (eds) (1992) *Talk at Work: Interaction in Institutional Settings*, Cambridge: Cambridge University Press.

Edge, J. (1992) *Co-operative Development*. London: Longman.

—— (2001) *Action Research*, Alexandria, VA: TESOL Inc.

Edwards, A. and Westgate, D. (1994) *Investigating Classroom Talk*, London: Falmer.

Ellis, R. (1990) *Instructed Second Language Acquisition*, Oxford: Blackwell.

—— (1994) *The Study of Second Language Acquisition*, Oxford: Oxford University Press.

—— (1998) 'Discourse control and the acquisition-rich classroom', in W.A. Renandya and G.M. Jacobs (eds) *Learners and Language Learning*, Anthology Series 39, Singapore: SEAMO Regional Language Centre.

—— (2000) 'Task-based research and language pedagogy', *Language Teaching Research*, 49: 193–220.

—— (2001) 'Investigating form-focused instruction', in R. Ellis (ed) *Form Focused Instruction and Second Language Learning*, Malden, MA: Blackwell.

——(2003)*Task-based Language Learning and Teaching*, Oxford: Oxford University Press.

Eraut, M. (1995) 'Schön shock: a case for reframing-in-action?' *Teachers and Teaching: Theory and Practice*, 1: 9–22.

Ferraro, J.M. (2000) *Reflective Practice and Professional Development*, ERIC Clearinghouse on Teaching and Teacher Education, Washington DC. ERIC Identifier: ED449120.

Firth, A. (1996) 'The discursive accomplishment of normality: On "lingua franca" English and conversation analysis', *Journal of Pragmatics*, 26: 237–259.

Firth, A. and Wagner, J. (1997) 'On discourse, communication, and (some) fundamental concepts in SLA research', *Modern Language Journal*, 81: 285–300.

—— (2007) 'Second/foreign language learning as a social accomplishment: elaborations on a reconceptualized SLA', *Modern Language Journal (Special Focus Issue on: The impact of the ideas of Firth & Wagner on SLA)*, vol. 91: 798–817.

Flanders, N.A. (1970) *Analyzing Teacher Behaviour*, Reading, MA: Addison-Wesley.

Foster, P. (1998) 'A classroom perspective on the negotiation of meaning', *Applied Linguistics*, 19: 1–23.

Gass, S.M. and Varonis, E.M. (1985) 'Non-native/non-native conversations: a model for negotiation of meaning', *Applied Linguistics*, 6: 71–90.

Glew, P. (1998) 'Verbal interaction and English second language acquisition in classroom contexts', *Issues in Educational Research*, 8: 83–94.

Goffman, E. (1981) *Forms of Talk*. Oxford: Oxford University Press.

Green, J. (1983) 'Exploring classroom discourse: linguistic perspectives on teaching-learning processes', *Educational Psychologist*, 18: 180–199.

Harmer, J. (1999) 'Abide with me: change or decay in teacher behaviour?' *IATEFL Teacher Trainer and Teacher Development Special Interest Group Newsletter*, 2: 23–27.

Hatton, N. and Smith, D. (1995) 'Reflection in teacher education: towards a definition and Implementation', *Teaching and Teacher Education*, 11 (1), 33–49.

ten Have, P. (2007) *Doing Conversation Analysis: A Practical Guide*, London: Sage.

Heritage, J. (1997) 'Conversational analysis and institutional talk: analyzing data', in D. Silverman (ed), *Qualitative Research: Theory, Method and Practice*, London: Sage Publications.

Heritage, J. and Greatbatch, D. (1991) 'On the institutional character of institutional talk: the case of news interviews', in D. Boden and D.H. Zimmerman (eds) *Talk and Social Structure: Studies in Ethnomethodology and Conversation Analysis,* Berkeley: University of California Press.

Howard, A. (2010) 'Is there such a thing as a typical language lesson?' *Classroom Discourse,* 1: 82–100.

Hymes, D. (1971) *On communicative competence,* Philadelphia: University of Pennsylvania Press.

——(1972) 'Models of the interaction of language and social life', In J. Gumperz and D. Hymes (eds), *Directions in Sociolinguistics: The Ethnography of Communication,* New York: Holt, Rinehart and Winston, pp. 35–71.

Jarvis, J. and Robinson, M. (1997) 'Analysing educational discourse: an exploratory study of teacher response and support to pupils' learning', *Applied Linguistics,* 18: 212–228.

Johnson, K. (1992) 'The instructional decisions of pre-service ESL teachers: new directions for teacher preparation programmes', in J. Flowerdew, M. Brock and S. Hsia (eds) *Perspectives on Second Language Teacher Education,* Hong Kong: City Polytechnic of Hong Kong.

——(1995) *Understanding Communication in Second Language Classrooms,* Cambridge: Cambridge University Press.

Kasper, G. (2001) 'Four perspectives on L2 pragmatic development', *Applied Linguistics,* 22: 502–530.

Kemmis, M. and McTaggart, R. (1992) *The Action Research Planner* (third edition), Geelong, Victoria, Australia: Deakin University Press.

Koester, A. (2006) *Investigating Workplace Discourse,* London: Routledge.

Kramsch, C. (1986) 'From language proficiency to interactional competence', *The Modern Language Journal,* 70 (4): 366–372.

Krashen, S. (1985) *The Input Hypothesis,* London: Longman.

Kumaravadivelu, B. (1999) 'Critical classroom discourse analysis', *TESOL Quarterly,* 33: 453–484.

Lantolf, J.P. (2000) *Sociocultural Theory and Second Language Learning,* Oxford: Oxford University Press.

Lantolf, J.P. and Thorne, S. (2006) *Sociocultural Theory and the Genesis of Second Language Development,* Oxford: Oxford University Press

Larsen-Freeman, D. (2010) 'Having and doing: learning from a complexity theory perspective', in P. Seedhouse, S. Walsh, C. Jenks (eds) *Reconceptualising Learning in Applied Linguistics,* London: Palgrave Macmillan.

Lee, W. and Ng, S. (2009) 'Reducing student reticence through teacher interaction strategy', *ELTJ,* 64(3): 302–13.

Legutke, M. and Thomas, H. (1991) *Process and Experience in the Language Classroom,* Harlow: Longman.

Leinhardt, G. and Greeno, J.G. (1986) 'The Cognitive Skill of Teaching', *Journal of Educational Psychology,* 78/2: 75–95.

Levinson, S. (1983) *Pragmatics,* Cambridge: Cambridge University Press.

Li, L. and Walsh, S. (forthcoming) ' "Seeing is believing": looking at EFL teachers' beliefs through classroom interaction', *Language Teaching Research,* 15/1.

Lin, A. (2000) 'Lively children trapped in an island of disadvantage: verbal play of Cantonese working-class schoolboys in Hong Kong', *International Journal of the Sociology of Language*, 143: 63–83.

Long, M.H. (1983) 'Native speaker/non-native speaker conversation and the negotiation of meaning', *Applied Linguistics*, 4: 126–141.

—— (1996) 'The role of the linguistic environment in second language acquisition', in W.C. Ritchie and T.K. Bhatia (eds) *Handbook of Second Language Acquisition*, San Diego: Academic Press.

Lyster, R. (1998) 'Recasts, repetition and ambiguity in L2 classroom discourse', *Studies in Second Language Acquisition*, 20: 51–81.

Markee, N. (2008) 'Toward a learning behavior tracking methodology for CA-for-SLA', *Applied Linguistics*, 29: 404–427.

Mann, S.J. (2001) 'From argument to articulation', *English Teaching Professional*, 20: 57–59.

McCarthy, M.J. (2003) 'Talking back: "small" interactional response tokens in everyday conversation', *Research on Language in Social Interaction*, 36: 33–63.

—— (2005) 'Fluency and confluence: What fluent speakers do', *The Language Teacher*, 29(6): 26–28.

McCarthy, M.J. and Carter, R.A. (2002) 'This that and the other: Multi-word clusters in spoken English as visible patterns of interaction', *Teanga*, 21, 30–52.

McCarthy, M. J. and Walsh, S. (2003) 'Discourse', in D. Nunan (ed), *Practical English Language Teaching*, San Fransisco: McGraw-Hill.

Mercer, N. (1994) 'Neo-Vygotskyan theory and classroom education', in B. Stierer and J. Maybin (eds), *Language, Literacy and Learning in Educational Practice,* Clevedon, Avon: Multilingual Matters/Open University.

Mortimer, E. and Scott, P. (2003) *Meaning Making in Secondary Science Classrooms*, Buckingham, UK: Oxford University Press.

Musumeci, D. (1996) 'Teacher-learner negotiation in content-based instruction: communication at cross-purposes?' *Applied Linguistics*, 17: 286–325.

Nassaji H. and Wells, G. (2000) 'What's the use of "triadic dialogue"?: An investigation of teacher-student interaction', *Applied Linguistics*, 21, 376–406.

Ng, M. and Lee, C. (1996) 'What's different about cooperative learning? And its significance in social studies teaching', *Teaching and Learning,* 17: 15–23.

Nunan, D. (1987) 'Communicative language teaching: making it work', *English Language Teaching Journal*, 41: 136–145.

—— (1989) *Understanding Language Classrooms*, London: Prentice Hall.

—— (1991) *Language Teaching Methodology*, Hemel Hempstead: Prentice-Hall.

—— (1996) 'Hidden voices: insiders' perspectives on classroom interaction', in K.M. Bailey and D. Nunan (eds), *Voices from the Language Classroom*, Cambridge: Cambridge University Press.

Nystrand, M. (1997) 'Dialogic instruction: when recitation become conversation', in M. Nystrand, A. Gamoran, R. Kachur and C. Prendergast (eds),

Opening Dialogue: Understanding the Dynamics of Language Learning and Teaching in the English Classroom, New York: Teachers College Press.

Ohta, A.S. (2001) *Second Language Acquisition Processes in the Classroom: Learning Japanese*, Mahwah, NJ: Erlbaum.

O'Keeffe, A. (2006) *Investigating media discourse,* London: Routledge.

O'Keeffe, A. and Farr, F. (2003) 'Using Language Corpora in Language Teacher Education: pedagogic, linguistic and cultural insights', *TESOL Quarterly* 37(3), 389–418.

O'Keeffe, A., McCarthy, M., Carter, R. (2007) *From Corpus to Classroom*, Cambridge: Cambridge University Press.

Pekarek Doehler, S. (2010) 'Conceptual changes and methodological challenges: on language, learning and documenting learning in conversation analytic SLA research', in P. Seedhouse, S. Walsh, C. Jenks (eds), *Reconceptualising learning in applied linguistics*, London: Palgrave-MacMillan.

Pica, T. (1997) 'Second language teaching and research relationships: a North American view', *Language Teaching Research*, 1: 48–72.

Psathas, G. (1995) *Conversation Analysis*, Thousand Oaks: Sage.

Rampton, B. (1999) 'Dichotomies, difference and ritual in second language learning and teaching', *Applied Linguistics*, 20: 316–340.

Richards, J.C. and Nunan, D (eds) (1990) *Second Language Teacher Education*, Cambridge: Cambridge University Press.

Richards, K. (2006) 'Being the Teacher': Identity and Classroom Conversation . . . A Response to Sheen and O'Neill (2005), *Applied Linguistics* 27: 135–141.

Röhler, L.R. and Cantlon, D.J. (1996) 'Scaffolding: a powerful tool in social constructivist classrooms', Online. Available HTTP: http://edeb3.educ.msu.edu./Literacy/papers/paperlr2.html (accessed 24 June, 2005).

Russell, T. (2005) Can reflective practice be taught? *Reflective Practice*, 6 (2), 199–204.

Sacks, H., Schegloff, E. and Jefferson, G. (1974) 'A simplest systematics for the organisation of turn-taking in conversation', *Language*, 50: 696–735.

Schön, D.A. (1983) *The Reflective Practitioner: How Professionals Think in Action*, New York: Basic Books.

—— (1996) *Educating the Reflective Practitioner Towards a New Design of Teaching and Learning in the Professions*, San Francisco, CA: Jossey-Bass.

Schmidt, R.W. (1990) 'The role of consciousness in second language learning', *Applied Linguistics*, 11(2): 129–58.

Schmidt, R. (1993) 'Awareness and second language acquisition', *Annual Review of Applied Linguistics*, 13: 206–226.

Scott, M. (2008) *WordSmith Tools (Version 5)*, Liverpool: Lexical Analysis Software.

Seedhouse, P. (1996) 'Learning talk: a study of the interactional organization of the L2 classroom from a CA institutional discourse perspective', unpublished thesis, University of York.

—— (1997) 'The case of the missing "no": the relationship between pedagogy and interaction', *Language Learning*, 47: 547–583.

—— (2004) The Interactional Architecture Of The Second Language Classroom: A Conversational Analysis Perspective, Oxford: Blackwell.

Seedhouse, P., Walsh, S. and Jenks (eds) (2010) *Conceptualising 'Learning' in Applied Linguistics*, London: Palgrave-MacMillan.

Sfard, A. (1998) 'On two metaphors for learning and the dangers of choosing just one', *Educational Researcher*, 27: 4–13.

Sinclair, J. and Coulthard, M. (1975) *Towards an Analysis of Discourse*, Oxford: Oxford University Press.

Slimani, A. (1989) 'The role of topicalisation in classroom language learning', *System*, 17: 223–234.

Spada, N. and Frohlich, M. (1995) *COLT Observation Scheme*, Sydney, Australia: Macquarie University, National Council for Educational Research and Training.

Sparks-Langer, G.M. (1992) 'In the eye of the beholder: Cognitive, critical, and narrative approaches to teacher reflection', in L. Valli (ed), *Reflective Teacher Education: Cases and Critiques*, Albany, NY: State University of New York Press, pp. 147–160.

Stubbs, M. (1983) *Discourse Analysis: The Sociolinguistic Analysis of Natural Language*, Oxford: Blackwell.

Swain, M. (1985) 'Communicative competence: some roles of comprehensible input and comprehensible output in its development', in S. Gass and C. Madden (eds), *Input in Second Language Acquisition*, Rowley, Mass.: Newbury House.

—— (2005) 'The output hypothesis: theory and research', in E. Hinkel (ed), *Handbook on Research in Second Language Teaching and Learning*, Mahwah, NJ: Lawrence Erlbaum.

Swain, M. and Lapkin, S. (1998) 'Interaction and second language learning: two adolescent French immersion students working together', *The Modern Language Journal*, 83: 320–338.

Taylor, C. (1985) *Human Agency and Language*, Cambridge: Cambridge University Press.

Thompson, G. (1997) 'Training teachers to ask questions', *English Language Teaching Journal*, 51: 99–105.

Thornbury, S. (1996) 'Teachers research teacher talk', *English Language Teaching Journal*, 50: 279–289.

Tsui, A.B.M. (1996) 'Reticence and anxiety in second language learning', in K.M. Bailey and D. Nunan (eds), *Voices from the Language Classroom*, Cambridge: Cambridge University Press.

—— (1998) 'The "unobservable" in classroom interaction', *The Language Teacher*, 22: 25–26.

van Lier, L. (1988) *The Classroom and the Language Learner*, London: Longman.

—— (1996) *Interaction in the Language Curriculum: awareness, autonomy and authenticity*, New York: Longman.

—— (2000) 'From input to affordance: social-interactive learning from an ecological perspective', in J.P. Lantolf (ed.) *Sociocultural Theory and Second Language Learning*, Oxford: Oxford University Press.

Vygotsky, L.S. (1978) *Mind in Society: the development of higher psychological processes*, Cambridge: Harvard University Press.

—— (1986) *Thought and Language* (new Edition by Kozulin, A.), Cambridge: MIT.

—— (1999) *Collected Works Volume 6*, R. Rieber and M. Hall (eds), New York: Plenum Press.

Wallace, M. (1991) *Training Foreign Language Teachers*, Cambridge: Cambridge University Press.

—— (1998) *Action Research for Language Teachers*, Cambridge: Cambridge University Press.

Walsh, S. (2001) 'QTT vs TTT: never mind the quality, feel the width?' *The IH Journal of Education and Development*, 10: 11–16. .

—— (2002) 'Construction or obstruction: teacher talk and learner involvement in the EFL classroom', *Language Teaching Research*, 6: 3–23.

—— (2003) 'Developing interactional awareness in the second language classroom', *Language Awareness*, 12: 124–142.

—— (2006) *Investigating Classroom Discourse*, London: Routledge

Walsh, S., and O'Keeffe, A. (2007) 'Applying CA to a modes analysis of third-level spoken academic discourse', in H. Bowles and P. Seedhouse (eds), *Conversation Analysis and Languages for Specific Purposes*, Bern: Peter Lang.

Walsh, S. and Lowing, K. (2008) 'Talking to learn or learning to talk: PGCE students' development of interactional competence'. Paper presented at the British Educational Research Association Conference, Herriot Watt University, Edinburgh.

Walsh, S., O'Keefe, A. and Morton, T. (2011) 'Analyzing university spoken interaction: a corpus linguistics/conversation analysis approach', International Journal of Corpus Linguistics [waiting for volume number].

Wells, G. (1999) *Dialogic Inquiry: Towards a Sociocultural Practice and Theory of Education*, Cambridge: Cambridge University Press.

White, J. and Lightbown, P.M. (1984) 'Asking and answering in ESL classes', *The Canadian Modern Language Review*, 40: 228–244.

Wilkins, D. (1976) *Notional syllabuses*, Oxford and New York: Oxford University Press.

Willis, J. (1996) *A Framework for Task-based Learning*, London: Longman.

—— (2001) 'Task-based language learning', in R. Carter and D. Nunan (eds) *The Cambridge Guide to Teaching English to Speakers of Other Languages*, Cambridge: Cambridge University Press.

Winter, R. (1996) 'Some principles and procedures for the conduct of action research', in O. Zuber-Skerritt (ed.), *New Directions in Action Research*, London: Falmer.

Wray, A. (2000) 'Formulaic sequences in second language teaching: principle and practice', *Applied Linguistics*, 21 (4): 463–489.

—— (2002) Formulaic Language and the Lexicon, Cambridge: Cambridge University Press.

Wu, B. (1998) 'Towards an understanding of the dynamic process of L2 classroom interaction', *System*, 26: 525–540.

Young, R.F. (2003) 'Learning to talk the talk and walk the walk: Interactional competence in academic spoken English', North Eastern Illinois University Working Papers in Linguistics, 2: 26–44.

—— (2008) *Language and Interaction: An Advanced Resource Book*, London: Routledge.

Zeichner, K., and Liston, D. (1996) Reflective Teaching: An Introduction, New Jersey: Lawrence Erlbaum Associates.

Zuber-Skerritt, O. (1996) 'Emancipatory Action Research for Organisational Change and Management Development', in O. Zuber-Skerritt (ed), *New Directions in Action Research*, London: Falmer.

Index

Related titles from Routledge

Introducing Applied Linguistics

Concepts and Skills

Susan Hunston and David Oakey

'For those of us involved in teaching postgraduate students where resources are limited, this is an ideal book to have at hand. The topics are varied and presented in such a way as to stimulate discussion in a very thought provoking way. I teach postgraduate courses in Thailand, Vietnam and China and this book will be "a must" on my reading list.'

Professor Joseph Foley, Assumption University, Thailand

Introducing Applied Linguistics provides in-depth coverage of key areas in the subject, as well as introducing the essential study skills needed for academic success in the field. Introducing Applied Linguistics:

* is organised into two Sections: the first introducing Key Concepts in Applied Linguistics; and the second devoted to the Study Skills students need to succeed.
* features specially commissioned chapters from key authorities who address core areas of Applied Linguistics, including both traditional and more cutting edge topics, such as: grammar, vocabulary, language in the media, forensic linguistics, and much more.
* contains a study skills section offering guidance on a range of skills, such as: how to structure and organise an essay, the conventions of referencing, how to design research projects, plus many more.
* is supported by a lively Companion Website, which includes interactive exercises, information about the contributors and why they've written the book, and annotated weblinks to help facilitate further independent learning.

Ideal for advanced undergraduate and postgraduate students of Applied Linguistics and TEFL/TESOL, Introducing Applied Linguistics not only presents selected key concepts in depth, but also initiates the student into the discourse of Applied Linguistics.

Susan Hunston is Professor of English Language and Head of the School of English, Drama, and American & Canadian Studies, at the University of Birmingham, UK.

David Oakey is an Assistant Professor in the Applied Linguistics Program at Iowa State University, USA.

Contributing authors: Svenja Adolphs, Aileen Bloomer, Zoltán Dörnyei, Adrian Holliday, Alison Johnson, Chris Kennedy, Almut Koester, Ruby Macksoud, Kirsten Malmkjaer, Kieran O'Halloran, David Oakey. Juup Stelma, Joan Swann, Geoff Thompson, Dave Willis, Jane Willis and David Woolls.

ISBN13: 978-0-415-44768-3 (hbk)
ISBN13: 978-0-415-44767-6 (pbk)
ISBN13: 978-0-203-87572-8 (ebk)

Available at all good bookshops

For further information on our English Language and Linguistics series, please visit
http://www.routledgelinguistics.com/

For ordering and further information please visit:
www.routledge.com

www.routledge.com/linguistics

Also available...

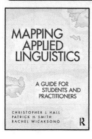

Mapping Applied Linguistics

A Guide for Students and Practitioners

Christopher Hall, Patrick H. Smith and **Rachel Wicaksono**

Mapping Applied Linguistics: A Guide for Students and Practitioners provides an innovative and wide-ranging introduction to the full scope of applied linguistics. Incorporating both socio-cultural and cognitive perspectives, the book maps the diverse and constantly expanding range of theories, methods and issues faced by students and practitioners alike. Practically oriented and ideally suited to students new to the subject area, the book provides in-depth coverage of:

- language teaching and education, literacy and language disorder
- language variation and world Englishes
- language policy and planning
- lexicography and forensic linguistics
- multilingualism and translation.

Including real data and international examples, the book features further reading and exercises in each chapter, fieldwork suggestions and a full glossary of key terms. An interactive Companion Website also provides a wealth of additional resources.

This book will be essential reading for students studying applied linguistics, TESOL, general linguistics, and education at the advanced undergraduate or master's degree level. It is also the ideal gateway for practitioners to better understand the wider scope of their work.

```
2011: 246x174: 448pp
Hb: 978-0-415-55912-6
Pb: 978-0-415-55913-3
eBook: 978-0-203-83242-4
```

For more information and to order a copy visit
www.routledge.com/9780415559133

Available from all good bookshops

Taylor & Francis

eBooks
FOR LIBRARIES

ORDER YOUR FREE 30 DAY INSTITUTIONAL TRIAL TODAY!

Over 22,000 eBook titles in the Humanities, Social Sciences, STM and Law from some of the world's leading imprints.

Choose from a range of subject packages or create your own!

Benefits for you
- ▶ Free MARC records
- ▶ COUNTER-compliant usage statistics
- ▶ Flexible purchase and pricing options

Benefits for your user
- ▶ Off-site, anytime access via Athens or referring URL
- ▶ Print or copy pages or chapters
- ▶ Full content search
- ▶ Bookmark, highlight and annotate text
- ▶ Access to thousands of pages of quality research at the click of a button

For more information, pricing enquiries or to order a free trial, contact your local online sales team.

UK and Rest of World: **online.sales@tandf.co.uk**

US, Canada and Latin America:
e-reference@taylorandfrancis.com

www.ebooksubscriptions.com

ALPSP Award for BEST eBOOK PUBLISHER 2009 Finalist

Taylor & Francis eBooks
Taylor & Francis Group

A flexible and dynamic resource for teaching, learning and research.